THE DIMENSIONS OF TIME AND THE CHALLENGE OF SCHOOL REFORM

SUNY series, Restructuring and School Change
H. Dickson Corbett and Betty Lou Whitford, editors

THE DIMENSIONS OF TIME AND THE CHALLENGE OF SCHOOL REFORM

edited by

PATRICIA GÁNDARA

State University
of New York
Press

Published by
State University of New York Press, Albany

© 2000 State University of New York

Production by Susan Geraghty
Marketing by Nancy Farrell

Printed in the United States of America

For information, address State University of New York
Press, State University Plaza, Albany, N.Y., 12246

Library of Congress Cataloging-in-Publication Data

The dimensions of time and the challenge of school reform / edited by
    Patricia Gándara.
        p.   cm. — (SUNY series, restructuring and school change)
    Includes bibliographical references and index.
    ISBN 0-7914-4357-4 (hc : alk. paper). — ISBN 0-7914-4358-2 (pb :
alk. paper)
    1. Schedules, School—United States. 2. Time management—United
States. 3. Educational change—United States. I. Gandara,
Patricia C. II. Series.
LB3032.D55 2000
    371.2'42—DC21   98-52441
                                                                 CIP

10 9 8 7 6 5 4 3 2 1

CONTENTS

INTRODUCTION

Patricia Gándara

All of our perceptions of self and world are mediated by the way we imagine, explain, use and implement time.

—Jeremy Rifkin, Time Wars

No single aspect of life is more fundamental to the way we, as humans, experience our existence than our concept of time, and no concept is more inclined to metamorphose across cultures—both macro-cultures and micro-cultures. While people living in the United States *generally* privilege time as measured by the clock, other cultures, even some that share space with us on this continent, privilege event time—time as measured by the passage of human events (Levine, 1997). A culture that privileges event time places greater importance on the consummation of an interpersonal activity—no matter how long that takes—than on an adherence to a schedule that orders a series of activities without regard to the interpersonal demands each might impose. Thus, while in the U.S., a high school principal may set up a series of meetings, scheduled at half hour intervals, with the expectation that people will take their leave at the appointed time, regardless of whether they assess their needs to have been met, a more event-oriented culture would find this practice simply abhorrent. However, modern cultures are not monolithic in this regard. Even within our own clock-oriented culture, there are occasions and places where event time is the more appropriate and "productive" way to organize experience, when the needs of people must be put ahead of the demands of the schedule. Likewise, modern event-oriented cultures can accommodate to the demands of clock-oriented business and commerce when necessary. However, the consequences of these very different ways of experiencing time can be great when applied to the organization of learning in cross-cultural contexts—whether they be the different macro-cultures of students and teachers or the different

1

micro-cultures that exist within institutions of learning.

Much has been written about the relationship between time and learning and a considerable body of knowledge now exists in this area. Likewise, the past decade and a half has spawned numerous studies on school reform—what works, what doesn't, and why. And, while many school reform studies have called attention to time as an important factor in school change, few have systematically investigated time as a critical element in school reform. Moreover, from study to study, time is typically talked about as though it were unidimensional and as if there were actually a shared understanding of *what* time is. Yet, time can take on radically different meanings across contexts and, in fact, there may be very little consensus about the nature of time from one context to the next.

To be sure, time is a social construct that marks the passage of events. Within mainstream American culture clocks are the metaphor for this kind of time, and the ticking of the clock represents the passage of time measured according to this metric. Cycles are another way of representing time, and the symbol of this kind of time is the calendar, marking the seasons as they come and go and reappear again. Time can also be a prism through which events are interpreted. Depending on one's perspective, the time associated with any particular event may weigh heavily or may be fleeting. Time is also a way of marking rhythms—the beating of a heart, or the sounds of a classroom as children move from silent reading to the excitement of a group science project. Hence, time can be an entity unto itself, a metric by which other things are measured, a way of organizing our thinking, and a perspective that can shape the way we experience the world around us. In addressing issues of time and school reform, there are at least two ways in which time can be conceptualized globally—as *content:* an entity that is managed and manipulated in school reform efforts, and as *process:* a factor that shapes how individuals experience efforts to create school change.

TIME AS THE CONTENT OF SCHOOL REFORM

To state the obvious, there is a relationship between the amount of time invested in learning and the quantity and quality of learning that occurs for any given group of students. Hence, at this level, the potential importance of time as an element in school reform is transparent—one way to increase student achievement is to manipulate time. However, the relationship between time and student achievement is not necessarily linear, and more time devoted to instruction does not always result in more learning. The reason for this is that time may take on many forms in instructional contexts: allotted time, engaged time, time on task, and academic learning time are but a few. Allotted time is the time that is provided for instruction in administrative plans; for example, fifty-five minutes per day are mandated for mathematics instruction. Engaged time refers to the time that students are actually engaged in doing mathematics in the math class. This may be only forty-five of the fifty-five allotted minutes, or even much less, after time spent on nonacademic tasks and activities is deducted (cf. Karweit, 1989). Time on task is the engaged time that is actually devoted to learning particular tasks—learning how to do long division, for example (Berliner, 1990). Academic learning time is the time that a student spends successfully engaged in on-task behavior that is aligned with achievement objectives (Berliner, 1990). Each form of learning time has some relationship to learning outcomes; however, the strength of these relationships remains a hotly debated topic.

It has been demonstrated that the relationship between allotted time and learning outcomes is relatively weak (Karweit, 1989), but the relationship between time on task or academic learning time and learning outcomes is almost certainly much greater (Berliner, 1990). Some investigators are optimistic that increased learning time can have a significant impact on learning outcomes (Wiley & Harnischfeger, 1974; Berliner, 1990; Walberg, 1993). Others are much less optimistic, citing the complexity of learning contexts, the ways in which multiple dimensions of time can conflict with each other, and the manner in which school structures place firm boundaries on how much can be learned independent of time (Karweit, 1989).

One important variable that is often neglected in the discussion of the effects of time on learning, however, is the concept of *time needed for learning*. J. B. Carroll (1963) proposed a model that took this into account. His model demonstrated that learning is a function of the amount of time needed to learn something divided by the time allotted for instruction. As the ratio approaches 1, optimal learning should occur. Either exceeding 1 or failing to attain it does not result in optimal learning. That is, neither insufficient time nor more time than is needed will produce optimal results. More time than is needed can prove wasteful, and even lead to boredom and a decline in performance (Kulik & Kulik, 1984). Berliner (1990) refers to Carroll's model as the result of a "moment of genius" in which aptitude/intelligence is converted into "a simple time variable," thereby obviating the usefulness of a theory of genetically driven intelligence.

In Chapter 1, Lorin Anderson links Carroll's model of learning with a model of school reform, elucidating how the Carroll model can account for time as a function of effective school reform. Anderson's analysis serves not only to organize our thinking about time and learning in the context of school reforms that purport to increase the achievement of students, but provides organizing principles for looking at the role of time in creating school reform itself. This provides us with one lens through which to understand time's impact, and its potential, on efforts at school change.

In Chapter 2, written by Susanna Purnell and Robert Reichardt, the authors show how schools participating in the New American Schools project defined their need for time and how they found the time to create the schoolwide reforms they had proposed. Here time is viewed as a commodity that must be bargained for and the authors, while making the argument that school reform is critically dependent on the availability of time for teachers to engage in the process of change, demonstrate the strategies that schools use in order to acquire that time. Interestingly, they conclude that districts that are more decentralized, and therefore grant more autonomy to local schools, are not necessarily at an advantage in finding time for reform.

Catherine Minicucci, in Chapter 3, reports on a national study of exemplary programs for English Language Learners and recounts how, in the most successful programs reviewed by the study, time was the critical variable that allowed these children to be included in reform initiatives. Minicucci asserts that the schools that successfully reformed to benefit English Language Learners devised inventive ways to maximize both the quantity and quality of time available for students to learn and for teachers to plan instruction. Four major strategies they employed included: (1) providing longer periods of time for in-depth study; (2) eliminating interruptions such as school bells and giving control of time over to the teacher; (3) extending time for learning through summer and intersessions and before and after school; and (4) providing the opportunity for students to remain with the same teacher(s) for more than a single year. Minicucci's chapter is especially valuable in detailing actual practices in a national sample of schools deemed to be highly successful with students learning English.

Chapter 4 recounts an experiment undertaken in three California schools to reorganize time with both student and teacher outcomes in mind. The great bulk of reform studies have focused on student outcomes as the critical dependent variable. This study pointedly looked at teacher working conditions—satisfaction, turnover, burnout, and salaries—as important indicators of successful reform. In this chapter Patricia Gándara argues that school reform will not be ultimately successful unless it takes into account not just the effectiveness of teachers, but also their needs and the satisfaction they feel with their jobs, and that this is a dimension of school reform that has received too little attention. The experiment reported on in this chapter provided the opportunity for teachers to simultaneously restructure their curricula and methods of instructional delivery, and to dramatically increase their salaries and improve their working conditions by reorganizing time.

In Chapter 5, Carolyn Kneese reports on a study of year-round schooling and its effects on the academic peformance of educationally "at-risk" students in one Texas school district. In this carefully designed study, Kneese attempts to answer the question of whether a year-round school calendar (reducing the length of out-of-school periods) can result in higher achievement for educationally "at-risk" (low-performing) students when compared to similar students on a regular school calendar. She also asks the question if the effects may be cumulative over time. Kneese reports that, based on her data, the year-round schedule did result in better achievement outcomes for the "at-risk" students. However, the differences between the YRE students and the traditional calendar students was not due to achievement gains of YRE pupils. Rather, it resulted from the fact that they did not suffer the achievement losses that the students in the traditional calendar schools experienced. While somewhat disconcerting, this is nonetheless further evidence to support the contention that summer learning losses can be especially detrimental for "at-risk" students. Kneese also reports evidence that the effects are cumulative over time for students in the YRE program. This study provides an interesting complement to some of the more ethnographic work reported in this volume in that it makes the argument, on more quantitative grounds, that time can be a potent variable in school reform efforts for special populations of students.

In Chapter 6, Judy Fish recounts the story of one district grappling with dual concerns: burgeoning school populations that cannot be accommodated in the existing space available, and a desire to institute radical reforms to drive up student achievement. Fish provides a real "on the ground" picture of how one district addressed these two concerns simultaneously, with interlocking reforms focused on the reorganization of time that were designed to serve both purposes. Her tale, however, is not one with a simple happy ending. While the district innovated in new and radical ways, and increased the satisfaction of both its parents and its teachers, changes in the demographics of the district have continued to require new responses and the rethinking of reforms that have already become outdated in some ways. Rather than a snapshot taken by a researcher who comes into a district for a period of time and documents a particular change effort, this is a moving picture of the challenge of creating change in the midst of a dynamic community. The lessons of this chapter are sobering for anyone who might have thought that school reform could be a completed act.

TIME AS PROCESS IN SCHOOL REFORM

Allan Pitman and Tom Romberg's chapter (7) serves as a bridge between the notions of time as content and time as process. They look at the content of reform in a series of case studies of mathematics reform efforts but conclude that process may be more important than content in understanding why some reforms take and others don't. The authors conclude that teachers' use of time is an important empirical indicator of their acceptance of reform, and quite possibly as a measure of the effectiveness of the reforms themselves. It is instructive that in four case studies involving six schools, only one of these schools actually used time differently to promote their reform objectives. Unfortunately, this is probably quite representative of the real challenge; it may be unrealistic to expect that more than 15 percent or 20 percent of schools, classrooms, or teachers will truly embrace change. Pitman and Romberg provide a key to why this may be in their analyses of the contexts in which teachers work. They suggest that the rhythms of lives of teachers affect their willingness to dedicate time to reflection on practice, and hence to reform. Teachers, like students, do not experience school in a vacuum. Time pressures and rhythms outside school affect what goes on inside of schools. This assertion also echoes Gándara's finding that teachers' enthusiasm for a radically redesigned year-round school schedule depended to a large extent on where they were in their career and life cycles. And, like Jon Wagner's findings on school reform in secondary schools in Chapter 8, these teachers were only willing to expend time on reform efforts if they believed that the reform was "real." While Pitman and Romberg have been at the forefront of curricular development in mathematics, their insightful comments remind us that school reform is not *just* about better instruction—it is also about understanding that schools and the people inside of them are complex, multilayered, and dynamic and that they actively construct their own interpretations of the reform efforts in which they are engaged.

Such constructivist interpretations of time help to explain its impact on school change and on the ways in which we go about trying to create change, or prevent it from occurring. Cambone (1995) has proposed that time can be constructed *rationally* (as in fifteen minutes will be allowed to complete the quiz), *phenomenologically* (as in the subjective experience of time—it "flies" for the student who is rushing to complete an assignment, and "drags" for the student who hates the material), and *cyclically* (as in the school year has always begun in September and any attempt to change that violates a strongly held value about the bounded space that school fills in our lives). Within these different constructions of time, Cambone argues that time is divided into many different dimensions, and is experienced in very different ways by the people in schools. In particular, he argues that while adminstrators may experience time as monochronic and sequential, with each task assigned its own time frame, teachers' work is framed polychronically, with several tasks being attended to at once and many having overlapping time frames. Moreover, the differing organizations of time in which, for example, teachers may protect "student time" or "class preparation time" from other intrusions can create different expectations about how time should be used. Failing to pay attention to these differences can result in a "clash between administrators and teachers over how teacher time will be used, and how quickly it is used, [that] highlights the role of power and politics in understanding time for teachers in school restructuring" (p. 521).

Thus, time is not just time, but a political resource as well. The use of time in schools requires that important decisions be made about how this resource will be distributed and who will wield the power over its distribution. As in all of politics, there can be very different ideas about the appropriate use of scarce resources, and when one group finds itself in a less powerful position, it can resort to tactics such as alliance building or even civil disobedience in order to make its case or protect its assets.

This more constructivist rendering of time helps to explain why, in spite of careful planning and strict adherence to tried and proven models, time continues to be a significant factor in realizing or failing to effect school change. Wagner's essay in Chapter 8 is an excellent accounting of such subjectively experienced time and how it intrudes on well-ordered notions of rational time in school restructuring. Wagner introduces his own taxonomy of time from the perspective of high schools attempting to reform themselves. He reflects on some of the ways in which school teachers and administrators use different conceptions of time in proposing and accounting for changes occurring in their schools. In certain ways, this essay echoes one of the observations made by Fish in Chapter 6 as she recounted the different "lenses" through which teachers, administrators, and community viewed their school restructuring efforts. While Wagner cites three different ways in which school personnel in reforming schools represent time (as a resource, as a template, and as a meaurement), he finds that in reality school change is highly dependent upon dynamic forces within schools—events that cannot be predicted but that shape the life of the school. Time and again, Wagner finds that teachers report change occurring as the result of particular "turning points," "crises," or "moments of special opportunity." Wagner suggests that describing phenomena of school change requires not only attention to different conceptions of time, but the different ways in which time is an actor in the school reform process—hence bureaucratic time (time organized for specific tasks within agreed-upon "frames") and dramatic time (evidenced by events that occur outside these organized frames) both play a role in defining the process of school change.

Mary Lee Smith and Audrey Noble's study of time in Chapter 9 reminds us that the success or failure of school reform efforts is not only dependent upon time allotted, but it is measured according to different clocks: the politicians' clock, the professionals' clock, and the teachers' clock. Depending on which clock one looks at, the pace will differ and the nature of "successful" outcomes will be defined differently. For the politician, Noble and Smith assert, change must occur within one term of office and must produce something like a tangible outcome—an improved test score, for example. For the professional, who is not immediately accountable for change, the clock may run at variable speeds, depending on the resources available and the size of the challenge. Change is measured as conceptual transformation. The teachers' clock is slow, recognizing the complexity of change when it involves many individuals with varying skills and abilities and varying levels of commitment to the process of change. It will depend on resources and the climate created for change. It will be measured in terms of differences in processes within the classroom. Hence, these authors argue that the success or failure of Arizona's and Delaware's statewide mandates to revamp standards and assessments was to be found in the eye of the beholder. In Arizona's case, politicians, needing a new issue and lacking the time and failing to provide the resources to realize the "old" initiative, deemed their reform a failure. In Delaware, where more resources were provided and political conditions were different, the clock was allowed to run a little longer, and politicians deemed the experiment a success. However, teachers in both states remained considerably more skeptical. Their clocks indicated that much more time was necessary to draw any conclusions about the reforms' effectiveness.

Another theme that is sounded in this volume is the difference between time experienced as clock-time—time passing, measured time, and time experienced as rhythms—the ups and downs, the denouements and the crescendos of life as it is lived. Both of these are ways of knowing time, but each yields a very different experience of time. They are hardly reconcilable, yet in efforts at reforming schools, we often pay little attention to these differing notions, and experiences, of time. John Lofty's essay (Chapter 10) is an intriguing look at the rhythms of life as experienced by students in a Maine fishing community and the rhythms of schooling—and how the two conflict. Lofty argues that the insensitivity to life rhythms experienced by some students, perhaps even by most, as they enter the world of schooling, can create great impediments to learning, and to learning to write in particular. He shows how the notion of "doing something until it is done" comes in conflict with the high school teacher's admonition to prewrite, edit, and rewrite—strategies that are central to the writing process but anathema to students who have been taught to earn their living by finishing a task quickly in order to move rapidly on to the next. Lofty also argues that the structuring of time for students reifies the power relationships between students and teachers, a situation that immediately puts the two at odds. In this insightful essay, Lofty raises questions about time that are not often articulated in the literature, but surely are at the heart of what the reform movement is trying to achieve.

In Chapter 11, Laurie Olsen and Ann Jaramillo describe a collaboration between California Tomorrow, a nonprofit organization dedicated to fostering positive intergroup relations among the diverse populations of that state, and the Mellon Foundation, aimed at restructuring a school that serves primarily immigrant students. Olsen and Jaramillo point out the special challenges of educating immigrant students—they enter American schools with vastly different levels of preparation, many come from war-torn countries and/or have experienced traumatic events in migrating to the United States; they typically move frequently in search of stable housing and employment, and sometimes they migrate back and forth from home country to the United States. Unique to this experiment, the researchers helped the school to find its own solutions to its particular dilemmas by putting together a group of teachers, administrators, and students to identify the issues and design the reforms to be instituted. Students had a major voice in the redesign of the school. It was their concerns that drove many of the changes—such as their desire for more time to study subjects in-depth and a redesigned calendar that allowed them to make up time if they came into the school after the official September school opening. Olsen and Jaramillo note the central importance of time in the students' perceptions of how the school needed to change to respond to their special needs, and alert us to the importance of listening to students, as well as teachers, when we invent school reform.

For most of us it would be impossible to imagine living our lives without a clock. The clock orders and organizes our days into all the compartmentalized spaces of time that allow us to function in a complex world with multiple demands. Likewise, the act of misplacing our calendars, with all the appointments, the places we must be, and the things we must do, slotted into circumscribed blocks of time, is tantamount to losing control of our lives. Why should we think that time is any less important in schools where the day is often broken into even smaller and more compact units, with dozens of goals to be met each day?

Unfortunately, while acknowledging that time may be a factor in school reform, most school reform efforts do not go any deeper into trying to understand how, when activities are reordered or new items are added to the agenda of the school, all of the content and the process of schooling are affected. When manipulating time *is itself the primary reform,* it is critical to understand the processes that such actions set in motion and it is necessary to pay attention to the different, and often conflicting, notions of time that people in schools hold. When the content of reform focuses on other aspects of schooling, it is nonetheless imperative that reformers consider the ways in which perceptions and experiences of time can become a key variable in the success or failure of their efforts. Our hope is that this book will make more explicit some of the multiple dimensions of time and challenge readers to think of time in the context of school reform in new and more complex ways.

REFERENCES

Berliner, D. C. (1990). What's all the fuss about instructional time? In M. Ben-Peretz and R. Bromme (Eds.), *The nature of time in schools* (pp. 3–35). New York: Teachers College Press.

Cambone, J. (1995). Time for teachers. *Teachers College Record, 96,* 512–543.

Carroll, J. B. (1963). A model of school learning. *Teachers College Record, 64,* 723–733.

Karweit, N. (1989). Time and learning: A review. In R. Slavin (Ed.) *School and classroom organization* (pp. 69–95). Hillsdale, NJ: Erlbaum.

Kulik, J. A., & Kulik, C. L. (1984). Effects of accelerated instruction on students. *Review of Educational Research, 54,* 409–425.

Levine, R. (1997). A geography of time, the temporal misadventures of a social psychologist. New York: Basic Books.

Rifkin, J. (1987). Time Wars. New York: Henry Holt (quote is from page 1).

Walberg, H. J. (1993). Productive use of time. In L. W. Anderson and H. J. Walberg (Eds.), *Timepiece: Extending and enhancing learning time.* Reston, VA: National Association of Secondary School Principals.

Wiley, D., & Harnischfeger, A. (1974). Explosion of a myth: Quantity of schooling and exposure to instruction, major educational vehicles. *Educational Researcher, 3,* 7–12.

PART I

Conceptualizing Time
and School Reform

CHAPTER 1

Time, Learning, and School Reform: A Conceptual Framework

Lorin W. Anderson

Time is related to school reform in at least two ways. First, time can be part of the *content* of reform. Arguably, the primary historical example of this is the attempt on the part of the board of trustees of the Carnegie Foundation for the Advancement of Teaching to regularize and quantify high school credits in terms of time (Pritchett, 1906). As a result of this effort, a four-year high school program was defined as the completion or acquisition of 14 Carnegie units (Krug, 1969). During the first third of this century, concerns for time were incorporated into the reform of curriculum (Bobbitt, 1918; Rugg, 1926), teaching and learning (Thorndike, 1913), and teacher preparation (Morrison, 1926).

Second, time, almost by definition, is an important aspect of the reform *process*. In Chapter 11 of this volume, Olsen and Jaramillo state the obvious: "Change takes time." Meaningful educational reform requires conceptualizing, planning, training, implementing, monitoring, and adjusting. In light of this, it is not surprising that Hall and Hord (1987) concluded that changes in education require two to three years before they yield results. However, because the "political clock" that is used to measure the success of reform efforts runs very rapidly (Noble & Smith, Chapter 9), many current reform programs do not have the luxury of this much time. Consequently, an increasing number of educational commentators have wondered whether meaningful educational reform is even possible (e.g., Sarason, 1990).

Whether as content or as process, the way in which time is allocated and used by students and by teachers is an important element of school reform. But time is only one piece of a very complex puzzle. Too often reform efforts, like modern political campaigns, are formulated around single issues (e.g., extending or restructuring the school year, lengthening the class period). The impact these changes have on teachers, students, administrators, and parents, and the ways in which these groups react to or act upon these changes are likely to be far more important to the success or failure of school reform than the mere shifting of time.

In order to understand the proper role of time in school reform, then, a conceptual framework is needed. One such framework, Carroll's (1963) Model of School Learning (MSL), has proven extremely useful in understanding the relationship between time and student learning. It has the potential of helping us understand the relationship between time and teacher learning, notably, the type of teacher learning that is essential to meaningful, enduring school reform.

THE CARROLL MODEL OF SCHOOL LEARNING

According to the MSL, the degree of learning is some function of the extent to which a student *actually spends* the amount of time he or she *needs to spend* in order to learn and learn well. Thus:

Degree of learning = f (time actually spent/time needed)

Furthermore, the time needed to learn is influenced by the student's aptitude for learning, his or her ability to understand instruction, and the quality of instruction he or she receives. In contrast, time actually spent learning is influenced by the student's perseverence and the opportunity to learn (i.e., the amount of time) he or she is provided.[1]

Although on the surface the model appears fairly simple, in reality it is quite complex. This complexity stems largely from the relationships among the factors that influence time spent and time needed. Beginning with the denominator of the fraction, Carroll argued that the best estimate of time needed to learn is the student's aptitude. In fact, he defined a student's aptitude as the minimum amount of time a student would need to reach some prespecified level of learning under ideal instructional conditions.[2] That is, the higher the student's aptitude, the less time he or she needs to learn.

Poor quality of instruction and difficulty understanding instruction both increase the amount of time a student will need to spend in order to learn beyond that required by virtue of the student's aptitude. There is, however, an inverse relationship between quality of instruction and ability to understand instruction. Students with lower abilities to understand instruction require a higher quality of instruction. Conversely, if instruction is of extremely low quality, students will need a great deal of ability to understand it (Carroll, 1963).

In terms of his model, Carroll hypothesized that if a student is able to understand the instruction provided (i.e., if there is a "match" between quality of instruction and ability to understand instruction), no additional time will be needed beyond that determined by the student's aptitude. At the other extreme, if a student completely lacks the ability to understand the instruction provided (e.g., instruction is given in English to a student who understands only Spanish), the student will need an infinite amount of time to learn (i.e., he or she will never learn). The total amount of time needed to learn, then, is equal to the amount of time needed because of the student's aptitude, adjusted, as necessary, for the discrepancy between the student's ability to understand instruction and the quality of the instruction provided.

Time spent learning is also determined by the interaction among the factors. In fact, time spent learning involves an interaction among all five factors. Specifically, Carroll (1963) stated that time spent learning "will be equal to the smallest of the following three quantities: (1) opportunity—the time allowed for learning, (2) perseverance—the amount of time the learner is willing to engage actively in learning, and (3) aptitude—the amount of time needed to learn, increased by whatever amount necessary in view of poor quality of instruction and lack of ability to understand less than optimal instruction" (p. 730). It must be emphasized that quantity (3) is identical to the denominator of the fraction (i.e., time needed).

Carroll provided a rationale for defining time spent in learning as the smallest of the three quantities. "(I)t is assumed that the individual will stop work as soon as he [or she] either (1) learns the task to the specified criterion of mastery (that is, spends the time needed), (2) spends an amount of time denoted by . . . [perseverance], or (3) is precluded from completing his [or her] learning because of the expiration of time as denoted by . . . [opportunity to learn], whichever of these events occurs earliest" (p. 731).

Part of the brilliance of Carroll's model stems from his definition of all factors in terms of time. These temporal definitions move the model out of the realm of the abstract into the arena of the empirically testable. In fact, a series of empirical tests of the model was conducted during the 1970s and early 1980s (see, for example, Anderson, 1973; Arlin, 1973; Block, 1970; Fisher, Berliner, Filby, Marliave, Cahen, & Dishaw, 1980; Gettinger, 1984a, 1984b, 1985; Gettinger & White, 1977, 1979; Millman, Bieger, Klag, & Pine, 1983; Powell, 1980). In combination, these studies yielded the following results.

- Both time needed to learn and time spent learning were related to student achievement. However, time needed to learn was a stronger predictor of student achievement than was time spent learning. In addition, time needed to learn was a stronger predictor of achievement than were scores on traditional intelligence tests.

- The more time students were engaged in learning, the higher their achievement. However, spending less time than was needed resulted in decreased student achievement. Furthermore, spending more time than was needed did *not* result in increased achievement.

- The more time allocated to a particular content area (e.g., word recognition skills, the whole number multiplication algorithm), the greater the student achievement in that content area. Also, the more time allocated to a particular content area, the more similar the achievement of different students in that content area.

- With high quality of instruction, the variation in time needed to learn across students decreased over a series of learning units. Quality of instruction is enhanced by (1) teacher's accuracy in diagnosing student knowledge and skill levels, (2) more substantive interaction between the student and his or her teacher, (3) the provision of specific feedback to students about their learning, and (4) engaging students in activities to correct their errors and misunderstandings.

THE CARROLL MODEL AND THE
CONTENT OF SCHOOL REFORM

In the Carroll model, the critical factors are directly or indirectly defined in terms of time. As I have written elsewhere (Anderson, 1985), time is simply a metric, that is, a unit of measurement. All of the factors included in the model must be taken into consideration if we are to understand and ultimately enhance student learning.

In terms of the Carroll model, current reform efforts pertaining to time generally focus on increasing students' opportunity to learn. Block scheduling, for example, increases the amount of time allocated to a specific subject matter during a given day. Year-round education either increases the number of days students spend in school or rearranges the school calendar so that the "number of school days is the same as in a traditional calendar school, but the spacing between school attendance periods is decreased" (Kneese, Chapter 5, this volume).

Within the Carroll model, opportunity to learn is only one of the two factors influencing time spent learning. Students must take advantage of that opportunity (i.e., they must persevere)! In this regard, Lofty (Chapter 10) comments on the difficulty he experienced when asking his students to work productively for a whole fifty-minute period. Far more attention needs to be paid by school reformers to what motivates students to pay attention and engage in learning for extended periods of time.

The other factors of the Carroll model—aptitude, ability to understand instruction, and quality of instruction—tend to be ignored in many reform efforts. However, they routinely are mentioned in calls for reform. Ability to understand instruction is a major problem in any attempt to educate students with limited English proficiency. As Olsen and Jaramillo (Chapter 11) write:

> While most immigrant students learn conversational English relatively quickly, they generally need four to ten years to become fluent enough to really comprehend the language and use it as a *medium of academic learning*. (emphasis mine)

And, in the Carroll model, inability to understand instruction can move the time needed to learn toward infinity.

Similarly, there is a general recognition that quality of instruction must be improved if time is to be used effectively and efficiently. As Pitman and Romberg (Chapter 7) assert:

> Any consideration of teachers' use of time must go beyond simple organizational aspects or whether a given teacher is employing certain materials or curricula. Such consideration must also explore teachers' interpretations of the curricular materials, their professional backgrounds, their school contexts, and their own concepts of [their subject matters].

Pitman and Romberg then go on to summarize studies in which teachers, "despite much use of the language of reform," adhere to their textbooks, adapt reform programs to their own beliefs by making "fundamental decisions about the allocation of their teaching time and about the character of that time," engage in the "routines of schoolwork," and find changes in classroom routines "unsettling." Furthermore, their emphasis on coverage of topics makes it unlikely that the amount of time many students need in order to learn well will be provided.

Redefining aptitude in terms of the amount of time a student needs in order to learn, rather than his or her capacity for learning, seems central to meaningful school reform. If aptitude is indeed capacity to learn, why change schools? No matter how schools are configured, no matter what curriculum is taught, no matter how teaching proceeds, students with the necessary capacity will learn while those without it will not. It is only when aptitude is defined in terms of time needed to learn that increasing opportunity to learn can be justified.

One final comment about the Carroll model in the context of the content of reform is needed. Even as early as the 1970s and 1980s, researchers struggled with the phrase "time spent learning." Some replaced it with "time-on-task"; others with "academically engaged time." While these are related, they are not synonymous. The phrase "time-on-task" focuses attention on the tasks on which students spend their time. Are the tasks relevant and meaningful? Do they emphasize rote learning or "higher-order" thinking? Are they the types of tasks students are likely to encounter on "high-stakes" tests?

In contrast, "academically engaged time" emphasizes what students "do" during that time. Do their minds wander? Do they attempt to memorize what is being said or read? Are they attempting to make sense of what they are being told? Quite clearly, academically engaged time is more in line with the current knowledge base of cognitive psychology. Furthermore, Lofty (Chapter 10) argues that what he terms "existential time" is "marked by a deep engagement in the activity at hand, whether in school or at home, that allows an individual to become a particular person."

Both emphases are essential for understanding "time spent learning." The tasks students are assigned or select must be worthwhile. At the same time, students must be "deeply engaged" in the process of learning. Inherent in these two interpretations of time spent learning is the opportunity to "transform learning to ensure that time in school will be much more meaningful than a monochrome 'succession of days' or the mere accumulation of credits toward graduation" (Lofty, Chapter 10). And as MacMullen (1996) has asserted: "The evidence is unequivocal that student learning must be at the center of reform efforts, and that schools involved in restructuring must maintain that focus consistently" (p. 55).

THE CARROLL MODEL AND THE
PROCESS OF SCHOOL REFORM

In addition to informing the content of reform, the Carroll model enables us to understand the process. As in the case of student learning, the model predicts that school reform will be successful to the extent that those involved in the reform process spend the time they need to spend in order to make the reform "work."

Before the Carroll model can be applied to school reform, however, two problems must be addressed. First, the language used in the reform literature has to be translated into the language of the model. Specifically, words such as "readiness," "vision," "commitment," "adoption," and "ownership" must be linked with the constructs included in the model. Once these linkages have been made, relationships of these constructs with time spent and time needed become obvious.

Second, unlike learning, school reform is a group endeavor. In order to understand the success or failure of reform efforts we must know something about teachers in general, not just about individual teachers. For example, commitment is a construct typically discussed in the reform literature (Louis & Miles, 1992; Thomas, 1994). While commitment is said to play an important role in reform efforts, little is known about the number or type of teachers who must be committed to making the change, the level of commitment that is needed, and/or the balance between teacher and administrator commitment that produces successful reform.

In light of this uncertainty, the Carroll model cannot be subjected to empirical examination. Rather, within the context of school reform, the model is best considered an heuristic framework. The *Random House College Dictionary* defines "heuristic" as "stimulating interest as a means of furthering investigation." Heuristic frameworks are valued for the thought and dialogue they stimulate—thought and dialogue that often lead to new insights and understandings. In this section, each of the factors in the Carroll model will be revisited, this time with an eye on the process rather than the content of school reform.

Aptitude

In the reform literature, aptitude can be equated with readiness. Like aptitude, readiness is a multifaceted construct—a combination of knowledge, skills, and beliefs. Readiness requires that expertise is or will be made available; that is, teachers and administrators either must possess or have access to the knowledge and skills they need to make and sustain the change (Thomas, 1994). In this regard, capacity building is frequently cited as a key component of successful school reform (Levin, 1995; Peterson, 1996; see also Olsen & Jaramillo, Chapter 11). But readiness for change also requires a formal recognition that change is needed (Rosenblum & Louis, 1979) and that it is desirable (Murphy, 1991). It also requires a belief that the reform effort, if successful, will result in substantial improvement (Fullan, 1994). As Nobel and Smith state in Chapter 9, "to make change is not a matter of simply acquiring new skills, but of requiring a change in ideological orientation."

There also are negative indicators of readiness. One of the most widely recognized is teachers' and administrators' previous experience with reform efforts that were not successful or were jettisoned before success could be determined. Fullan (1994) has summarized the impact of this experience in the following terms: "The more teachers or others have had negative experiences with previous innovation in the district or elsewhere, the more cynical or apathetic they will be about the new change presented, regardless of the merit of the new idea or program" (p. 2842).

Within the Carroll model, readiness predicts the amount of time needed to successfully implement school reform. Schools in which large numbers of teachers fail to understand the need for change or view change as desirable, see little if any possibility that the specific program being implemented will result in meaningful change, and do not possess the type or level of expertise required to carry out the change will require a substantial amount of time to make reform a reality. Conversely, where all these readiness elements are present, a shorter period of time will be needed.

Ability to Understand Instruction and Quality of Instruction

In the context of school reform, ability to understand instruction is analogous to the ability to understand the reform as it is experienced by those responsible for adopting, implementing, and/or sustaining it . Many reforms are difficult to understand. This difficulty stems in part from aspects of the reform itself (e.g., complexity) and in part from the way the reform is presented (e.g., lack of clarity).

As defined by Thomas (1994), complexity refers to the "number of different elements of the educational system that are involved in the change" (p. 1852). Many reform efforts are quite complex. Consider reforms conducted under the auspices of the Coalition of Essential Schools, for example. There are nine Common Principles. Four of the principles express the Coalition's beliefs about the intellectual purpose of schools. Similarly, four principles express beliefs about the relationships among members of the school community and are intended to promote a sense of community in the school. The ninth principle speaks more to implementation than belief (MacMullen, 1996). Nine principles of three different "types" makes for a fairly complex reform. And the greater the complexity, the more difficult it is to understand the reform.

A lack of clarity about the reform also impacts negatively on the ability to understand it. This lack of clarity may pertain to the desired ends, the means to these ends, or both (Fullan, 1994). Clarity is problematic in many reforms because of the catch phrases and special terminology necessary for understanding. Those associated with Accelerated Schools use phrases such as "unity of purpose," "empowerment coupled with responsibility," and "building on strengths" (Levin, 1995), which have quite specific meanings within this reform effort. At the same time, the phrases are reasonably abstract and thus subject to multiple interpretations. Multiple interpretations result *from* a lack of clarity and result *in* an inability to understand the reform.

In the Carroll model, quality of instruction is highly interrelated with the ability to understand instruction. Thus, an examination of quality of instruction should begin with the results of the analysis of ability to understand instruction. In this regard, it seems obvious that the solution to the lack of clarity problem is clarity. What is not obvious is what clarity means from an instructional perspective within the context of school reform. The literature does provide some clues, however.

Little (1986) suggested that clarity can be enhanced through explicit "shared agreements." These agreements pertain to the "promise of the program ideas, . . . the nature of the roles and relationships required of teachers and principals, and the adequacy of the description [of the reform effort] to reflect an actual sequence of implementation" (p. 31).

Clarity also requires that teachers and administrators have access to written material about the reform and engage in dialogue about what they have read (Gibboner, 1994). When those involved in school reform engage in a meaningful dialogue of what they have read, they are more likely to gain "shared understanding [and] shared investment," which will result in "thoughtful development and the fair, rigorous test of selected ideas" (Little, 1986, p. 35).

Finally, clarity is enhanced when teachers and administrators have opportunities to see the program or programs in operation. Site visits, then, contribute to clarity (Ward & Pascarelli, 1987).

In summary, clarity, like change, takes time. In the California Tomorrow project described by Olsen and Jaramillo (Chapter 11), teachers

- went on a retreat before school began;
- engaged in voluntary after-school meetings;
- had a professional development coach who observed in the teachers' classrooms;
- visited schools noted for innovative approaches to curriculum and instruction; and,
- participated in eight sessions after school let out for the summer.

All of these activities quite likely enhanced clarity.

As mentioned earlier, complexity is a second problem associated with difficulty in understanding reform. What aspect of quality of instruction can address complexity? One answer to this question appears to be the communication of "vision" (Louis & Miles, 1992: MacMullen, 1996). Louis and Miles (1992) emphasize that vision involves two dimensions:

> the first is a sharable, and shared vision of what the *school* could look like; it provides direction and drive power for change, and criteria for

> steering and choosing. . . . The second type is a shared vision of the
> *change process* . . . what will be the general game plan or strategy for
> getting there? (p. 187)

Vision reduces complexity in part because it is visual. Visions can be expressed in terms of pictures, models, figures, and graphs—all of which allow the simultaneous processing of the multiple facets of the reform. A picture is indeed worth a thousand words. But as the Louis and Miles quote reminds us, both dimensions of vision, the *could* and the *how*, must be portrayed.

There are other aspects of quality of instruction. Teachers need opportunities to "try out" the new program in a supportive environment; to learn by doing. Thus, the creation of collaborative work environments (Louis & Miles, 1992; Fullan & Hargreaves, 1991; see also Noble & Smith, Chapter 9) and interactive work structures (MacMullen, 1996) are aspects of instructional quality, as is the role of the principal (MacMullen, 1996).

According to the Carroll model, when the quality of instruction is inadequate in light of teachers' and administrators' ability to understand, instruction time needed to learn is increased. In terms of the process of school reform, the greater the lack of fit between the quality of professional development provided and the ability to understand the reform effort, the more time that will be needed to successfully implement the reform program.

Perseverance

Two concepts used fairly frequently in the reform literature are directly related to perseverance: commitment and relentlessness. Commitment can be defined as the time, energy, and effort that people are willing to devote to the reform effort and the extent to which they remain faithful to that effort in the face of opposition (Thomas, 1994). Louis and Miles (1992) suggested that one of the keys to successful implementation of school reform is the presence of teams of interested persons who are willing to invest time and energy in the effort.

If commitment is lacking, ways must be found to motivate teachers to participate in the reform efforts. Gándara (Chapter 4) identified four such motivating factors: salary, the belief that the program was better for students, enjoyment in working in the school, and a sense of autonomy.

Relentlessness, as defined by Slavin et al. (1996), involves zero tolerance for failure.

> Although the particular elements of [the program] may vary from
> school to school, there is one feature we try to make consistent in all
> schools: a relentless focus on the success of every child. . . . Success

does not come from piling on additional services, but from coordinating human resources around a well-defined goal, constantly assessing progress toward that goal, and *never giving up until success is achieved*. (pp. 49–50) (emphasis mine)

There are several factors that apparently increase the perseverance of school reform efforts. Among the most frequently mentioned are encouragement (Firestone & Corbett, 1988), empowerment (Louis & Miles, 1992), collective responsibility (MacMullen, 1996), and a relatively stable school community (Fullan, 1994; Thomas, 1994).

In the Carroll model, perseverance is defined as the amount of time the learner is willing to engage actively in learning. In terms of the process of school reform, perseverance refers to the amount of time teachers and administrators are willing to engage actively in the reform process. The higher the perseverance, the more time spent on reform; the lower, the less time spent. And, the less time that is spent, the less likely the reform will be successful.

Opportunity to Learn

Carroll defines opportunity to learn simply as the amount of time allowed for learning. This is easily translatable as the amount of time allowed for the reform to work. Insufficient time for school reform has been widely documented. More than a decade ago, Huberman and Miles (1984) concluded that the shorter the time span between the adoption and the implementation of an innovation, the greater the number of problems that arose (Huberman & Miles, 1984).

Fullan has contended that "deeper meaning and solid change must be borne over time" (Fullan, 1994, p. 2841). In this regard, he argued that ongoing, interactive, cumulative professional development is required to develop the new concepts, skills, and behavior needed to make and sustain change in schools.

To complicate matters, however, different groups apparently use different clocks to keep time (Noble & Smith, Chapter 9). As mentioned much earlier, the political clock runs fast. Because of the speed of this clock, politicians emphasize mandated change. Professionals (e.g., leaders of professional associations, members of commissions, consultants, and service providers) have their own clock. The professionals' clock keeps its own time, usually varying by project and issue. Finally, the teachers' clock runs slowly. It measures years, rather than projects (professionals) or terms (politicians).

In the Carroll model, a lack of opportunity to learn restricts the amount of time spent learning. Similarly, insufficient time allowed for school reform decreases the likelihood of success. The political clock would likely measure inadequate time. At the same time, however, too much time (defined in the Carroll model as more time than is needed) does not result in greater likelihood of success. Thus, the teachers' clock may also contribute to the failure of school reform.

Interactions among the Constructs

As was mentioned in an earlier section of this chapter, the complexity of the Carroll model stems primarily from the interaction among the constructs. Similar interactions can be found in the school reform literature. Consider "ownership," for example. Fullan (1994) suggested that ownership requires clarity, skill, and commitment. Using Carroll's terminology, ownership is some combination of ability to understand instruction, aptitude, and perseverance. Thus, skill reduces the time needed to make the reform. Clarity ensures that no additional time is needed beyond that required in light of the skill level. Commitment ensures that those involved in the reform will spend the time needed to spend in order to achieve success.

In the context of the Carroll model, then, ownership implies that the ratio of time spent to time needed approaches 1. As this ratio approaches 1, the likelihood that the reform will be successful likewise approaches 1. Fullan's (1994) closing statement about ownership is consistent with this interpretation. "True ownership is not something that occurs magically at the outset, but rather is something that emerges at the conclusion of a successful change process" (p. 2846).

CLOSING COMMENTS

Understanding time in relation to schooling is difficult because time itself has no inherent meaning. As Olsen and Jaramillo (Chapter 11) conclude: "Time in and of itself is not the answer. It is a resource to use." In developing his model, Carroll (1963) initially selected time "in order to capitalize on the advantages of a scale with a meaningful zero point and equal units of measurement" (p. 724). As humans we attribute meaning to time. When things are slow, time drags; when we are having a good time, time flies. Sometimes time is not even time, as when, for example, time is money. When all is said and done, time is important to us because, as Jackson (1977) reminds us, "it marks the expenditure of a precious commodity—human life" (p. 38).

Teachers spend most of their in-school time in their classrooms teaching. Consequently, they have little time to spend making sweeping changes in the way they teach or the way their schools are run. If their efforts are to be successful, then, reformers must find ways of minimizing the time needed to successfully implement the reform while maximizing the time those involved in the reform will spend on it (Gándara, Chapter 4; Olsen & Jaramillo, Chapter 11).

Several factors are likely to reduce time needed. Among the most promising are a clear understanding of the vision, shared agreements as to the roles and responsibilities of teachers and administrators, shared agreements as to the sequence of steps to be followed during the implementation process, the possession of a "reading knowledge" of the reform, opportunities for professional dialogue based on those readings, opportunities for visits to other schools in which the reform is being implemented successfully, and the presence of a collaborative work environment in the school.

Likewise, several factors can potentially increase the time spent on the reform by teachers and administrators. These include empowerment, encouragement, the acceptance of collective responsibility, the presence of a relatively stable school community, and sufficient time for adoption, preparation, implementation, and institutionalization.

To the extent that time spent is equal to time needed, the Carroll model predicts success. The use of the model as an heuristic framework, then, provides an opportunity for educators to design, analyze, and modify reform efforts that are increasingly likely to achieve their desired ends—to enable all children to learn and learn well.

NOTES

1. A reviewer of an earlier draft of this chapter suggested that the Carroll model was "outdated." I would argue that the model is as relevant today as when it was developed. Certainly, new terminology has been introduced and new measures are available. But they all "fit" within the conceptual framework advanced by Carroll. For example, multiple intelligences are aptitudes. Learning styles quite likely affect ability to understand instruction. Perseverance has been replaced by motivation. In terms of the model, then, multiple intelligences and learning styles would influence the time needed to learn, while motivation would affect the time actually spent learning.

2. In defining aptitude in terms of time needed to learn, Carroll set the traditional definition of aptitude on its head. Traditionally, aptitude has been defined as the ability to learn something in a certain amount of time. For example, musical aptitude is the ability to learn music quickly. When time is held constant, achievement varies in direct proportion to aptitude. But what would happen if rather than holding time constant we held the level of achievement constant? Then time would vary in direct proportion to aptitude. In this case, aptitude would reflect the time needed to learn.

REFERENCES

Anderson, L. W. (1973). *Time and school learning.* Unpublished doctoral dissertation, University of Chicago.

Anderson, L. W. (1985). *Perspectives on school learning: Selected writings of John B. Carroll.* Hillsdale, NJ: Lawrence Erlbaum Associates.

Arlin, M. (1973). *Learning rate and learning rate variance under mastery learning conditions.* Unpublished doctoral dissertation, University of Chicago.

Block, J. H. (1970). *Student learning and the setting of mastery performance standards.* Unpublished doctoral dissertation, University of Chicago.

Bobbitt, F. (1918). *The curriculum.* Boston: Houghton Mifflin.

Carroll, J. B. (1963). A model of school learning. *Teachers College Record, 64,* 723–733.

Firestone, W. A., & Corbett, H. P. (1988). Planned organizational change. In N. J. Boyan (Ed.), *Handbook of research on educational administration.* New York: Longman.

Fisher, C. W., Berliner, D., Filby, N., Marliave, R., Cahen, L., & Dishaw, M. (1980). Teaching behaviors, academic learning time, and student achievement: An overview. In C. Denham & A. Lieberman (Eds.), *Time to learn* (pp. 7–32). Washington, DC: National Institute of Education.

Fullan, M. (1994). Implementation of innovations. In T. Husen & T. N. Postlethwaite (Eds.), *International encyclopedia of education* (2nd ed., pp. 2839–2847). Oxford, England: Pergamon.

Fullan, M., & Hargreaves, A. (1991). *What's worth fighting for in your school? Working together for improvement.* Toronto, Ontario: Public School Teachers Foundations.

Gettinger, M. (1984a). Achievement as a function of time spent in learning and time needed for learning. *American Educational Research Journal, 21,* 617–628.

Gettinger, M. (1984b). Measuring time needed for learning to predict learning outcomes. *Exceptional Children, 51,* 244–248.

Gettinger, M. (1985). Time allocated and time spent relative to time needed for learning as determinants of achievement. *Journal of Educational Psychology, 77,* 3–11.

Gettinger, M., & White, M. A. (1977). *Time-to-learn: A behavioral analysis for evaluating curriculum fit with class ability.* Unpublished manuscript, Teachers College, Columbia University.

Gettinger, M., & White, M. A. (1979). Which is the stronger correlate of school learning? Time to learn or measured intelligence? *Journal of Educational Psychology, 71,* 405–412.

Gibboner, R. (1994). *The stone trumpet: A story of practical school reform 1960–1990.* Albany, NY: State University of New York Press.

Hall, G., & Hord, S. (1987). *Change in schools.* Albany, NY: State University of New York Press.

Huberman, M., & Miles, M. B. (1984). *Innovation up close: How school improvement works.* New York: Plenum.

Jackson, P. W. (1977). Looking into education's crystal ball. *Instructor, 87,* 38.

Krug, E. A. (1969). *The shaping of the American high school, 1880–1920.* Madison: University of Wisconsin Press.

Levin, H. M. (1995). Learning from accelerated schools. In J. H. Block, S. T. Everson, & T. R. Guskey, (Eds.), *School improvement programs.* New York: Scholastic.

Little, J. W. (1986). Seductive images and organizational realities in professional development. In A. Lieberman (Ed.), *Rethinking school improvement* (pp. 26–44). New York: Teachers College Press.

Louis, K. S., & Miles, M. B. (1992). *Improving the urban high school: What works and why?* London: Cassell.

MacMullen, M. M. (1996). *Taking stock of a school reform effort.* Providence, RI: Brown University, Annenberg Institute for School Reform.

Millman, J., Bieger, G. R., Klag, P. A., & Pine, C. K. (1983). Relation between perseverance and rate of learning: A test of Carroll's model of school learning. *American Educational Research Journal, 20,* 425–434.

Morrison, H. C. (1926). *The practice of teaching in the secondary school.* Chicago: University of Chicago Press.

Murphy, J. (1991). *Restructuring schools: Capturing and assessing the phenomena.* New York: Teachers College Press.

Peterson, P. L. (1996). Learning from school restructuring. *American Educational Research Journal, 33,* 119–153.

Powell, M. (1980). The Beginning Teacher Evaluation Study: A brief history of a major research project. In C. Denham & A. Lieberman (Eds.), *Time to learn* (pp. 1–5). Washington, DC: National Institute of Education.

Pritchett, H. S. (1906). *First annual report of the president and treasurer.* New York: Carnegie Foundation for the Advancement of Teaching.

Rosenblum, S., & Louis, K. (1979). *Stability and change: Innovation in an educational context.* Cambridge, MA: Abt Associates.

Rugg, H. (1926). Curriculum-making and the scientific study of education since 1910. *The foundation and technique of curriculum-construction.* Twenty-sixth yearbook of the National Society for the Study of Education, Part I (pp. 67–82). Bloomington, IL: Public School Publishing Company

Sarason, S. (1990). *The predictable failure of educational reform.* San Francisco: Jossey-Bass.

Slavin, R. E., Madden, N. A., Dolan, L. J., Wasik, B. A., Ross, S., Smith, L., & Dianda, M. (1996). Success for all: A summary of research. *Journal of Education for Students Placed at Risk, 1,* 41–76.

Thomas, R. M. (1994). Implementation of education reforms. In T. Husen & T. N. Postlethwaite (Eds.), *International encyclopedia of education* (2nd ed.). Oxford, England: Pergamon.

Thorndike, E. L. (1913). *Educational psychology: The psychology of learning* (Vol. 2). New York: Teachers College.

Ward, B. A., & Pascarelli, J. T. (1987). Networking for educational improvement. In J. I. Goodlad (Ed.), *The ecology of school renewal, Eight-sixth yearbook of the National Society for the Study of Education* (pp. 192–209). Chicago: University of Chicago Press.

PART II

Time as the Content of School Reform

CHAPTER 2

Time and Resources: The Early Experience of New American Schools

Susanna Purnell and Robert Reichardt

The provision of time for teacher participation is vital to any school reform effort. And yet this aspect of change is often ignored or slighted even though the time demands are substantial. Because restructuring education puts additional demands on a staff that must keep the school open and functioning while simultaneously making changes, principals and teachers often refer to the experience as trying to "rebuild the airplane while in flight" or "change the tires while driving down the highway." This chapter explores issues related to the creation of time for teachers to learn, implement, and ultimately incorporate reforms aimed at every aspect of the school. In particular, we examine how schools and districts create and reconfigure time and resources to support restructuring.

There is a broad consensus in the literature that effective reform requires rethinking the use of time.[1] For example, Fullan and Miles found that "every analysis of the problems of change efforts that we have seen in the last decade of research and practice has concluded that time is the salient issue."[2] The retooling of schools emphasizes teachers adopting new skills and approaches as well as a new paradigm of professional development. Staff development changes of any kind are incremental. Districts and schools must provide a consistent supply of time for training and practice, not just "one shot doses."[3] In addition, teachers who normally work in isolation need time to work together on those changes whether learning, planning, teaming, or observing each other.

31

Fullan has argued that only when teachers meet together can they form the quality working relationships that are "strongly related to implementation."[4]

Using the early experience of the New American Schools (NAS) reform initiative, we identified the time creation strategies and resources used by twenty-four schools in three school districts during the 1995–96 school year.[5] We found that schools used a variety of methods for teachers to attend both outside training events and common planning venues within the school. However, some approaches cost more than others. In comparing the jurisdictions we found that some were more successful at reassigning and reallocating existing time and resources in support of the implementation. Others created more time through additional funding or asking teachers to volunteer their time. Interestingly, the most centralized district created the most training time, illustrating that strong district support of an initiative can provide effective focus and resources in support of implementation.

NEW AMERICAN SCHOOLS (NAS)

Begun in 1991, New American Schools (NAS) is an ambitious private-sector initiative to influence the shape of school reform. Believing that schools and their jurisdictions had become mired in their own bureaucratic rules and traditions, NAS aimed at promoting high-performing schools by introducing "break-the-mold" school designs rather than a more piecemeal program or school-within-a-school approach. They believed that the design vision would provide an organizing focus for the school, thus promoting commitment and willingness to make changes. NAS was not looking for a one-size-fits-all approach, but sponsored a number of designs to entice more schools to implement reform.

To accomplish their agenda, NAS set a demanding schedule. They issued an RFP (request for a proposal) for "break-the-mold" designs and in 1992 funded eleven design teams for a year to develop the design and demonstration strategy. A year later NAS decided to continue funding nine of those teams for a two-year demonstration phase. Finally, in 1995 NAS sponsored seven of the design teams in a coordinated scale-up phase, affiliating ten school jurisdictions with the New American Schools effort for a three-year period. Thus within a six-year period design teams were tasked with creating a K–12 school design, successfully demonstrating that design in at least two sites, and then providing adequate training and support to implement that design in a significant number of schools.[6]

Key to understanding the NAS effort is the past experience of its backers. Funded primarily by businesses and foundations that had already poured a lot of money into demonstration programs, the New American Schools leadership brought a lot of skepticism to funding yet one more model school program. They had seen past programs disappear from schools as soon as the outside grants expired. It didn't matter how successful the program proved, there seemed to be no will or capacity on the part of the education jurisdictions to continue funding the effort, let alone replicating a "success story" in other schools.

As a result, the NAS leadership was willing to provide the seed money or transitional funds, but their major agenda was rapid self-sufficiency and replication. In their view the success of the enterprise ultimately will be measured by the number of schools that use the designs after NAS has ceased funding the initiative. Thus NAS willingly funded the efforts at the initial schools to promote speedy implementation as demonstration sites, but at the end of the two-year demonstration phase funding to schools for the most part stopped. The burden of funding the scale-up phase fell on the jurisdictions and schools using the design. Indeed NAS expected the design teams themselves to become substantially self-sufficient (primarily through fees for services) by the end of the fifth year and that NAS itself would cease to exist after six years.

To promote the scale-up of the designs, NAS affiliated with ten jurisdictions in 1995.[7] In searching for appropriate sites, NAS looked for jurisdictions willing to provide strong public support from the leadership, an investment strategy to support the costs of implementation, and a commitment that at least 30 percent of the schools in the jurisdiction would be implementing NAS designs within three years. NAS devised the strategy as a means to encourage jurisdictions to become more supportive of reforms. They believed districts would be more likely to remove bureaucratic impediments and actively facilitate the implementation if a substantial portion of their schools were involved. In addition, the strategy provided the design teams with a marketplace and some economies of scale since they could work with a number of schools in the same geographic location.

COMPARING APPROACHES TO TIME CREATION AND RESOURCES IN THREE NAS JURISDICTIONS

To discover how the New American Schools jurisdictions created and funded time for the staff to work on the implementation of the designs, we examined the experiences of twenty-four schools in three school districts, referred to as Districts A, B, and C. Selection was based on the three districts that had schools using the greatest number of NAS designs. In the 1995–96 school year, schools implemented five NAS designs in District C, four designs in District A, and three designs in District B. We consulted with each district to identify two schools per design for our fieldwork. Districts were asked to include secondary schools in the selection that resulted in a high school and at least one middle school being visited in each district. (The overall distribution was sixteen elementary schools, five middle schools, and three high schools.)

We visited and interviewed the NAS design teams, district officials, and school administrators and staff of two schools per design in each jurisdiction during the spring of 1996 and conducted follow-up telephone interviews that summer. We asked how many teachers from each school had attended the training events as well as the frequency and duration of any planning time. In all cases we asked for staff time spent working specifically on the NAS design. Teacher training time spent for other purposes was not included. Also, special education and elementary resource teachers (music, art, physical education) were excluded from the survey. For each district we used the information to calculate an average amount of training and planning time provided a classroom teacher in each school. The result was then averaged for the two schools using each NAS design in the jurisdiction.

We also used the interviews and documentation to identify what kind of resources each jurisdiction used to create that time. We asked how each school provided time for teachers and staff to attend training or hold team meetings. Did it require hiring substitutes or paying stipends to the attendees? Did teachers meet as teams on their own time, or was their planning time provided during the school day? The results reflect only the resources needed for the teachers' time and not other costs, such as design team fees for the trainers and materials or travel expenses for the staff.

We analyzed the results in several ways. First, we used the data, to get some idea of the amount and type of time involved. Throughout this examination of the NAS implementation a theme emerged that resembled almost every other implementation study in schools: a plea from teachers and administrators alike that there is simply never enough time. This effort solicited concrete data on the time spent by teachers. It does not capture all the time spent, especially all that teachers did on their own time, but patterns begin to emerge that help us understand the time demands associated with change.

Second, we wanted to understand the trade-offs between the various strategies used to create time. We were interested to what extent time was created using existing resources and how schools used time both inside and outside the school day. Third, the information collected also shed some light on the ability of a district to support and encourage reform.

Districts often are pictured as throwing impediments in the way of reform and indeed the whole charter school movement was established on the premise that the schools can make the necessary changes if they are free of their controlling bureaucracies. Because the three districts in this study granted schools varying degrees of control over resources, it was possible to compare how centralized and decentralized (i.e., site-based) districts created time and support for implementation.

In a perfect world this study would be controlled with all things being held constant except which strategies each jurisdiction chose to adopt. However, there were some differences in circumstances that should be noted. First, as already discussed, the NAS initiative set a very demanding schedule for the design teams. As the scale-up phase began the design teams were still transitioning into fee-for-service assistance organizations. Most had little or no experience in pricing their services and with only two years in demonstration schools most design teams were still grappling with the extent of training needed to implement each element of the design. As a result, when the teams negotiated with each of the three jurisdictions they were not totally consistent in their pricing and training requirements. Also, there were some differences in the start-up times of the designs in two districts. In three schools the design teams had begun implementation the previous year and in another two schools implementation did not begin until the second term. However, when the total training days of these five schools were compared to schools that began implementing the design at the beginning of the year, there were no significant differences.

Some of the same caveats apply to the district's role. The quick start-up meant that districts and schools had a very limited time to reconfigure their schedule and budget to accommodate the time demands associated with the implementation of these school designs. This essay looks at only the first year of this experience; one would expect changes as districts and schools gained more knowledge of the time needed and ways to create that time.

Finally, there were similarities and differences among the jurisdictions used in the study. All are urban districts serving inner-city populations. In 1995 all three were under pressure from their state education agencies to improve both the overall performance of the district as well as the test results and related indicators of the poorest performing schools. All three districts supported ongoing reform agendas that included the affiliation with New American Schools, although District C made this affiliation a more central part of their strategy than the two other districts. Table 2.1 details selected characteristics of the three districts and indicates that District C had the largest proportion of schools joining a NAS design.

TABLE 2.1
Characteristics of Districts
(1995–96 school year)

	Districtwide per Pupil $ (1993)	Student to Teacher Ratio in the Sample	No. of Nonstudent Contract Days	% of District's Schools Using NAS Design
District A	$6,698	20.6	11	9
District B	$6,444	13.3	5	16
District C	$3,945	18.5	7	18

Table 2.1 also offers some comparisons of the resources in each district. The higher per pupil costs in Districts A and B reflect to some extent the stronger union environment in those districts as compared to District C. Teacher contracts also varied in terms of the number of non-classroom days provided for such activities as staff development, classroom setup at the beginning of the year, or parent–teacher conferences.

TIME NEEDED TO IMPLEMENT THE NAS DESIGNS

The time demands for implementing a whole-school design are extensive. In exploring the experiences of twenty-four NAS schools we found that even though they were adopting five different designs, the different kinds of time needed were very similar.[7] Several characteristics of the designs and implementation strategies contributed to this. First, these were whole-school designs so time had to be found for the entire faculty to work on the implementation. All the design teams initiated the implementation with a schoolwide meeting to provide orientation on the design and implementation plan. Although in subsequent training and planning faculty might be grouped or regrouped according to task, the nature of the whole-school design was that every teacher had to put in a significant amount of time.

The nature of the designs also contributed to the time demands. All but one of the designs asked the faculty to mold aspects of the design to their particular school and classroom. All four designs required teachers to create at least some of the curriculum. The designs espoused a constructivist approach to instruction and therefore teachers were told to abandon textbooks and use project-based approaches with a lot of hands-on learning. The necessity to search for appropriate materials and resources for these curriculum units added to the time demands. In addition, most designs asked teachers to crosswalk their curriculum units with the design and/or jurisdiction standards. Two designs required all teachers to join a task committee to work on specific aspects of the design, such as a technology plan, community/business relations, or social services support for the students.

Teaming was the key to implementing all these tasks. Since developing the curriculum was tied to a grade-level or multi-age cluster group, the implementation required time for those teachers to meet together. Often in schools the classrooms for a particular grade were already housed in the same part of the school and the classes were on the same lunch schedule. But this really required common planning time. More difficult to arrange during the school day were the task committee meetings because these drew teachers from across the school, a configuration somewhat alien to the school schedule and usual patterns of interaction.

Implementation also required training in basic skills assumed in the design. Two designs that emphasized integration of technology in instruction had to bring faculty computer skills up to speed. Most of the design teams gave training in team building and conflict resolution. A design emphasizing school autonomy got the local jurisdiction to train the leadership team on how to make a school budget. Almost all teams provided training in instruction skills such as cooperative learning and using learning centers.

The designs also emphasized professional development as an integral part of the school. The design teams used a number of strategies to facilitate teacher access to the tools, knowledge, and experiences of the profession. Most important of all from the teachers' point of view, the teams devised opportunities for them to break out of the isolation of their own classroom and school. Design teams often put a premium on staging events that invited interaction with other schools trying the design. Four teams sponsored events that brought together teachers from all the jurisdictions. These usually lasted several days and often were hosted by one of the schools. One team held summer seminars on a particular curricular topic, another did a series of televised videoconferences hooking up teachers from three geographic locations, and a third held a national conference that several teachers from every school attended. Two designs sponsored visits of teachers as critical friends to view what other schools were doing and provide feedback. While all these events involved only selected faculty from each school, it was anticipated that over time almost all the teachers would have an opportunity to participate.

Finally, all the teams arranged for design team member(s) visits to each school. How this time was used varied greatly. Two teams employed their own local facilitator, who usually spent one day a week in the schools and played the role of trouble shooter, logistics facilitator, and trainer to the school. Others sent members of the national design team on fairly regular visits to the school, usually every four to six weeks. One team used such visits to conduct implementation checks in every classroom and another met with each of the teacher teams. Another team used the visit to send a specialist in a particular element of the design and others just used it as a communication device, responding to any concerns of the principal and teacher leaders.

In summing up the time requirements of the designs, two general categories of requirements emerge. The first characterized as training time includes all the more formal events conducted under the direction or advisement of the design team. Planning time, on the other hand, refers to the time provided for teachers to actually carry out the implementation at the school level. Planning time was more likely to be ongoing instead of a single event and conducted by the internal staff rather than being directed from outside the school.

Using these two categories of time, Table 2.2 provides a listing of the kinds of time used in the implementation of the NAS designs. It not only identifies the length or frequency of the time used but also to what extent staff participate in each format. The final column, labeled "resources used," identifies which of five general strategies were used to create that particular time slot. As can be seen, schools and jurisdictions used different approaches to create similar blocks of time.

TIME CREATION STRATEGIES

Interviews with district and school administrators revealed that the NAS schools basically used five approaches to creating time for teachers to work on the implementation.[8]

1. Nonstudent contract days. Districts employ teachers for a given number of days during the year. The contracted days almost always include some noninstructional days to give teachers time to set up and dismantle their classroom at the beginning and end of the school year and to attend staff development, known as in-service, during several days throughout the year. Some jurisdictions also use these days for parent–teacher conferences and for the paperwork associated with grades at the end of the semester. In most districts NAS design teams were able to use at least some of the in-service days for training events. Some design teams also used some of the contract time given teachers to set up or pack up their classrooms by scheduling a summer institute at the start or end of school.

TABLE 2.2
Types of Time Needed to Implement NAS Designs

	Event	Attendees	Time Length	Resources Used
Training Time				
5 Design Teams	Summer Institutes	Most/all of faculty	Multiple days	Contract days Stipends Volunteer
5 Design Teams	In-service training	All faculty	Half day or more	Contract days
4 Design Teams	Pull-out training	Partial faculty (by grade, design committee, etc.)	Half day or more	Substitutes Reallocate
4 Design Teams	Cross-jurisdiction meetings	Selected faculty	Multiple days	Substitutes Volunteer Stipends
5 Design Teams	Team member(s) visit school	Various configurations	Usually one day	Substitutes Reallocate Volunteer
Planning Time				
5 Design Teams	Common planning time	Grade level, cluster teachers	Daily/weekly	Reallocate Volunteer
3 Design Teams	School-level design team	Across faculty	As needed	Reallocate Substitute Volunteer

This approach has a number of advantages and few drawbacks. It involves no extra cost. Because the school is closed to students, all the teachers can attend without the distractions of the school day. The major trade-off concerns how the faculty would use the time otherwise. For example, some teachers complained that using some of their setup days for the summer institute made it very difficult for them to be ready for the opening of school. However, for the most part, appropriating these nonstudent days contributes to making the implementation the focus of the school.

2. **Reallocation of time and positions.** Schools already have resources of time, personnel, and budget funds that have been allocated in certain ways as evidenced by the master schedule, the staff roster, and the discretionary budget. Reallocation of these resources can be used to create time for the implementation. For example, the master schedule can be redone to accommodate the need for common planning time. Many elementary

schools do this by scheduling resource teachers and school library visits to free up targeted groups of classroom teachers simultaneously.

In addition, schools can change the mix of staff positions to allow teachers more flexibility. An assistant principal slot can be traded in for several teacher aides or for a design team facilitator. These individuals can fill in for classroom teachers as they attend planning meetings or training events. Staff can be given different assignments during the day. For example, kindergarten teachers with early release classes can free up other classroom teachers the final hour of the school day. A secondary teacher can be assigned fewer classes in exchange for extra free periods to act as the design team facilitator for part of the school day.

Finally, the nonsalary discretionary budget can be reallocated to buy time by adding personnel to the roster. For most schools this is a relatively small portion of the school budget and, depending on what pots of money the school controls, usually includes the funding for textbooks, materials, athletics, and professional development. Many of the schools in this sample reported discretionary budgets of less than $25,000. However, schools qualifying for Title I schoolwide funding generally had a much larger discretionary budget and used it to create facilitator, teacher aide, and tutoring positions. In fact, one design team geared the marketing of their design to Title I schools.

Reallocation of resources has the advantage of providing teacher time without requiring additional funding. The drawbacks are that most school administrators have little experience in making such changes particularly since they don't always have control over the resources. Reallocation can be painful, particularly if it involves changing personnel. Also, school and jurisdiction administrators often feel constrained by local and state regulations, union contracts, and traditional practices. In our interviews administrators often cited state requirements for class size and seat time as barriers to making significant changes in the master schedule or staff roster.

3. Volunteer time. Schools in this sample also added time simply by soliciting teacher willingness to spend their own time to attend training and do the necessary planning. Teachers attending summer events might get reimbursed for their travel and registration expenses, but basically they went on unpaid time. In schools with no common planning time teachers still must coordinate curriculum development; they often added time to meet before or after school or on weekends.

While volunteer time is free, requiring no additional resources, there are penalties associated with overuse of this approach. Teachers will tell you that no matter how much time is actually provided they are going to have to spend their own time also. However, excessive volunteer time can lead to either burnout or limited commitment and participation in the initiative. Teachers tend to be more skeptical than usual about the seriousness of an initiative that is underresourced.

4. Substitutes. This is one of the most widespread devices for freeing teachers for training or planning during the school day. The drawback it that although substitutes are relatively cheap laborers they do add cost to the time being created. In addition, administrators often complain about the quality and size of the substitute pool. This was a real problem in one of the districts we looked at because the schools were so large that to free up even a significant subset of the faculty involved too high a demand on the subpool.

Teachers and parents often complain about this approach if it is overused. Teachers feel guilty if they are absent from the classroom too long, and parents worry about the adverse effects on their children's education. As one parent put it, "It's fine to want to improve the school in the future but my child is in class now."

5. Stipends. Stipends can be used to buy time beyond the existing teacher contract and are often given to teachers who attend weekend or summer training or meetings. Stipends usually cost more than hiring substitutes but add incentive for teachers to participate on their own time rather than being absent from the classroom.

Although all these strategies create time, there are trade-offs attached to their selection. As noted, using nonstudent contract days or reallocation of existing resources to create time does not add to the cost. On the other hand, using substitutes or stipends does. Relying on teachers' volunteer time is free but when overused can be costly in terms of teacher burnout and limited commitment to the implementation. These time creation devices also vary in terms of when teachers work on the implementation. Using substitutes or reallocation of personnel and school schedules frees up teachers during the school day. The use of in-service days, stipends, and volunteer time occurs outside the instructional day. Moreover, stipends and volunteer activities actually create additional time beyond the teacher contract.

The jurisdictions studied used all five approaches to create significant amounts of teacher time. However, individual schools had varying levels of control over employing these devices, in particular, the authority to reassign or reallocate resources. Table 2.3 identifies whether the schools rather than the school district had control over in-service days and the resources associated with the reallocation strategy.

The table shows the districts fell along a continuum of school versus district control. District A was the most decentralized, with schools having site-based budgeting, including control of the personnel budget. In contrast, District C was very centralized, with the schools having little say over the budget or other resources. District C schools had a small nonpersonnel budget but for the most part could not reallocate the funds from one category to another. Although schools in District B had a small discretionary budget, the bulk of the budget remained under central control. The schools in all the districts had at least some influence over their scheduling within the confines of such factors as the bus schedule. In District A schedule changes required the approval of 90 percent of the faculty. Likewise, faculty influenced how schools used in-service days in District A and District B.

COMPARISONS OF TEACHER TIME FOR TRAINING

Based on data gathered in interviews and documentation, Table 2.4 describes the average amount of training time provided classroom teachers implementing NAS designs in twenty-four schools. The average time does not necessarily mean that every teacher spent the same amount of time in training. Within a school some teachers attended events or worked on planning the implementation more than others. Such teachers might have been more enthusiastic and less distracted by other

TABLE 2.3
School Control Over Time Resources

	District A	District B	District C
School Schedule	Yes	Yes	Yes
In-Service Day	Yes	Yes	
Discretionary Budget	Yes	Yes	
Personnel Budget	Yes		

TABLE 2.4
Teacher's Average Number of Training Days per Year
(1995–96 school year)

	District A	District B	District C
Design Team 1	4.2	N.A.	10.1
Design Team 2	4.5	7.7	13.0
Design Team 3	N.A.	6.7	11.7
Design Team 4	5.0	N.A.	6.5
Design Team 5	3.0	2.9	2.7

N.A.: Not applicable because the design teams had no schools in that district.

demands or required more training time due their role in the implementation. What the average time does provide is a good measure of the capacity of the jurisdiction and design team to create time.

In looking over Table 2.4, it is immediately evident that training time varied greatly both across jurisdictions and designs, with District C generating the most time. As already noted, design teams were not always consistent in their negotiations with each district and this to some extent explains why training days for a particular design varied by jurisdiction. However, the rank order of the largest to the smallest amount of training days per design is almost identical within each jurisdiction. This would indicate that some of the variation is tied to more basic differences in the designs and implementation strategies. For example, in all three districts Design Team 5 teachers received the least amount of training time. This is the most specified of the five designs and the only one that provides teachers with a very detailed curriculum rather than requiring the teachers to create curriculum units. As a result, the design team required relatively less training time.

While these factors account for some of the differences they do not explain why District C appears to have been so much more successful than the two other districts in providing training time. The picture becomes clearer when we compare the time creation strategies employed by each school jurisdiction.

Table 2.5 illustrates that the three jurisdictions employed significantly different strategies to provide training time. Most of the training in District C took place outside instructional time, either during the non-student contract days used for in-service or during the summer and weekends paid for by stipends. In contrast, the schools in District A held most of the training during the school day by either reallocating time and positions, or using substitutes to release teachers from classroom

TABLE 2.5
Composition of Training Time by Creation Strategy
(1995–96 school year)

	District A	District B	District C
% In-Service	20	0	41
% Reallocation	25	13	13
% Volunteer	0	41	6
% No Added Cost	45	54	60
% Stipend	12	9	35
% Substitute	43	37	5
% Added Cost	55	46	40

instruction. Finally, District B relied heavily on teachers volunteering their own free time during or beyond the school day, an approach that the two other districts hardly used.

A key factor in creating such a difference in the actual number of training days was District C's extensive use of in-service days. This strategy guaranteed training time for the entire faculty, while all the other approaches were more likely to garner a smaller number of participants.

A fundamental contrast between the lowest amount of time created in District A versus the two other districts is the eschewing of approaches that actually increase the time available. Thus although the schools in District A were much more adept at reallocating time and positions within the school day, they showed little or no inclination to extend the time available for training through stipends or volunteer activities. The differences between Districts B and C also reflect how each district extended time. In District C teachers were rewarded with stipends for spending more time on training whereas in District B they were asked to spend added time without compensation—an approach that probably lowered the participation rate.

The contrasts between Districts A and C are especially interesting because the schools in District A had site-based budgeting while District C was highly centralized. The central office in District C was much more successful in creating time even though the schools in District A had more experience reallocating resources in support of a program. The difference appeared to be that District C was willing to focus its resources on the implementation, dedicating more in-service time to the design teams even though it had fewer in-service days than District A. The centralized district was also able to invest additional resources in the form of stipends to buy more time.

The focus and commitment of the schools and jurisdictions to the implementation may have been a factor. The fact that the schools in Districts A and B dedicated few or none of their staff development days to the designs suggests that they were not willing to abandon competing programs and interests. This was particularly true in District B, where the staff of a number of schools in the sample had to participate in another major district initiative during the same time period. The substantial reliance on teachers volunteering time to attend training may also have limited the commitment and focus of the schools in District B.

COMPARISONS OF TEACHER TIME FOR PLANNING

The inclusion of planning time within the school can be a powerful tool in promoting the implementation. Planning time is more likely to occur regularly and more frequently than the training events. Moreover, because the attendees are usually the same team members they can more easily keep building on past work even when the allotted time is fragmented. In the case of the NAS schools, two designs required schools to create a facilitator position. Part of the job description was to meet regularly with each grade-level team and keep the group focused on working through the implementation of the design curriculum and instruction.

The difference between training and planning time is underscored by how we measured it. The training time represented a cumulative total for the year and was measured in days. The planning time appears much smaller because it was measured in hours per week and therefore represents only a fraction of the total time accumulated over the thirty or more weeks in the school year. The small numbers displayed in Table 2.6 represent the average weekly time spent on planning, but these can be misleading. For example, one hour a week for planning time totals to about three to four days over the course of the school year. A school generating over three hours a week planning provides the equivalent of over 5 percent of that teacher's 180-day contract.

District and design team factors influenced the provision of planning time. Several of the schools in Districts A and B did not join the designs until the summer preceding the schools. This made it more difficult for them to realign schedules and budgets to support planning time. In District A it was common practice for secondary schools to save personnel costs by paying teachers to teach an extra class during their free period. One principal estimated that about 30 percent of the staff did this. This may explain the relatively low average planning time for Design Teams 1 and 2 in District A since almost all were secondary schools.

In another example, Design Team 4 employed an implementation strategy that designated the first year as a planning year. Training and

TABLE 2.6
Teacher's Average Number of Planning House per Week
(1995–96 school year)

	District A	*District B*	*District C*
Design Team 1	0.45	N.A.	1.00
Design Team 2	1.70	2.37	3.55
Design Team 3	N.A.	1.38	2.21
Design Team 4	0.46	N.A.	0.68
Design Team 5	3.26	2.26	1.61

N.A.: Not applicable because the design teams had no schools in that district.

planning time was vested in getting the structural underpinnings of the design in place. This meant establishing a series of task force committees that in turn worked on developing an implementation plan for each element of the design. The design team postponed asking the teachers to do the more time-consuming job of writing the curriculum until the second year of the implementation. This implementation strategy contributed to teachers from those schools spending the lowest levels of planning time on the design implementation across the jurisdictions.

As with the training time we looked at the strategies used to create the planning time by jurisdiction. The results, shown in Table 2.7, show an unwillingness across the jurisdictions to pay any added cost to create this kind of time. Both districts and schools reserved the use of substitutes or stipends in support of "one-shot" training events rather than routine meeting time. Virtually all the planning time was created at the school level by rearranging the master schedule and/or positions, or by asking teachers to volunteer time beyond the school day. As might be expected, District A schools, which had the most control over reallocation, used that approach most of the time. But interestingly, the schools in District C, which was the most centralized, also relied on reallocation, reflecting the control those schools had over the master schedule. District B again showed the most limited capacity to create time, relying again on teachers to schedule such activities in their free time.

IMPLICATIONS FOR REFORM

While this essay has focused on the time needed for teachers to implement reform, time is just one of a number of factors influencing successful change. By concentrating on just one issue, the complicated world of reform has been oversimplified. In the subsequent tracking of these twenty-four schools, we found that implementation progress was influenced by such factors as the district's and school's commitment to

TABLE 2.7
Composition of Planning Time by Creation Strategy
(1995–96 school year)

	District A	District B	District C
% Reallocation	80	41	77
% Volunteer	18	59	23
% No Added Cost	98	100	100
% Added Cost (substitutes)	1		

the design, the capacity of the design teams to provide technical support, a conducive operating environment, and the lack of any competing crises. We also found there generally was a positive correlation between the amount of training time and implementation progress.[9]

The following are some generalized conclusions drawn from this analysis.

- *Schoolwide reform requires a substantial amount of training and planning time that involves the whole staff in a variety of formats, not just traditional staff development workshops.* In the twenty-four schools studied the total amount of training and planning time ranged from about six to twenty days per teacher.
- *Districts and schools can employ a number of time creation strategies but these have implications for when the training occurs and how much it costs.* Schools and jurisdictions in this study used three different approaches that emphasized creating reallocated and release time during the school day, using reimbursed time outside the school day, and asking teachers to volunteer their own time.
- *Planning time is created at the school level without the use of additional resources.* While schools and jurisdictions may have been willing to pay substitutes and stipends for sporadic training events, teachers used only reallocated or volunteer time for the more routinized planning time.
- *Planning time may be the more lasting form of time for reform.* Although planning time appeared fairly small, it had a cumulative impact over the course of the school year. In contrast to episodic training events, schools appeared more likely to sustain planning time over a long period by incorporating it as part of the school's master schedule.
- *Districts do not have to be the boogeymen of school reform.* In this study, the most centralized jurisdiction provided the greatest amount of time to teachers and the most decentralized district provided the least amount of time. A district can constructively support a school-level initiative by providing focus and extra resources. Schools experienced in site-based management, however, may be more adept at the reallocation of resources needed to sustain the reform once the district has moved on to other initiatives.

NOTES

1. For example, see Michael G. Fullan & Matthew B. Miles (1992), Getting reform right: What works and what doesn't, *Phi Delta Kappan, 73* (10);

National Education Commission on Time and Learning (1994), *Prisoners of time*; Paul Hill & Susanna Purnell, *Time for reform* (1992), Rand, R-4234–EMC; Stewart C. Purkey & Marshall S. Smith (1983), Effective schools: A review, *The Elementary School Journal*, 88 (4).

2. Fullan & Miles, op. cit., p. 750.

3. Purkey & Smith, op. cit.

4. Michael G. Fullan (1991) *The new meaning of change* (New York: Teachers College Press), p. 77.

5. RAND provided New American Schools with ongoing research and analytic support. Public documentation of RAND's analyses include the following: Susan Bodilly et al. (1994), *Designing New American Schools: Baseline observations on nine design teams*, MR-598–NASDC; Susan Bodilly (1995), *Lessons from New American Schools development corporation's demonstration phase*, MR-729–NASDC; Karen Mitchell (1996), *Reforming and conforming: NASDC principals discuss school accountability systems*, MR-716–NASDC; Susan Bodilly (1998), *Lessons from New American Schools' scale-up phase*, MR-942-NAS; and Thomas K. Glennan Jr. (1998), *New American Schools after six years*, MR-945–NAS.

6. Seven design teams participated in the scale-up phase of New American Schools. These included ATLAS Communities, Audrey Cohen College System of Purpose-Centered Education, Co-NECT Schools, Expeditionary Learning/Outward Bound, Modern Red Schoolhouse, National Alliance for Restructuring Education, and Roots and Wings. Unlike the others, Roots and Wings was geared to elementary schools only.

7. The ten jurisdictions included Cincinnati, Dade County (Florida), Kentucky, Maryland, Memphis, Philadelphia, Pittsburgh, San Antonio, San Diego, and the Washington Alliance.

8. For a more extensive inventory of time creation devices, see Hill & Purnell, *Time for reform*, op.cit.

9. See Susan Bodilly, *Lessons from New American Schools' scale-up phase*, op. cit.

CHAPTER 3

Effective Use of Time
in the Education of
English Language Learners

Catherine Minicucci

Time is a powerful resource in the education of English Language Learners.[1] This was the conclusion of a study for the U.S. Department of Education, Office of Education Reform and Improvement.[2] The Student Diversity Study was one of eight studies commissioned by the Department of Education to assess the impact of school reform on the nation's schools. The study identified and described eight exemplary schools with high-quality math, science, or language arts programs for language minority students. "At these [exemplary] schools, time and collaboration are viewed as resources equally as valuable as money and personnel in providing [LEP] students with a good education. These schools have devised inventive ways to maximize both the quantity and the quality of time available for students to learn and for teachers to plan instruction"[3] (McLeod, 1996, p. iv).

This essay summarizes how the Student Diversity Study was carried out, describes the innovative use of time in the eight exemplary schools and provides a short description of how the exemplary schools were organized for learning.

STUDENT DIVERSITY STUDY

The goal of the Student Diversity Study was to synthesize elements of exemplary programs in school reform for language minority students in grades 4 through 8. The study team identified, studied intensively, and wrote case studies of eight exemplary schools that offer state-of-the-art curriculum and instruction in language arts, math or science in a restructured school. This research identified theory-based and practice-proven strategies to effectively teach language arts, mathematics, and science to students from linguistically and culturally diverse backgrounds (Minicucci et al., 1977, p. 78).

Case study schools were selected to reflect a variety of demographic and geographic contexts. Exemplary schools selected for the study demonstrated innovative, high-quality curriculum in a reformed school context, as well as excellent language development programs for English Language Learners. In addition, case study sites implemented innovative school reform approaches beyond the standard observed in excellent but otherwise traditional school settings.

The schools chosen for intensive field examination were selected after an extensive nationwide search. To locate candidates for exemplary schools, the study team solicited nominations from knowledgeable people at the national, state, and local levels. From the twenty states with the largest populations of English Language Learners, 156 schools were nominated, The research team found it much more difficult to locate exemplary math or science programs than language arts programs. Of the 156 nominated sites, approximately two-thirds were language arts sites and one-third were math and/or science sites (McLeod, 1996, p. 3).

The study team screened seventy-five of the most promising nominated sites using telephone interviews. Each school was assessed using six indicators of excellence: (1) *Innovation*: the school departed from standard instruction, scheduling, organization, and/or curriculum segmentation in order to facilitate program goals. (2) *Embeddedness*: the practices for English Language Learners were not isolated, but were part of the entire school program and were articulated with the type of practices used in earlier and later grades. (3) *High standards*: school staff embraced and articulated the philosophy of the program which includes a vision of quality education for English Language Learners. (4) *Longevity*: the school's use of the identified practices was a serious long-term effort. (5) *Qualified staff*: staffing and training of staff were appropriate to the practices being implemented with English Language Learners. (6) *Generalizability*: the school served students who were fairly typical of English Language Learners nationally and its situation (e.g., funding) was not so special as to preclude other schools learning from it (Institute for Policy Analysis and Research, 1995, p. 1.6).

Results of the telephone interviews were used to reduce the number of sites for in-depth study to twenty-five. From that pool, demographic, geographic, and programmatic variables were used to select fifteen schools for a one-day preliminary field visit to determine which programs would become the final case study sites. One-day visits by one or two fieldworkers to each of the fifteen sites provided the research team with information that allowed the selection of case study sites (Institute for Policy Analysis and Research, 1995, p. 1.6).

Based on the preliminary visits, eight schools were selected for more intensive study. Data on student outcomes that are comparable across the sites were not available, in large part because English Language Learners are often not given the standardized tests (in English) that districts or states require of most students (Berman et al., 1992). Therefore, the research team cannot demonstrate quantitatively that the eight case study sites are exemplary in the sense of demonstrated evidence of significantly higher student achievement scores. Nevertheless, the nomination, screening, and field visits all led to the conclusion that these schools were highly innovative and followed practices that are considered by researchers to provide outstanding learning opportunities for LEP and all students (Berman et al., 1992).

At each case study site, a team of three to four researchers spent three to four days at the school, interviewing the principal and site administrators, interviewing teachers, conducting classroom observations, and conducting focus groups with English Language Learners and parents of English Language Learners. District-level officials were interviewed at each site as were members of an external partner if the school had one. External partners included nonprofit organizations, federally funded science projects, private curriculum and staff development organizations, corporate-sponsored organizations, and Schools of Education.

Three areas were identified for specific inquiry: design of effective instructional strategies for culturally and linguistically diverse students, implementation of those strategies under various conditions, and impact of those strategies on students. At case study sites, researchers examined the context for reform. That is, what factors helped to initiate, develop, and sustain reform? What were the barriers, and how were they overcome? The role of research-based information on the reform was explored, as well as the resources required to design and implement the reform.

USE OF TIME FOR LEARNING

One of the consistent features found in the exemplary case study sites was their innovative uses of time to support learning. In traditional schools, learning is usually subservient to a rigid time schedule in which time is divided up into equal, pre-set segments for instruction. In the typical departmentalized high school, for example, the school day is divided up into fifty-minute periods; bells ring to mark off each period and students move on to their next class. Traditional use of time in such a schedule has an impact on how teachers work with each other and interact with students. Short periods of fifty minutes inhibit project work or extensive laboratory experiments. Departmentalized structures and six- or seven-period days means that the typical secondary school student sees six or seven teachers per day and the typical secondary school teacher sees 120 to 180 students per day (twenty to thirty per period). In this structure, there are rarely opportunities for teachers teaching the same group of students to plan curriculum and instruction together.

In the case study schools, time was the servant of learning. The exemplary sites organized time

> so that the academic schedule would respect the flow of learning units within classes. Such flexibility provided students with protected time to learn and allowed them to engage in self-directed learning activities within cooperative groups. Blocks of time were allocated appropriately for the pedagogic needs of different subject matters or themes. The school day and year were structured or extended to accommodate teacher planning, collaboration and professional development, and to provide extra support for LEP students' transition to English and the incorporation of newcomers into the LEP program. In short, creative uses of time helped to tailor the educational program to the students' strengths and needs. (Institute for Policy Analysis and Research, 1995, p. 10.5)

It is important to stress that the innovative uses of time were implemented within a context of (1) smaller school organizations created to allow more contact between a small number of students and teachers, (2) ample opportunities for teacher collaboration to plan curriculum and instruction, (3) investment in professional development of staff, (4) high-quality programs for English Language Learners staffed by qualified personnel fluent in the language of the students and knowledgeable about their culture, and (5) an inclusive vision of high expectations for all students, including English Language Learners.

Organization of Time

The case study schools organized time in a deliberate fashion to further student learning, by designing longer blocks of time for in-depth study and/or by designing ways for students to spend more than one year with a single teacher.

Block Schedules   Block schedules were used by both elementary and middle schools in the study as a means to create longer periods of time for learning. Linda Vista Elementary School in San Diego, California, had a time block for language arts of ninety minutes' duration and shorter blocks for social studies and mathematics each day. Del Norte Elementary School in Ysleta, Texas, had three-hour language arts blocks Monday through Thursday and on Friday the three-hour block was devoted to science. Monday through Thursday afternoons, Del Norte students studied math for nearly two hours; on Friday afternoon they studied social studies for two and a half hours (McLeod, 1996, p. 21). Teachers at these elementary schools structured time into longer time blocks to allow for longer cooperative projects, more sustained attention to literacy, time for science experiments, and protected blocks of time without interruption.

The middle schools utilized block schedules as well. At Hanshaw Middle School in Modesto, California, students were enrolled in two core classes of ninety minutes' duration for language arts/social studies and math/science. Horace Mann's block schedule allowed for one spanning the first two periods of the day, another spanning the final two periods (McLeod, 1996, p. 21).

In addition to creating longer blocks for sustained attention to core subject matter, these schools created smaller time segments for electives, music, and enrichment.

Extended Time with the Same Teacher   Several of the exemplary schools organized classes so that students would have more than one year with the same teacher or team of teachers. Hollibrook Elementary School in Spring Branch, Texas, utilized continuum classes in which a teacher would remain with a group of students for a period of years. A class was formed at kindergarten and stayed together with the same teacher until third or fourth grade. The teachers had flexibility in deciding when they want to end the continuum, whether at third grade or beyond. At Hollibrook Elementary School, one fourth-grade bilingual class had been together with the same teacher since kindergarten. One combined second-grade bilingual class taught by two teachers had been together since kindergarten. In continuum classes, the students and the teacher knew one another very well. The goal was to introduce stability in the children's lives in contrast to the mobility and social instability in the surrounding neighborhood. Also, continuum classes, it was hoped, would foster parent involvement as parents got to know the teachers well over a period of years. Parental consent was required for students to be in continuum classes.

Continuum classes offered unique advantages to students learning English as a second language. Transition to English literacy can be tailored to fit the student and the usual gaps between elementary school teachers were eliminated. The first-grade teacher knew how far her students got in kindergarten and so on. At Hollibrook School, continuum class students learned to be competent members of cooperative groups. The capacity of students to work alone or in pairs for extended time periods was developed in the continuum class. This freed up teachers' time and energy to devote to other learning activities (Institute for Policy Analysis and Research, 1995, pp. 3.1–3.23).

Graham Parks School in Cambridge, Massachusetts, had ungraded classes in their Haitian Creole bilingual program at every grade level (pre-K, 1–2, 3–4, and 5–8). Students stayed with the same teacher for two years up to grade 4 and for up to four years in grades 5 through 8. In the upper elementary grades, there was a grade 5 through 8 ungraded class taught by two bilingual teachers. One bilingual teacher was a native speaker of Creole, the other bilingual teacher was a native speaker of English who speaks Creole. Ungraded classes allowed the teacher to tailor instruction to fit students' need. This was particularly helpful in Graham Parks school because of the variation in previous levels of schooling the Haitian immigrant children brought with them into the American public school.

Protection of Time

The exemplary schools protected time to learn by eliminating distractions in the classroom. The schools were free of buzzers, bells, students being pulled out, and interruptions from messages being brought into the classroom. The teachers could rely on uninterrupted instructional time. Teachers had a defined role in deciding how to use time, and how to create opportunities for common planning time among faculty members. At Hollibrook Elementary School in Spring Branch, Texas, for example, teachers set the schedule for the music and art teacher to allow teachers time to plan together across grade levels or programs. For classes taught in a team-teaching format, the teachers had the freedom to determine their own schedules for music, physical education, and lunch breaks.

The concept of time as a key resource was fundamental in these schools. Use of time was an explicit decision by teachers and administrators, not a default to some "norm" of dividing up the day into little segments punctuated by loud buzzers and bells. Time was the servant of learning, not the reverse as typically seen in traditional school formats.

Extensions of Time

English Language Learners face unique challenges—they must learn English and subject matter such as math, science, and social studies. In programs that foster primary language literacy, English Language

Learners must also maintain and enhance literacy in their native language. Extended time is a powerful resource for English Language Learners, giving students a way to accomplish the daunting learning challenges they face. In case study schools, extensions of time were accomplished through after-school programs, summer school, year-round school, and intersession programs.

Del Norte Elementary School in Ysleta, Texas, offered a four-week summer program of four hours per day to English Language Learners. Six of the eight exemplary schools offered after-school programs for English Language Learners. After-school homework centers afforded students assistance with their homework, often with tutors or teachers fluent in their native language. This was especially important in the middle grades (6–8) as students were making the transition to English instruction. At Graham Parks school, for example, three eighth-grade Haitian Creole bilingual students were mainstreamed into science with a monolingual English class. They relied upon the homework center after school, staffed with Creole-speaking tutors, to assist them with the reading and writing demands of mainstream science in English. In student focus groups, English Language Learners told the study team that after-school homework centers and tutorials had been one of the most helpful aids to learning English and core subjects such as math, science, and social studies. "Linda Vista operates on a single-track, year-round schedule. The school is open for four nine- to ten-week sessions; the academic year begins in July and ends in June, with four three- to four-week breaks during the year. The year-round schedule diminishes the need for review at the beginning of the year, and avoids long summer breaks which can impede the progress of English-language learners. During the breaks, the school offers half-day two-week intersessions funded with summer school money. Linda Vista moved to the year-round schedule five years into the restructuring process" (Institute for Policy Analysis and Research, 1995, p. 4.18).

The chart on the next page summarizes the use of time in the case study schools.

PROFILES OF EXEMPLARY SCHOOLS

The eight exemplary schools are described briefly below. The full case studies are available from the National Clearinghouse on Bilingual Education, *School Reform and Student Diversity: Case Studies of Exemplary Practices for LEP Students*, The Institute for Policy Analysis and Research, in collaboration with the National Center for Research on Cultural Diversity and Second Language Learning, August 1995.

USES OF TIME IN CASE STUDY SCHOOLS

School	Organization of Time	Time Extensions
Elementary Schools		
Del Norte Heights Elementary School, Ysleta, Texas	Block schedule	After-school program; summer school
Linda Vista Elementary School, San Diego, California	Block schedule	After-school program; year-round single-track schedule intersession program
Hollibrook Elementary School, Spring Branch, Texas	Extended block for language arts; continuum classes	After-school activities program
Inter American School, Chicago, Illinois		After-school tutoring
Middle Grades (6–8)		
Graham Parks School, Cambridge, Massachusetts	Block schedule; ungraded classes	After-school tutoring
Hanshaw Middle School Modesto, California	Block schedule	After-school program
Horace Mann Middle School San Francisco, California	Block schedule	After-school program
Harold Wiggs Middle School El Paso, Texas	Advisory period	

Del Norte Heights Elementary School, Ysleta, Texas

Del Norte Heights in the Ysleta Independent School District in El Paso, Texas, is a K–6 school enrolling 650 students. Spanish-speaking English Language Learners comprise 40 percent of the student body. Teachers and the principal share a vision that includes a well-defined transitional bilingual program and the use of consistent learning strategies throughout the school. Teachers, the principal, district staff, students, and parents believe that bilingualism and biliteracy are important and that English Language Learners can achieve them. Their vision also includes high expectations for all students, involvement of parents, and the coordination of the school program and staff development activities in order to meet those expectations.

The bilingual program begins at kindergarten with 90 percent of instruction in Spanish; that percentage was reduced to 60 percent in third grade and to 20 percent in fourth grade. By the end of the fourth grade, most English Language Learners who entered at kindergarten or first grade were ready to be redesignated fluent English-proficient. Parents could choose between an all-English or bilingual environment for the fifth and sixth grades.

Del Norte's school structure included site-based management, innovative and flexible uses of time, and extensive parent involvement. "The school has reorganized the way time is used during the week to allow for larger blocks of time for core subjects. From Monday through Thursday, students have a block of time devoted to language arts and a block devoted to mathematics; individual teachers choose whether to teach mathematics in the morning or in the afternoon. On these days, students also have a 40 minute period for instruction in art, music, drama, or library research. Enrichment Time (described below) is a part of the language arts block.

"On Fridays, the day is again divided into two instructional blocks, with students spending the full day studying science and social studies. Teachers have discretion about which subject to teach in the morning and which in the afternoon. The longer time blocks allow teachers to plan more complex lessons and provide students with more problem-solving activities. They are able to plan science labs, get students engaged in social studies research, and allow students time for sustained reading and writing." After-school activities included tutoring and a special reading program (Institute for Policy Analysis and Research, 1995, pp. 2.18, 2.3–2.25).

Hollibrook Elementary School, Spring Branch, Texas

Hollibrook School, located on the west side of Houston, in the Spring Branch Independent School District, is a pre-K to fifth-grade school of one thousand students. The student population is 67 percent Spanish-speaking English Language Learners. The school is surrounded by large apartment complexes, most of which have major security and drug problems. The critical building blocks of this program are Spanish bilingual continuum classes, the use of cooperative learning, and freedom for individual teachers to structure school time in flexible ways. Hollibrook developed a unique learning environment by placing a group of students with the same teacher over a number of years. The goal of these continuum classes was to introduce greater stability into students' lives. Parents, teachers, and students got to know one another very well and built strong and effective working relationships. Continuum classes were especially effective in transitioning students to English instruction because losses or gaps in learning between grades were effectively eliminated. The flexible nature of continuum classes allowed teachers to tailor long-term instructional goals to students as they moved toward transition and literacy. Another factor that contributes to the success of the program is the school's efforts to connect with students' families and with the community at large. Hollibrook had a parent center on campus, bilingual social workers, teacher outreach to apartment buildings, and bilingual office staff. Parents took ESL classes on campus.

The program has been strengthened in vital ways by the concept of Accelerated Schools and district support for site-based decision making and bilingual education programs. Accelerated Schools, developed by Professor Henry Levin of Stanford University, is based on the premise that all students need enriched accelerated learning rather than remediation. Accelerated Schools promotes an inquiry method in which faculty members form committees or cadres to examine questions developed by faculty, administrators, parents, and students. The ungraded continuum class developed out of the inquiry method. Creation of full-day kindergarten, use of social workers in lieu of school counselors, and investment in technology also originated through inquiry and was supported by the Spring Branch Independent School District's site-based decision-making policies (Institute for Policy Analysis and Research, 1995, pp. 3.3–3.23).

Inter-American School, Chicago, Illinois

Inter-American School is a pre-K–8 public school serving 650 students in the Chicago Public School District. It was founded in 1975 by a small group of parents and teachers as a bilingual preschool under the auspices of the Chicago Public Schools. The parents and teachers envisioned a multicultural school where children were respected as individuals and where their languages and cultures were respected as well. Today the school is a citywide magnet school whose students are 70 percent Hispanic, 13 percent African American, and 17 percent white. The developmental bilingual program at the school has the goal of bilingualism and biliteracy for both English Language Learners and monolingual English-speaking students. At all grade levels, English-dominant and Spanish-dominant students are assigned to classrooms in roughly equal proportions. In pre-kindergarten, all core subjects are taught in Spanish to all students. Spanish-dominant students take English as a second language and English-dominant students take Spanish as a second language. The 80:20 ratio of Spanish to English instruction remains through third grade; English instruction then increases gradually to reach 50:50 English to Spanish by eighth grade. Students enrolled in the fifth and sixth grades at Inter-American are fully bilingual and biliterate in Spanish and English.

Much of the school's curriculum is integrated across disciplines and built around themes that reflect the history, culture, and traditions of students. The school emphasizes the study of the Americas and Africa, especially how African history and culture have influenced the Americas. Grade-level teachers work together to develop their curriculum around themes. For example, fourth-grade teachers use a thematic unit on Mayan civilization to integrate content across the curriculum. In social studies, students study the geographic spread of Mayan civilization, Mayan religion, and cultural traditions. In science, students study Mayan architecture and agricultural systems. In language arts, students read and write stories about the Mayans. A volunteer parent taught an art lesson in which students paint Mayan gods. The unit began with a visit to the Field Museum to see an exhibit on Mayan culture, architecture, and religion.

Teachers spanning two grade levels work intensively with each other throughout the school year. The teachers at pre-kindergarten and kindergarten, grades 1 and 2, and so on, plan together, exchange students across grade levels and classrooms, and work together on thematic units.

Like other Chicago schools, Inter-American School has a local school council that sets school policies, hires and evaluates the principal, interviews prospective teachers, and controls the school budget. The professional personnel advisory committee, made up entirely of faculty members, sets priorities and takes responsibility for the instructional program (Minicucci et al., 1995, p. 79).

Linda Vista Elementary School, San Diego, California

Linda Vista Elementary School is a pre-K to grade school with one thousand students in the San Diego Unified School District. The English Language Learners at the school come from a variety of linguistic backgrounds. Fifty percent are Spanish speakers, 22 percent speak Hmong, 16 percent speak Vietnamese, and 6 percent speak Lao. Linda Vista has experienced rapid and dramatic shifts in student populations over the past ten years and its restructuring has focused on adjusting the school organization and program to better meet the changing needs of students.

There are four developmental ungraded "wings" at the school: early childhood, primary, middle, and upper. The wings function like four schools within a school, each composed of students within a relatively close age range with mixed levels of English language fluency and previous schooling. Within each wing, the school groups students by home language or English language level for language arts, ESL, and social studies instruction. The remainder of the school day students are mixed into heterogenous groups for math, science, art, music, and physical education. A two-hour block of time is devoted each morning to language arts for all students. The use of oral language, literature, writing that reflects real-life situations, research-based writing, directed and free journal writing, and dramatic interpretations of literature promotes language development in a natural manner. Cooperative learning is featured prominently in Linda Vista classrooms. By the time students reach fourth grade, they are expert cooperative learners, able to accomplish learning tasks on their own, freeing time for teachers to work one on one with students.

Spanish-speaking English Language Learners are placed in bilingual language arts classes. Non-Spanish-speaking English Language Learners are grouped according to English language ability and instructed using sheltered techniques. The levels of ungraded classes for speakers of languages other than Spanish include Sheltered A and B, and Transition A and B.

Linda Vista adopted a year-round, single-track calendar to eliminate long summer breaks that can impede the progress of English Language Learners. A year-long schedule diminishes the need for review at the beginning of the year. A flexible daily schedule allows Linda Vista teachers to have two prep periods per week for common planning time. A strong feature of Linda Vista's reform effort is the teacher collaboration. Teachers engage in peer observation, using their "pre" time to visit other teachers' classes and observe instruction.

Linda Vista is developing an authentic portfolio-based assessment to record students' growth as they progress toward specified learning outcomes. Student work is scanned into computers and the records are maintained in electronic portfolios. Linda Vista teachers are entrepreneurial in spirit; they have a number of grants and partnerships. Their partnership with Apple Classrooms of Tomorrow and the National Alliance for School Restructuring, and their Restructuring Demonstration Grant, enhanced the program, by supporting staff development, technology, alternative assessment, and additional teacher planning time (Institute for Policy Analysis and Research, 1995, pp. 4.3–4.25).

Graham and Parks School, Cambridge, Massachusetts

Graham and Parks School is a K–8 school enrolling 365 students from throughout the city of Cambridge. Seventeen percent of the students are

LEP. Most English Language Learners are Haitian immigrants. The district's desegregation plan shapes the school's program: parents of English-speaking students choose the school through a lottery system and parents of Haitian Creole-speaking students choose the school for its Creole bilingual program.

Graham and Parks' Creole bilingual program serves Haitian immigrant students from kindergarten through eighth grade. Most of the Haitian students at the school immigrated to the United States with or without their immediate families as a result of the political upheaval in their native country. When these children enter Graham and Parks School, some are malnourished, and most are unschooled. As a rule, they have no literacy in Creole or English. The school provides special services for students and their families. For example, the Student Support Team, made up of the principal, parent liaison, assistant principal, nurse, school psychologist, and interns, meets every Monday and takes a case study approach to students who are referred by staff. Counseling is also available at Cambridge Hospital and through a Haitian community counseling program. Graham and Parks is also staffed with a bilingual parent coordinator, Haitian resource room teacher, and Haitian mediation specialist.

The Haitian Creole bilingual program is organized into multi-grade classes taught by bilingual teachers fluent in Creole and English (pre-K, 1–2, 3–4, and 5–8). The program goals for language development include the acquisition of literacy in both Creole and English. Each pre-K through third/fourth bilingual class is teamed up with a monolingual English class and team teaching, allowing flexible mixing and grouping of students. There is a multi-age class for Creole speakers in grades 5 through 8 composed of twenty-three students and taught by two bilingual teachers.

Graham and Parks has a steering committee for school decision making, comprised of staff, counselors, parents, community representatives, and the principal. The committee makes decisions on the design of programs and how to structure team teaching. Staff selection is done by faculty and parents.

The science program at Graham and Parks was collaboratively developed by TERC (a nonprofit educational research firm located in Cambridge) and Graham and Parks teachers under grants from the National Science Foundation and the U.S. Department of Education, Office of Bilingual Education and Minority Language Affairs, and Office of Educational Research and Improvement. Graham and Parks and several other schools in the Boston area serve as living laboratories for the development of TERC's "sense-making" approach to learning science (Minicucci, 1996, pp. 4–6).

Hanshaw Middle School, Modesto, California

Hanshaw Middle School is a grade 6–8 middle school serving 860 students from a predominantly low-income Latino community in Modesto, California. It opened in the fall of 1991. Hanshaw students are 56 percent Hispanic, 26 percent white, 11 percent Asian, and 5 percent African American. After interviewing five hundred families in their homes, the principal and faculty agreed on four principles for the foundation of Hanshaw's program: high expectations for all students, support for the Latino and Chicano experience, a meaning-centered curriculum, and a conscious effort to impart life skills as part of the curriculum. The principal recruited teachers from industry—a former carpenter teaches math, a former museum director teaches science, and a former wildlife biologist teaches science.

Hanshaw is organized into five houses, each named for a campus of the California State University system. Each house contains six to nine teachers led by a team leader. Teams of two teachers (one for math/science core and one for language arts/social studies core) teach a group of thirty to thirty-five students. All students take two ninety-minute core classes, one for math/science and one for language arts/social studies. Each year students visit the college campus their house is named after, meet college students from various ethnic backgrounds, hear lectures, and receive a T-shirt and diploma. Students identified strongly with the college campus, which provided them with an alternative to gang affiliation. Life skills such as patience, flexibility, integrity, initiative, and effort are taught at the start of each school year. Students are rewarded throughout the year for demonstrating life skills. Teachers within each house make decisions about the school's budget.

Hanshaw teachers' curriculum design decisions are based on a simple principle: The lesson or skill must be relevant to the students' lives. Teachers strive to help students know the "why" of an answer, or multiple answers, or multiple ways of getting to an answer rather than one single answer. Teachers build on students' own experiences in thematic instruction. Themes unify instruction across science, math, language arts, and social studies, incorporating topics from the curriculum frameworks of the state of California.

Hanshaw offers several programs for English Language Learners: instruction in Spanish in core curricular areas, sheltered instruction for advanced Spanish-speaking English Language Learners and students who speak other primary languages, and mainstream English instruction for clusters of English Language Learners speaking the same primary language. When English Language Learners are considered ready to transition, they are clustered together in mainstream classes. Many of the mainstream class teachers have special training and credentials in second language acquisition. English Language Learners receive challenging content in math and science taught in Spanish or in sheltered English.

Hanshaw's program is supported by an external partner, Susan Kovalik & Associates from Washington State, which works with Hanshaw faculty in intensive summer and weekend retreats. A Kovalik coach assists the school on a monthly basis, designing curriculum, providing instructional coaching, and helping the faculty identify problems and solutions. Hanshaw has a comprehensive health and social services center on campus staffed with social workers and counselors bilingual in Spanish and English (Minicucci et al., 1995, pp. 79–80).

Horace Mann Middle School, San Francisco, California

Horace Mann Middle School, in the San Francisco Unified School District, enrolls 650 students in grades 6 through 8. Students enroll in the school in accordance with a districtwide open enrollment policy aimed at desegregating schools by limiting the enrollment of students from any one ethnic group. Spanish-surname students make up 38 percent of the school, Chinese students are 14 percent, other white make up 20 percent, other non-white make up 13 percent, African American students are 9 percent, and Filipino students are 6 percent of the school population.

All Horace Mann students are placed into one of six "families," two at each grade level, of approximately one hundred students and four core teachers. Students take all of their core classes (language arts, social students, science, and mathematics) and some of their electives with the family; other electives and PE are offered outside the family structure. All families are comprised of heterogeneous student populations. Within the family, the students are clustered into "strands" of approximately twenty-five students for core content courses. Spanish-speaking English Language Learners are served within the family structure via Spanish bilingual strands. The Spanish bilingual program promotes English language development and Spanish language maintenance for LEP and bilingual students; the goal is biliteracy for all students. Students enrolled in the bilingual program receive half of their core course instruction (science and social studies) in Spanish and half in English (language arts and mathematics). Newcomer Chinese English Language Learners are served in a self-contained class that is not part of a family. All programs for English Language Learners are supported by bilingual and language development specialist (LDS)-trained teachers and aides.

Horace Mann uses a block schedule in which students have two academic blocks each day; each academic class meets every other day. The block schedule provides time for students to carry out in-depth research and project-based work without interruption. Each family also offers an after-school program for students who need extra help. The daily schedule provides built-in time every day for teacher collaboration.

At Horace Mann, Project 2061 supports cooperative project work of students in the form of learning challenges. Learning challenges incorporate skills and knowledge from math, science, social studies, and language arts in a thematic approach. Students work as members of a heterogenous team to meet the learning challenge. Project 2061 supports staff development, design of the learning challenges, and assessment of the success of student learning in challenges. English Language Learners participate fully in the learning challenges for Project 2061 at Horace Mann Middle School (Minicucci, 1996, pp. 8–9).

Wiggs Middle School, El Paso, Texas

Wiggs Middle School, in the El Paso Independent School District, enrolls one thousand students in grades 6–8. As the first middle school in the El Paso district, and one of the first in Texas, Wiggs has been at the forefront of the statewide movement for implementing the middle school model since the school opened in 1987. Harold Wiggs Middle School student body and staff are organized into two families at each grade level, and groups English Language Learners into two additional families called LAMP families (Language Acquisition for the Middle School Program). The five teachers from each family meet on a daily basis to discuss various topics, including planning collective activities, problems with and rewards for individual students, and school-wide activities. Teachers have in-depth knowledge of their students, their school progress, and their family situations and are alert to signs of problems in any arena. Students at Wiggs have seven academic periods, a homeroom period, and an advisory period. Teachers have an individual period each day that they can use for conferences or for preparation. The final period of the day is the advisory period for all students in the school.

Wiggs has site-based management, supported by Texas's new accountability system. The school-level governing body, the Campus Improvement Committee, is comprised of representatives of the faculty, staff, parents, and the community. The Committee prepares a yearly Campus Improvement Plan and makes decisions on the school's discretionary budget, school policies and activities, partnerships with the community, and strategies for involving parents and community members as partners in the school.

Located near the Mexican border, Wiggs accommodates a constant influx of students from Mexico, most of whom arrive literate in Spanish with consistent previous schooling. In order to incorporate the new-comers, the Language Acquisition for the Middle School Program (LAMP), which consists of a sheltered English program, an intensive ESL component for newcomer English Language Learners, and Spanish language classes. The teachers are trained in ESL, sheltered English, and their content area. Most of the teachers in the program are fluent in Spanish. LAMP classes are smaller than regular classes, averaging between fourteen and fifteen students per class. Small class sizes allow teachers to provide intensive instruction to English Language Learners and to monitor individual student progress.

The LAMP program is housed in two families—one for beginning English Language Learners, the other for intermediate English Language Learners. Students in the LAMP families span the three grade levels at the school. The program's structure allows staff the flexibility to move students from the beginning LAMP family to the intermediate LAMP family when they are ready.

The LAMP science curriculum thematic units allow students to explore science topics from their real lives in greater depth and from a variety of angles. Students also learn to make connections between traditional academic disciplines and how various disciplines can provide different perspectives on a question (Institute for Policy Analysis and Research, 1995, pp. 9.3–9.20).

SUMMARY

Time is a critical resource in the education of all students, particularly English Language Learners whose native language is other than English. English Language Learners must learn academic content and English in school. In programs that foster native language literacy, these students must also build reading and writing skills in their native language. The Student Diversity Study, conducted under the auspices of the U.S. Department of Education Office of Education Reform and Improvement, identified and described eight exemplary schools using a case study approach. The schools identified through an extensive national search met three criteria: they were engaged in substantive school reform, they offered high-quality programs for English Language Learners, and they presented high-quality program curriculum and instruction in math and science (grades 6–8) and language arts (grades 4–6) for English Language Learners.

The eight case study schools were identified through an extensive process of nomination and screening. Study researchers found that the exemplary sites used time carefully and purposefully to advance student learning. These schools:

1. Organized time in flexible ways to provide longer time periods for in-depth study. Both elementary and intermediate schools utilized block schedules.
2. Protected learning time by eliminating bells, interruptions, and students pulled out of class. Teachers in these schools had control over the use of instructional time.
3. Extended time by after-school programs, summer school, and intersessions for year-round schools. This afforded the English Language Learners additional opportunity to learn English, maintain their native language, and master academic content.
4. Several elementary schools in the study kept students with teachers for more than a single year. These schools extended the time students spend with a teacher from one to two to five years. This eliminated instructional gaps and created smoother continuity between grade levels, fostered parent involvement, and helped students become self-directed learners in cooperative groups.

Innovative uses of time were found to support student learning and help English Language Learners meet the unique challenges they face in school.

NOTES

1. English Language Learners are students whose native language is other than English. They have limited proficiency in English, which requires a special program of instruction for them to benefit from schooling. The term "Limited English Proficient," or LEP, is the common descriptive term used in both educational research and state laws governing language development programs. English Language Learners is a less pejorative term that is increasingly being used in research and practice.
2. The Student Diversity Study was part of the Studies of Education Reform program, supported by the U.S. Department of Education, Office of Research, under contract No. RR91–172003.

REFERENCES

Berman, P. Chambers, J., Gándara, P., McLaughlin, B., Minicucci, C., Nelson, B., Olsen, L., & Parrish, T. (1992). *Meeting the challenge of language diver-*

sity: An evaluation of programs for pupils with limited proficiency in english (Vols. 1–5). Berkeley, CA: BW Associates.

The Institute for Policy Analysis and Research, in collaboration with the National Center for Research on Cultural Diversity and Second Language Learning. (1995). *School reform and student diversity: Case studies of exemplary practices for LEP students*. Washington DC: National Clearinghouse for Bilingual Education.

McLeod, Beverly. (1996). *School reform and student diversity: Exemplary schooling for language minority students*. Resource Collection Series, No. 4. National Clearinghouse for Bilingual Education.

Minicucci, Catherine. (1996). *Learning science and english: How school reform advances scientific learning for limited English proficient middle school students*, Educational Practice Report 17. Santa Cruz, CA, and Washington DC: National Center for Research on Cultural Diversity and Second Language Learning.

Minicucci, Catherine, Berman, Paul, McLaughlin, Barry, McLeod, Beverly, Nelson, Beryl, & Woodworth, Kate. (1995). School reform and student diversity. *Phi Delta Kappan, 77* (1), 77–80.

Nelson, Beryl. (1996). *Learning English: How school reform rosters language acquisition and development for limited English proficient elementary school students*. Educational Practice Report No. 16. Santa Cruz, CA, and Washington, DC: National Center for Research on Cultural Diversity and Second Language Learning.

CHAPTER 4

Rethinking Time and Teacher Working Conditions

Patricia Gándara

The most recent school reform movement was launched in the 1980s with an initial focus on curriculum, assessment, and governance (Firestone, 1994; Gándara, 1994). Numerous reports were issued that provided blueprints for reorganized and more rigorous curricula; the call for minimum competency testing was heeded by most states in the nation; and "restructuring" and "school based management" became the anthems of many school districts. Only after the initial flurry of activity at the more macro level of schooling did the focus shift to what actually happens inside the classroom between students and teachers, and to issues of pedagogy and teacher preparation. The result of this new focus has been increased interest in providing teachers with more knowledge and training about how students learn, and hence on how to teach better.

School districts all over the country have dedicated themselves to increased in-service training of teachers with the often unarticulated assumption that more knowledge will result in better teaching outcomes, which in turn will increase the satisfaction of teachers. In all of the rhetoric, however, little attention has actually been paid to how schools can work better not just for students, but for teachers, and concomitantly, how student performance is integrally linked to teacher satisfaction. Moreover, recent studies show that in spite of the new attention focused on strengthening teachers' skills and preparation, teacher satisfaction is actually on the decline. The source of much of the declining satisfaction of teachers is their perceived loss of support from both parents and principals (National Center for Education Statistics, 1997a). In a critique of the reform movement's failure to take teacher working conditions into account, Seymour Sarason noted, "From their inception our public schools have never assigned importance to the intellectual, professional, and career needs of their personnel . . . it is virtually impossible to create and sustain over time conditions for productive learning for students when they do not exist for teachers, [thus] the benefits sought by educational reform stand little chance of being realized" (1990, p. 145).

Of the major education reports of the 1980s, nearly every one touched on the need to recruit the most able students into teaching and to provide the proper incentives to retain them. Yet data have shown that half of the teachers in the United States leave the profession every seven years (Anthony, 1988; Darling-Hammond, 1984). Recent data on teacher mobility also show that an increasing percentage of teachers are leaving teaching before retirement age—from 27.2 percent of all leavers in the period between 1987 and 1989 to 30.7 percent in the 1993–95 period (National Center for Education Statistics, 1997b). This creates an obvious impediment to fostering and sustaining real change if the teachers who are trained to institute reforms do not stay in their jobs long enough to realize these goals. In response to these concerns, teachers' salaries rose during the decade of the 1980s from a national average of $15,970 in 1980 to $31,331 in 1990—a 20 percent increase in real dollars (National Center for Education Statistics, 1991). Unfortunately, this increase was not sustained into the 1990s, as salaries plateaued, and even declined slightly, with a real dollar decline in salaries of a little more than 1 percent between 1991 and 1996 (National Center for Education Statistics, 1997a). Thus, even with such a substantial increase in salaries during the 1980s, the earnings of teachers remain considerably below those of other professionals for whom similar preparation is required (Anthony, 1988; Murnane et al., 1991). This is due in part to the fact that teachers typically hold nine- to ten-month contracts, unlike other professionals who work year-round.

The hardship that a truncated work year poses for many teachers is evidenced by the fact that nearly half of all teachers hold a second job, and as many as 72 percent of all male teachers do (Anthony, 1988). The majority of these second jobs are in nonprofessional occupations, requiring teachers to further divide their energies and demean their status as educators (Wisniewski & Kleine, 1984). It therefore should not be surprising that male teachers, and those teachers with the highest level of preparation, are the most likely to leave teaching early in their careers (Anthony, 1988).

Firestone (1994) looked at the issue of teacher salary systems and proposed three different ways in which teacher compensation can be structured to fairly reward increased skill and/or output and serve as an incentive to retain competent teachers. The three include knowledge or skill-based pay, job enlargement, and collective incentives. Both skill-based and collective incentives are based on qualities of individuals or outcomes that do not require a new definition of the job of teacher. Job enlargement, however, is based on a redefinition of the work role and may include expansion of remunerated time. Firestone found the job enlargement proposal to be especially promising.

This essay reports on a study that sought to test out a job enlargement option that would significantly increase teacher salaries, but that would do so in the context of a fundamental structural change in the school. Time would be manipulated to increase salary options, but just as important, to force changes in the way that teachers teach, and in the ways that they relate to each other.

Among the characteristics of teacher working conditions that have been written about extensively is the phenomenon of isolation (Lortie, 1975; Goodlad, 1984; Fullan, 1991). Many researchers have documented the lack of time or opportunity for teachers to interact professionally within the context of the school. Individual teachers are essentially on their own, and new teachers often find this to be one of the most difficult aspects of their job—having no one to turn to (Fullan, 1991). With distant professional relationships, and few opportunities to collaborate, it not surprising that coordinating school reform efforts among teachers who have never really worked together would be daunting, and often unsuccessful (Sarason, 1990).

A second axiom of educational practice is that the overwhelming majority of time (from 70 to 80 percent) in most classrooms is spent in whole-class instruction dominated by teacher talk (Flanders, 1970; Goodlad, 1984). Advances in cognitive research, however, suggest that time spent in active engagement with the subject matter, and opportunities to co-construct knowledge with peers and teachers is often a more effective, yet infrequently used approach in many classrooms (Perkins, 1992). Many school reform efforts have emphasized the importance of teacher collaboration (Little, 1988) and opportunities to work jointly on "polished lessons" (Stevenson & Stigler, 1992), yet most reform efforts do not create structural incentives to support and reward this collaboration. Too often teachers are simply exhorted to improve their practice and "shown" how to do so in a series of inservice workshops scheduled for nonteaching days. Fundamental change in how schools organize time and how they compensate their personnel are seldom considered.

The study reported here, which became known as the Orchard Plan Experiment,[1] set out to create fundamental structural changes in participating schools through the manipulation of calendars and time to:

1. provide opportunities for teachers to substantially increase their salaries through job enlargement; that is, to extend their nine-month

teaching contract to an eleven-month contract (with approximately three additional weeks of vacation during the spring and winter breaks in addition to the one month off in the summer)

2. break down old structures so that new pedagogies and instructional reorganization become a necessary response to change

3. create incentives for teacher collaboration and team teaching

4. make it impossible to continue whole-class, teacher-centered instruction as a routine method of instruction

ELEMENTS OF THE EXPERIMENT

This experiment was begun in 1988 in the context of an enormous demographic shift in California in which schools were receiving well in excess of one hundred thousand new students annually, a large percentage of whom were low-income, immigrants, and ethnic minorities. In response to the severe overcrowding that resulted from this large influx of students, year-round schooling went from a novel experiment in a few schools to encompassing one-fourth of all the schools in the state as a way of accommodating the burgeoning school population. We viewed that this rapid shift in the way schools were organized for instruction could serve a greater purpose than just accommodating more students; it could provide an important laboratory to experiment with "radical" school reform. Moreover, we considered that the expanded school calendars could provide the opportunity for teachers to expand the time they spent in their jobs by 20 percent, serving more students over this extended period, and hence providing the opportunity to increase their salaries commensurately, *without adding any extra costs to school budgets*. See Figure 4.1 for a graphic representation of the experimental school calendar.

A request for proposals was released by the State Department of Education, and three schools, representative of the diversity of schools in the state, were selected to participate in the study. Key elements of the experiment are described in Table 4.1. The experiment continues to date, though formal data collection ended after five years of implementation.

Key to the involvement of schools was the requirement that not only the district superintendent, school board, and site principal agree to participate, but that the teachers' bargaining unit sign a contract with the state as well. This meant that teachers and their bargaining representatives had to be full and willing partners in the experiment. This limited substantially the number of sites from which we had to choose, but increased the chances for success of the experiment. In 1988–89, the

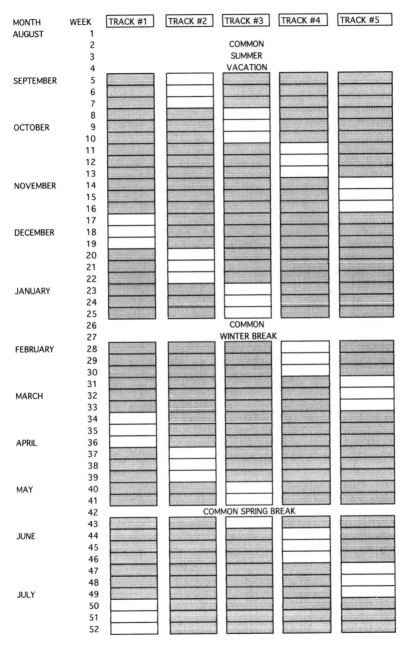

FIGURE 4.1
Proposed Year-Round School Schedule

TABLE 4.1
Elements of the Orchard Plan Experiment

1. An extended year calendar in which approximately 223 days are available for instruction.

2. A reorganization of categorical funding (e.g., Chapter One, Economic Impact Aid, Special Education, Gifted and Talented) to shift these funds into intersession enrichment courses, thereby providing extra days of instruction, with emphasis on "at-risk" students.

3. A reduction in class size by at least two to three students per classroom, achieved through a rotation of five tracks of students in which only four tracks are present at any one time. (Teachers have 20 percent more students on their rolls, but about three students fewer in their class at any time.)

4. The accommodation of 20 percent more students at the site.

5. The opportunity for teachers to extend the length of their contracts by 20 percent, resulting in 20 percent higher salaries.

6. The restructuring of the curriculum into smaller units with built-in review and more careful monitoring of student progress. (Team teaching, small-group learning experiences, and mastery-learning orientation expected to result from this restructuring.)

7. Voluntary participation on the part of schools, teachers, and families with all having a stake in the planning of the program.

three schools were each given a $60,000 planning grant to study, along with their communities, how they might restructure their schools to include the educational reform initiatives that are outlined in Table 4.1. Implementation of the program would not begin until teachers and communities had a full year to study and plan jointly. The Year I grant money was typically used for teacher release time, travel to visit other innovative schools, and computer equipment to help teachers to better keep track of student progress and to manage the data they would be collecting.

The three participating schools, which were from vastly different parts of the state with very different student populations, were asked to adopt a 60/15 year-round schedule. This required that students be grouped into five heterogeneously composed tracks that would attend school on a staggered basis for sixty days then vacation or attend intersessions for fifteen. This cycle was to repeat itself three times during the school year. Hence, although some students cycled out of school at regular intervals, teachers remained in their same classrooms. (This is an important feature of the experiment because most other year-round programs require teachers to change classrooms with each track change.

Not surprisingly, this is an element of year-round schools that many teacher do not like.) All students and teachers, however, would share a common summer break of approximately four weeks, plus two weeks in winter and a one-week spring vacation. Hence, significant "down" time was built into the schedule to give everyone—teachers and students—a sense that there was a beginning and an end to the school year.

Although five tracks (of approximately seven students each) were assigned to each teacher and all eventually had contact with each other, only four tracks of students were present in the classroom at any one time. This configuration resulted in a three-student reduction in class size. For example, as was common in California's overcrowded classrooms, where a teacher typically had thirty-one students before the experiment, now there were twenty-eight in the class at any one time ($35/5 = 7$; $7 \times 4 = 28$), still a large number, but a noticeable difference for most teachers.

With different tracks of students moving in and out of the classroom every three weeks, creating a whole new composition of students—some having been exposed to the previous weeks' instruction, and others not—we predicted that whole-group instruction would lose its viability. Teachers rapidly concluded this as well, and they turned to team teaching and cooperative learning strategies as the most effective strategies for instructional delivery. Although the experiment did not specify *how* teachers were to implement the plan, one of the objectives was to encourage teachers to use team building. In other words, the teachers came to the same conclusions that the researchers had, but independent of any outside intervention. While the idea that the composition of the classroom would change every three weeks was initially unattractive to many teachers, ironically, when teachers were surveyed after only one year, this was found to be among the most desirable features of the program. I return to this point later.

THE SAMPLE

The three schools that participated in the study were vastly different in terms of size as well as student composition. *Lark* is a small rural school serving a very economically disadvantaged student population, about half of whom were ethnic minorities; the largest group being Hmong. This school had only seven teachers on staff, with a total school population of about two hundred. *Brady* is a medium-sized urban/suburban school near the California–Mexico border. Its student population is largely lower-income and working-class; the single largest group of students was Hispanic; however, there was considerable ethnic mix. There were nineteen classroom teachers and three resource teachers serving a student population of about 570. *Palm* is a very large (about 850 students) K–8 school located in a suburb of southern California. Its student population was mostly white when the study began, but has seen a dramatic increase in Latino students over the past few years. There were thirty-two classroom teachers in this school and six resource teachers. Demographic characteristics of the teachers are shown in Table 4.2.

After the teachers bargaining unit had voted to join the Orchard Plan experiment, any teacher who did not want to participate was given the opportunity to take a similar position in any other school in the district that had an opening. A number of teachers decided to take positions in other schools, and opportunities became available for new teachers to join the faculties of the experimental schools. (Two of the principals noted that teachers who were most likely to seek other positions were those who had already "burned out," and the principals were quite happy with this turn of events.) At Lark, six of the seven teaching slots became available; however, at the two other schools, only a few positions became open, and each had long lists of teachers who were interested in applying. Applicants were disproportionately male, and hence the faculties of the schools included a higher percentage of male teachers than is typical for elementary schools (22%). It is also notable

TABLE 4.2
Teacher Characteristics

	LARK	BRADY	PALM	TOTAL	%
Number of Teachers in School	7	19	32	58	100
Gender					
Female	5	13	27	45	78
Male	2	6	5	13	22
Age					
Under 30	3	1	13	17	29
30–45	1	10	12	23	43
Over 45	3	8	5	19	33
Average Years' Experience	11	19	7		$\bar{X} = 12.3$
Number with More Than Five Years College	4	19	24*	47	81

*This number was extrapolated from 65 percent of the teachers because of missing data.

that the average years of teaching experience for all schools was quite high (mean = 12.3 years); at Brady the average was nineteen years and all classroom teachers claimed to have completed more than five years of college; in fact, many held master's degrees, and two had J.D. or Ph.D. degrees. In sum, teachers who were willing to undertake such a radical change in the organization of their work tended to be teachers with substantial experience and advanced degrees and were disproportionately male.

METHODS

Because this study sought to understand the impact of the experiment on the school as a whole, on the individual students and their families, as well as on the teachers, data were collected and analyzed that are not reported in detail here; these included extensive analyses of test score data on total school performance and that of subsets of students in both reading and mathematics, student absenteeism, sociometric data on students' attitudes toward their peers, and surveys of parent satisfaction. Specific to the impact on teachers and their practice, data were collected through group interviews of teachers in the experimental schools, individual interviews with principals and other district personnel, anonymous surveys of teachers, including teaching practices in both experimental and control classrooms, and district and school records. Each experimental school was paired with a control school in the same district whose demographic features and test score data closely paralleled those of the experimental schools in the baseline year. Data on student performance, pupil sociometrics, and teacher absenteeism were collected for all of the schools, both experimental and control.

Teachers in each of the experimental schools were convened in groups of varying sizes at least twice during the study period to share with the researcher their impressions of the program and its strengths and weaknesses. Administrative personnel were excluded from these meetings to increase the likelihood that teachers would feel free to comment openly. General questions, such as "What aspects of the program work for you, and what needs to be rethought?", "How has your teaching changed as a result of this experiment?", and "How have classroom dynamics changed as a result of the experiment?" were posed to the groups. Teachers were quite outspoken and anxious to share their feelings, and this provided information that was critical to understanding the data that were collected through the surveys.

In addition to the focus groups, teachers were given anonymous surveys and asked to return them directly to the researcher. These were distributed in the spring of the first year of operation (about nine months into the academic year), during the fall of the second year (about two months after returning to school from summer break), and again in the spring of the third year (about nine months after commencing the year). Return rates for the surveys are reported in Table 4.4. They were generally high, ranging, with one exception, between 86 percent and 100 percent of the teachers at the schools. Surveys included a number of questions about level of job satisfaction, reasons for agreeing to participate in the experiment, and assessment of the educational value of the experiment. The final survey, which was distributed at the end of the third year of the extended contracts, asked several questions relating to teacher burnout. These data are reported in Table 4.5. Considerable opportunity was also provided in the surveys for teachers to comment freely on any aspect of the experiment that they chose. As always, the teachers were not reluctant to express their thoughts and these are included in the findings section.

Finally, data were also collected from district records on teacher salaries and absenteeism.

FINDINGS

Teacher Salaries

Table 4.3 shows the average salaries earned by teachers at each of the experimental schools, compared to the average salaries for their district, the state, and the nation in 1991–92 school year. Each year thereafter, these teachers' salaries rose at the same percentage increase as all other teachers in the district; since the Orchard teachers' base was the larger beginning in 1991–92, the gap between themselves and all other teach-

TABLE 4.3
Teacher Salaries, National, State, District,
and Experimental School Means, 1991–92

	National Mean*	State Mean*	District Mean	School Mean	School's Highest Salary
	$34,413	$41,811	—	—	—
Lark	—	—	$28,000	$42,586	$47,958
Brady	—	—	$41,911	$54,735	$64,883
Palm	—	—	$37,298	$45,058	$67,623

*National Education Association, 1991–92 estimates of school statistics.

ers continued to widen over time. Also included in the table is the highest salary earned at that school by a regular classroom teacher. In each case the highest salary was earned by teachers with more than twenty years of teaching experience and most held at least a master's degree; a similarly qualified teacher teaching at a traditional school in the same district earned 20 percent less.

The disparity among district salaries is notable, with the rural district in northern California paying considerably less than the urban/suburban districts to the south. Nonetheless, within each of these contexts the opportunities for earning what teachers referred to as a "professional salary" are dramatic.

Consistent with other studies that have shown that the short teaching year can be stress-producing when it means having to seek a second job to make ends meet, several teachers commented candidly about the way in which the extended contract reduced stress in their lives.

> *For the first time in years I've had a full-time job. Now I am employed in a position where I don't have to seek employment when the children are on break.*

> *I enjoy the four-week break in the summer, two weeks at Christmas, and a week in spring. As a single parent I would have to work in the summer anyhow.*

> *I no longer have to find a summer job to support my household.*

Not surprisingly, teachers expressed a high degree of satisfaction with their compensation, but this also appeared to be related to an increased sense of professionalism. As one teacher put it, "Now we are being paid what teachers really deserve. In addition, our schedule is now comparable to other professionals." Moreover, teachers also expressed a similar level of satisfaction with their jobs.

Teacher Satisfaction

In response to the question, "How satisfied are you with your job?" 98 percent of the teachers in 1991–92 reported being "moderately satisfied" (19%) or "very satisfied" (79%). As noted in Table 4.4, the level of satisfaction increased steadily from an overall of 74 percent in 1989–90, the first year of implementation, to 92 percent in the second year, and 98 percent in the third year (see Table 4.4).

The consistent increase in satisfaction was no doubt affected to some extent by the exiting of unhappy teachers. However, over the three-year period, only five teachers (or less than 3 percent per year) left the schools, and of these, at least half left because of family relocations rather than any dissatisfaction with their job. Some of the increase in job

TABLE 4.4
Teacher Satisfaction, Number of Teachers Responding to Each Category, 1989–90, 1991–92

	LARK			BRADY			PALM		
Year	89–90	90–91	91–92	89–90	90–91	91–92	89–90	90–91	91–92
N	6	7	6	19**	19	22	17	37	36
% Response	86	100	86	86	86	100	56	100	97
Very Satisfied	5	1	3	11	13	20	10	29	26
Satisfied	1	4	2	4	6	2	3	6	10
Neutral*	0	2	0	2	0	0	1	2	0
Unsatisfied	0	0	1	0	0	0	3	0	0
Very Unsatisfied	0	1	0	1	0	0	0	0	0

*The neutral category was removed from the 1991–92 survey to force teachers' responses. "Satisfied" and "Unsatisfied" were consequently changed to "Moderately Satisfied" and "Moderately Unsatisfied."
**One teacher responded to the survey, but did not answer this question.

satisfaction could also have been due to an artifact of the data because Palm had a relatively low rate of return on teacher surveys in the first year of implementation. Nonetheless, teacher satisfaction did increase over time and evidence for this was also found in many teacher comments.

> *We're still working the bugs out of our program and feel we have a more dynamic program each year.* [First-grade teacher]

> *Initially, the [experiment] appeared overwhelming. However, working the Orchard Plan is not as complicated as it sounds. Each year gets easier and better.* [Second-grade teacher]

> *Pacing is important and you learn this in your first year.* [Third-grade teacher]

Teachers attributed their satisfaction to a number of factors: the opportunity to do something different, changes they perceived in their students, greater satisfaction with the pay they were receiving, but in small focus groups, teachers commonly talked about the opportunity to team and share with other teachers and the camaraderie that had been built during the months of joint planning. Because the only viable way to make the experiment work was through team teaching at least part of the time (teachers "specialized" in particular areas, allowing them to plan for several "tracks" of students who were at different places in the curriculum) the collaboration that was begun in the planning year continued throughout the implementation of the program. Teachers also felt tremendous ownership for the programs they had put in place because they had designed them, made the decisions about how they would be implemented, and had been given considerable autonomy in deciding how the grant funds would be spent. Teachers who had traveled to other schools (sometimes out of state) to talk with teachers and administrators who were also trying to innovate commented especially on the sense of professionalism and competence this engendered in them.

Motivation to Participate

Why had teachers chosen to participate in this experiment? When asked this question in the first year of implementation, 35 percent of the teachers stated that salary was their most important consideration. At the end of the third year, a similar percentage of teachers, 38 percent, gave salary as their primary reason for staying with the experiment. However, 24 percent stated that they had stayed because they felt the program was better for the students. In order of importance, teachers also noted that they "liked this school," and they enjoyed "more autonomy." Hence, while salary was ranked as the number one motivation for joining the experiment and staying with it, the majority of teachers cited another reason, one having more to do with school climate and conditions, as the reason for their participation. An important feature of the school climate was the collaboration that was fostered among teachers as they team-taught and worked together to build new curricula that could be taught in three-week chunks.

Teacher Burnout

While the Orchard Plan experiment provided the opportunity for teachers to enlarge their jobs and receive commensurately higher salaries as a result, to participate in the design and implementation of a total reorganization of their schools, and to work collaboratively with each other in ways they never before envisioned, we nonetheless worried about the issue of burnout. Would teachers be able to continue teaching up to 225 days per year over a multiyear period? And what would the effects be on students? This was measured in several ways.

On the surveys that were administered toward the end of the third year of the experiment, teachers were asked, "Are you getting burned out from working an extended contract?" and "Do you intend to return to this school next year?" We also asked if teachers wanted to return to a nine-month contract. Table 4.5 displays the responses to these questions.

There is an interesting, apparent discrepancy in the percentages of teachers who say they are burned out and those who want to return to a nine-month contract. For example, 18 percent of teachers claimed to be burned out at the end of their third year in the program, yet only 7 percent said they wanted to return to a nine-month contract. Some teachers commented on this question by saying that although they felt burned out (the survey was administered in the ninth month of teaching), they were no more so than they would be on a traditional calendar—suggesting that this was a "time of year" phenomenon rather than a reflection on their satisfaction with the program. Additionally, one of the teachers who reported being burned out was of retirement age, and planning to retire at the end of the year. She was evidently burned out with teaching in general, rather than specifically with the eleven-month contract. The remaining teachers who reported being burned out were the same four who also marked that they wanted to return to a nine month contract. In most cases, these were younger teachers who wanted to start a family; none of these teachers was in the 45+ range. Teachers were anxious to comment on the burn-out issue and had strong opinions:

> *My personal belief is that burnout is more a personality problem of boredom. I've not had that problem. I always find new ideas to try.*
> [First-grade teacher]

TABLE 4.5
Teacher Burnout, 1991–92

Question	LARK (n = 6) no. yes responses	(%)	BRADY (n = 19) no. yes responses	(%)	PALM (n = 32) no. yes responses	(%)	TOTAL (n = 57) no.	(%)
. . . burned out?	3	(50)	0	(0)	7	(22)	10	(18)
. . . like to return to nine-month contract?	0	(0)	0	(0)	4	(13)	4	(7)
. . . plan to return next year?	5	(83)	19	(100)	30	(94)	54	(95)

Even on an extended contract, I work less than the general public and I don't feel the whole general public is burned out. [Third-grade teacher]

The way we team in the fifth grade has eliminated problems of burnout. We teach a track for no longer than twelve weeks at a time. [Fifth grade teacher]

In our district all the discussion/concern over burnout on the five track has come from outside the building! I wish people would just ask us first if there is even a cause for concern. [Fourth-grade teacher]

Another measure of teacher burnout or stress is increased absenteeism (Farber, 1991; Hammen & DeMayo, 1982). Teacher absenteeism was charted for the baseline year (1988–89) and the two subsequent years of implementation for both the experimental and the control schools. Table 4.6 displays these results.

The data in Table 4.6 suggest that teachers did not experience significantly increased stress over the three-year period, at least not at levels that would lead to high rates of illness or absenteeism. Although absences rose by a small amount at two of the schools (Lark and Palm), this increase was over an extremely low base and represented rates considerably lower than at the control schools, where teachers were working a shorter year. Moreover, in the case of Palm, the increase was only slightly more than would be expected as a percentage of the increased number of days worked. At Brady, where the initial rate of absenteeism was higher than at the other schools, teacher absences actually declined slightly over the three-year period.

A fourth measure of teacher burnout or stress can be student achievement. Farber has suggested that "the impact of teacher stress and burnout may be greatest in terms of its potentially devastating effects on pupil education, particularly those in lower socioeconomic groups" (1991, p. 85). The logical link between student achievement and teacher

TABLE 4.6
Teacher Absenteeism, Orchard and Control Schools
(average number of days absent per teacher, 1988–89 to 1990–91)

	LARK	CONTROL	BRADY	CONTROL	PALM	CONTROL
1988–89	2.0	7.8	7.8	7.8	1.2	2.7
1989–90	3.0	6.1	8.1	7.3	1.8	3.2
1990–91	3.7	5.7	7.6	N/A	2.0	4.0
1989 to 1991 Difference	+1.7	−2.1	−0.2		+0.8	+1.3

attitude can be viewed from the perspective of studies on teacher expectation effects.

Teachers' expectations have been demonstrated to affect student achievement (Brophy & Good, 1986), and a "don't care" attitude about the individual needs of students is one of the hallmarks of burned-out teachers (Farber, 1991). Hence, if teachers are truly feeling burned out, one could expect to see these effects in a decline in student achievement. However, this did not occur at any of the experimental schools. On standardized measures of student achievement over the three years, 1988–89 to 1990–91,[2] none of the experimental schools showed a loss in achievement compared to its control, and all experimental schools showed significant gains in achievement in particular areas, and for particular groups of students.[3]

In sum, there was little evidence of increased stress or burnout for the great majority of teachers who opted to work the extended year. At the same time, high levels of job satisfaction were reported. After three years, 95 percent of teachers planned to return to the extended contract and 93 percent said they did not want to return to a nine-month schedule. From teachers' comments it was evident that older, more experienced teachers were the most enthusiastic supporters of the reorganization of time and the opportunity for extended teaching contracts.

Because of the three-week periods I am better organized and this automatically makes me feel less stressed. I am able to fit in more units that appeal specifically to me which makes it more interesting. [female, twenty-seven years' experience]

I have adjusted my teaching and other activities to conform to an extended year contract. I love it! Never would I return to a nine-month contract if I had the choice. [male, forty years' experience]

I'm excited about teaching. I would encourage others to try this program. [female, sixteen years' experience]

The best teaching experience I have had in thirty years of teaching! [female]

These comments from the teachers are consistent with other studies that suggest that burnout is not so much a function of the amount of time worked as the attitudes one has about one's job and its compensations (Farber, 1991).

In the same way that the rethinking of the teaching calendar had resulted in new roles and relationships for teachers, the five-track program had also resulted in new roles and relationships among students. Echoing Sarason's (1990) sage admonition, the effects on teachers' attitudes toward their work appeared to be mirrored in the attitudes of students. At least this was widely reported by teachers. In the first focus groups with teachers, a major theme that emerged was the teachers' fondness for the rotation of students every three weeks. This was more than surprising, since it had originally been a difficult feature of the experiment to sell. Teachers commented, at every school, that classroom disruptions were down, fewer students were being sent to the office for behavioral difficulties, and students who had never before participated in class were participating. They explained this by saying that the rotation of students tended to reduce frictions among students that normally tend to increase over time when students are in constant contact with each other, and that the cycling out of academic "stars" provided more opportunities for students who had not participated as much to fill those now vacant roles. Moreover, they reported that every three weeks there was a "first day of school" phenomenon that increased the enthusiasm of students and created excitement about being reunited with classmates they had missed seeing.

Unfortunately, it was impossible to test the difference in behavioral difficulties empirically because the schools had not kept good data on office referrals prior to initiating the experiment; there was no baseline against which to compare the current situation. We did, however, test the issue of greater participation on the part of students by comparing sociometric data for both the control and experimental schools, and by surveying teachers in both control and experimental classrooms, looking for evidence that more students were actively participating, perceived by their peers to be leaders, or were academic stars in experimental classrooms. We were unable to confirm this, based on student data, though the teachers in the experimental classrooms continued to insist that it was an important phenomenon in their classrooms, and their explanations of the phenomenon appeared logical. This remains an unresolved issue in the research, but nonetheless speaks to the teachers' attitudes about their work conditions: They experienced their classroom environments as improved and they were, almost without exception, happier in their teaching.

The Orchard Plan experiment attempted to test a host of reform ideas and their impact on students, communities, and schools. However, most fundamentally, it concerned itself with the problem of retaining good teachers in schools who would be willing to innovate and to stay at a school long enough to create and sustain change. The principle behind the experiment was that in order to force *real* change, school structures needed to be modified in ways that would not permit teachers to do what they had always done, but that would also provide opportunities for career enhancement that would not otherwise be available to them. By manipulating time, and opening the entire school calendar to new ways of organizing time, possibilities were introduced for both students and teachers that did not exist in a rigid 180-day September to June schedule, and almost no one was interested in going back to the way things had been done before.

However, the future of this reform remains uncertain. As teacher turnover occurs, which is inevitable, will new teachers be as committed to the reform agenda as their predecessors? Without the advantage of a year spent in planning with other teachers, and without lengthy school breaks during which such collaboration could occur outside school hours, will the new teachers develop the same camaraderie with their peers as the first set of teachers, who were the designers of the experiment? Without the enthusiasm that accompanies ownership of a program that is the product of one's own work, will new teachers tend to burn out sooner? And will the communities continue to support schools that are "out of sync" with other schools in their districts? Erosion of community support has been a factor in the demise of many other allegedly successful experiments (Willis,1993). If we have learned anything from the reform efforts of the past fifteen years, certainly we now know that reform is not something that happens and is completed—it requires sustained attention and renewal. The challenge for the Orchard Plan schools will be to regularly re-create the enthusiasm and collaborative spirit that accompanied their initial efforts, and find ways to continue innovating in these schools.

NOTES

1. The experiment was named after the Orchard School, a school in Utah that had successfully experimented with a calendar like that adopted for this study.

2. Achievement data were also collected for the 1991–92 school year; however, student attrition was so high at this point that firm conclusions could not be drawn from these drastically reduced samples.

3. For a fuller discussion of the achievement data associated with this study, see Gándara and Fish (1994).

REFERENCES

Anthony, P. (1988). Teachers in the economic system. In K. Alexander & D. Monk (Eds.), *Attracting and compensating America's teachers* (pp. 1–68). Cambridge, MA: Ballinger.

Brophy, J., & Good, T. (1986). Teacher behavior and student achievement. In M. Wittrock (Ed.), *Handbook of research on teaching* (pp. 328–375). New York: Macmillan.

Darling-Hammond, L. (1984). *Beyond the commission reports.* Santa Monica, CA: RAND.

Farber, B. (1991). *Crisis in dducation: Stress and burnout in the American teacher*. San Francisco, CA: Jossey-Bass.

Firestone, W. (1994). Redesigning teacher salary systems. *American educational research journal, 31*, 549–574.

Flanders, N. (1970). *Analyzing teacher behavior*. Reading, MA: Addison-Wesley.

Fullan, M. (1991). *The meaning of educational change*. New York: Teachers College Press.

Gándara, P. (1994). The impact of the educational reform movement on Limited English Proficient students. In B. McLeod (Ed.), *Language and learning: Educating linguistically diverse students*. Albany: State University of New York Press.

Gándara, P., & Fish, J. (1994). Year round schooling as an avenue to major structural reform. *Educational Evaluation and Policy Analysis, 16*, 67–86.

Goodlad, J. (1984). *A place called school: Prospects for the future*. New York: McGraw-Hill.

Hammen, C., & DeMayo, R. (1982). Cognitive correlates of teacher stress and depression symptoms: Implications for attributional models of depression. *Journal of Abnormal Psychology, 91*, 96–101.

Little, J. W. (1988). *Conditions of professional development in secondary schools*. Stanford, CA: Center for Research on the Context of Teacher Education.

Lortie, D. (1975). *School teacher: A sociological study*. Chicago: University of Chicago Press.

Murnane, R., Singer, J., Willet, J., Kemple, J., & Olsen, R. (1991). *Who will teach?* Cambridge, MA: Harvard University Press.

National Center for Education Statistics (NCES). (1991). *Digest of education statistics, 1991*. Washington, DC: U.S. Department of Education.

National Center for Education Statistics (NCES). (1997a). *Condition of education, 1997*. Washington, DC: U.S. Department of Education.

National Center for Education Statistics (NCES). (1997b). *Digest of education-statistics, 1997*. Washington, DC: U.S. Department of Education.

National Education Association. (1991). *1991–92 Estimates of School Statistics*. Washington, DC: Author.

Perkins, D. (1992). *Smart schools, From training memories to educating minds*. New York: The Free Press.

Sarason, S. (1990). *The predictable gailure of educational reform*. San Francisco: Jossey-Bass.

Stevenson, D., & Stigler, J. (1992). *The learning gap*. New York: Summit Books.

Willis, S. (1993). Are longer classes better? *ASCD Update, 35*, 1–3.

Wisniewski, R., & Klein, P. (1984). Teacher moonlighting: An unstudied phenomenon, *Phi Delta Kappan, 65*, 353–355.

CHAPTER 5

Increasing Achievement for Elementary Students, Including Those At-Risk, Through the Manipulation of Time and the School Calendar

Carolyn Kneese

Many educators today are considering a reorganization of the school calendar from the traditional nine-month model to a year-round model, for they believe that achievement can be increased for all students (Brekke, 1992a), in particular for those considered at-risk (Mutchler, 1993), through the manipulation of time and the school calendar.

In 1983 the Task Force on Education for Economic Growth recommended that states extend the duration and intensity of academic learning time in schools in order to improve the academic achievement of America's youth. Proposals for educational reform similarly have called for extending the school year from 180 to 200 days (Brekke, 1992b). These proposals are supported by consistent research findings of an association between the time a student spends learning and the amount of learning that occurs (Bradford, 1992).

These findings, however, do not mean that simply extending the school year will improve student achievement. After reviewing studies that found the length of the school day or class period was not related to student achievement, Stallings (1980) concluded that student learning depends on how the available time is used, not just the amount of time available. If this is true, it is questionable whether the marginal extension of the school day or the school year would have a significant impact on student achievement (Hazelton, Blakely, & Denton, 1993).

Thus two conceptions of year-round education (YRE) are found in the literature. One views year-round education as an extended year for the student, who attends school for more days than a student on a traditional school calendar of 180 days, or who attends an intersession for academic enhancement. The other conception involves a rearrangement of the school calendar, such that the number of school days is the same as in a traditional calendar school, but the spacing between school attendance periods is decreased (Pelavin, 1977). Proponents of this type of year-round education believe that retention of learning is increased by simply spacing school attendance into shorter academic learning periods (Hazelton, Blakely, & Denton, 1992). The present study involves an investigation of the effect of this type of year-round education on student achievement.

Goren and Carriendo (1986) identified two organizational arrangements for year-round education: multi-track and single-track. The single-track organization involves year-round attendance with all students on the same schedule, whereas in the multi-track organization some students are in attendance while others are on vacation. Each track is generally implemented for different purposes. The single-track organization is usually voluntarily implemented by a school district for purposes of reform, because it is thought to enhance student learning by providing a schedule that minimizes learning loss (Hazelton, Blakely, & Denton, 1992). On the other hand, the multi-track organization is usually mandated by a school district in order to increase capacity (Bradford, 1992), but can also be utilized to reduce class size (Brekke, 1992b).

One might conclude that since the year-round program with spaced learning approximates the same total number of days (generally 180) as that of the traditional calendar year, it would have a similar effect on achievement. Additionally, one would surmise that both year-round education tracks would perform in an identical manner, given an equal opportunity to learn (Kneese, 1996). However, because multi-track programs were originally implemented to increase capacity, they were typically found in high-growth, poor, and inner-city areas. These students were generally low-income, transient, minority, and limited English-proficient (Quinlan, George, & Emmett, 1987). Single-track programs, on the other hand, were generally found in lower-growth, suburban, and more middle-class districts. These students were less difficult to educate and typically performed relative to other students with similar background characteristics (Quinlan et al., 1987). Therefore, because single-track YRE is generally implemented with the express intent of maximizing student outcomes by spacing learning in shorter intervals (Morse, 1992) versus simply increasing capacity, one would expect the single-track program to outperform the multi-track YRE (Kneese, 1996). However, it has been found that multi-track, when instituted for school reform purposes, appears to show increases in achievement as well (Gándara & Fish, 1994).

The effect of the traditional calendar schedule on the learning retention of at-risk students is of particular concern to educators, for at least one-third of elementary and secondary students in the United States can be identified as high-risk (Levin, 1987; Pallas, Natirello, & McDill, 1985). One indicator of an at-risk student is limited English proficiency (LEP). Because an increasing number of students come from homes where English is not the primary language, three months away from formal instruction seems likely to hinder their second language acquisition. For most of these students, the language of summer is the language of the family, which for LEP students is likely to be a language other than English. Furthermore, students who are experiencing learning difficulties in a traditional calendar school must usually go through nine months of failure and frustration before they can attend summer school, which is far too late for effective remediation to occur. In contrast, intermittent intersession periods accommodate more frequent remediation periods in direct response to student needs.

Many studies have found that the gains made during the school year are not sustained over the summer vacation and this loss is greater for at-risk students (Pelavin & David, 1977). A 1978 study supported by the New York State Board of Regents (reported in Brekke, 1992a) found that advantaged students advance academically an average of one year and three months in school and then learn an additional month's worth during the summer, whereas disadvantaged students advance an average of one year and one month during the year and then lose three to four months during the summer. Hayes and Grether (1969) found that upwards of 80 percent of differences in reading level between economically advantaged white schools and African American and Puerto Rican ghetto schools could be explained by differential progress made during four summers between second and sixth grades.

Gándara and Fish (1994) found that there were few achievement differences for all students in the multi-track year-round program in their study. The targeted at-risk students, however, did increase achievement when an intensive intersession program was provided for them.

It seems reasonable to expect that the effectiveness of YRE in improving student academic achievement would build over time. It is reported that meaningful change is a process taking two to three years to show results (Hall & Hord, 1987). The ten schools in this study had been on the YRE calendar for three different periods of time. One school was in its fourth year of YRE; five schools were in their third year of YRE; and four schools were in their second year of YRE. Therefore, it was expected that the school in its fourth year of YRE implementation would produce greater student academic achievement than the schools in their third year of YRE implementation, and that these schools in turn would produce greater student academic achievement than the schools that had been implemented YRE for only two years.

As the purpose of the present study was to determine whether all elementary school students or those at-risk in a single-track YRE program would achieve greater academic growth than their peers in a traditional calendar school, the following questions were asked: After matching for initial reading and math achievement, is there a significant difference in the reading and math achievement of the general population of YRE and TCS students after one year of instruction? After matching for initial reading and math achievement, is there a significant difference in the reading and math achievement of the specific population of YRE and TCS at-risk students after one year of instruction? After matching for initial reading and math achievement, does the difference in the reading and math achievement of YRE and TCS students increase as a function of the number of years of program implementation?

The participants were selected from YRE and TCS classes in ten schools in a suburban school district located near a major city in the Southwest. The district encompasses 345 square miles and serves a diverse population in a variety of residential settings: a traditional urban community, a rural community in the eastern section of the district, and a surburban community in the southern section. The district serves approximately 25,500 students, whose ethnic makeup is 81.9 percent white, 10.7 percent Hispanic, 6.1 percent African American, and 1.3 percent other. The socioeconomic level of students in schools in the district for 1992–93 was reported to be 26.4 percent economically disadvantaged and 3.7 percent limited English proficiency. The other 70 percent ranged from middle to high socioeconomic level.

In 1989, the board of trustees for the school district made the decision to implement YRE for the purpose of determining whether student achievement would be enhanced if students had continuous instruction throughout the year. In 1989, the district implemented a closely monitored pilot program involving fifty-four students on a dual track, 30/10 calendar at one elementary school. A dual-track system is one in which both year-round single-track and traditional calendars are employed in the same school. The 30/10 design is one in which thirty days (six weeks) of instruction are followed by ten days (two weeks) of vacation, except for longer breaks (approximately four weeks) in December and August. Participation by students and teachers in the YRE program was strictly voluntary, and students in all attendance zones of the school districts were eligible to participate.

The pilot program was expanded in 1990–91 after a survey of parents confirmed a high interest in participation. The parents of more than one thousand students requested to be in the program. Six elementary schools were selected as sites. Approximately 850 students and forty classroom teachers were involved that year in the YRE program.

The YRE program was expanded for the 1991–92 school year to ten K–6 schools, because of increasing demand by parents throughout the district. Approximately 1,200 students were served that year in the YRE program. For the 1992–93 school year, another campus was added and the enrollment was up to 1,462 students. The program for the 1993–94 school year was available in four of the six intermediate schools and in seven of the seventeen elementary schools in the district.

YRE and TCS students attended school the same number of days (175), and were taught by teachers who followed the same district-adopted curriculum. However, because the TCS students followed the September to June calendar, they had approximately four more weeks of learning time between the same initial school day (September) and test day (April) as did the YRE students, whose learning followed the 30/10 design. In many YRE programs, the ten day intersession might be utilized for enrichment and remediation, but the intersession in this school district was used for vacation time only and not for academic advancement for the YRE students. For those reasons, the TCS students should have had an increased academic advantage over that of the YRE students at the April testing date.

Because YRE students were self-selected, as is the case in many single-track YRE programs, class size varied from fifteen to twenty-three. Class size in the TCS is set by the state and is larger, ranging from twenty to twenty-five.

Selection of the schools for the present study was limited to those that had year-round education classes and whose students had taken the criterion achievement test (the NAPT in 1992 and 1993, explained below). Therefore, one of the eleven dual-track schools was not included in this sample, as it had been in operation for only one year. As explained above, the ten schools had implemented their YRE programs over a three-year time period. One school began in August 1989, and therefore the YRE program had been implemented in that school for four years. In August 1990 five more schools began the program, and so they had a three-year implementation period. The remaining four schools began their year-round education programs in August 1991, and so they had a two-year implementation period.

The total enrollment in the YRE classes consisted of 1,114 students, with a fairly equal gender distribution. The students were largely white, with less than 10 percent African American, Hispanic, and Asian Pacific students. Although only seventy-three students were classified as Chapter 1, approximately 20 percent were on the school's free lunch program. In the district, an at-risk student is designated by the Texas Education Agency 1993–94 Public Education Information Management System Data Standards as a student who: (1) did not perform at a satisfactory level on a beginning-of-school readiness test or an achievement test (which can be the NAPT from the previous spring); (2) failed at least one reading, writing, or math section of the recent third- through fifth-grade versions of the Texas Educational Assessment of Minimum Skills or Texas Assessment of Academic Skills (TEAMS/TAAS) tests; (3) has limited English proficiency (LEP); (4) has been a victim of abuse, as determined by the Texas Department of Human Services; or (5) engages in delinquent conduct as described by the Texas Family Code 51.03(a).

Because of the fact that SES level was not included in the definition of at-risk, the subsample came from across all three SES levels—low, middle, and high. This at-risk YRE subsample of forty-three was comprised of fourteen white females, two Hispanic females, and three black females; twenty-two white males and two black males. We could assume that these were low-achieving students who were simply performing below standard, and for whom LEP was most likely not an issue.

The district's test results on the NAPT for 1992 and 1993 were obtained from district records. Samples were drawn from the population of YRE and TCS students in the school district by the following stratified sampling and matching procedure:

1. A total of four hundred fourth-, fifth-, and sixth-grade YRE students were identified by the school district who were enrolled in 1993, and previously in 1992 as third-, fourth-, and fifth-grade students in each of the ten dual-track schools. Each record contained 1992 NAPT percentile ranks in reading and math, 1992 and 1993 NCE scores for the reading and math subtests, student ID, demographic information, grade, and campus.

2. A total of three thousand fourth-, fifth-, and sixth-grade traditional calendar students were identified by the school district who were enrolled in 1992, and previously in 1992 as third-, fourth-, and fifth-grade students in each of the same ten dual-track schools.

3. A total of 311 YRE students were subsequently identified who were present and had taken the reading and math subtests of the NAPT in 1993 and previously in 1992. Within each grade and within each school 311 TCS students were individually matched to the 311 YRE students by percentile rank on the reading and math subtests. When more than one student from the traditional calendar pool qualified, a student was randomly selected from that group.

To summarize, there were two samples of matched pairs of students in the study: one sample for math and one for reading. Each YRE student (N = 311) was matched twice. First, each YRE student was matched to a TCS student in the same school and grade on their 1992 NAPT reading percentile rank. Second, the same YRE student was matched with another TCS student in the same school and grade on their math percentile rank. An overlap in sampling could occur if a particular TCS student was matched with one YRE student on the math test and a different YRE student on the reading test.

The achievement measures were the reading and mathematics subtests of the Norm-Referenced Assessment Program for Texas (NAPT) of the Iowa Test of Basic Skills. This nationally used standardized test was administered to both the YRE and TCS groups, as well as to the entire population of students in all grades in the school district.

The NAPT was designed and constructed by professional staff at the University of Iowa. NAPT test reliabilities are high, with interpretations aided by carefully developed norms (Norm-Referenced Assessment Program for Texas, 1993). The Kuder-Richardson 20 reliability coefficients for grades 3, 4, and 5 in reading comprehension are 0.92, 0.91, and 0.91, respectively. The coefficients for grades 3, 4, and 5 for mathematics problem solving are 0.87, 0.87, and 0.86, respectively.

This study focused only on the use of the reading and mathematics portions of the NAPT. In 1992 Form 1 was given to all students in the populations, containing the eleven basic skills tests, plus social studies and science. In 1993 only the reading and math subtests, Form 2, were administered. The reading comprehension test scores and the problem-solving test scores from the mathematics test comprised the data set for the statistical analyses.

The scores of the NAPT are equal-interval, normalized standard scores called Normal Curve Equivalents (NCE) and have a mean of 50 and a standard deviation of 21.06. An NCE of 50 is at grade level. With one year of gain in one school year, a student will maintain the same NCE. In other words, from year to year the pre-test NCE (obtained at the end of school year 1) is the expected post-test NCE (obtained at the end of school year 2). Therefore, any gain in a NCE score from one year to the next constitutes an improvement in academic achievement.

The mean was used as a measure of central tendency to represent the entire group of scores. The standard deviation was calculated to determine the variability of the comparison and control group test scores in the study.

In order to compare the post mean scores of the YRE and TCS groups, tests of statistical significance (*t* tests for related samples) and effect size analysis were utilized. The Bonferroni inequality for determining the critical value of *t* was employed (Glass & Hopkins, 1984), simultaneously encompassing all ten comparisons. Thus the mean score differences were ultimately tested for significance at an alpha level of 0.005 rather than 0.05.

Effect sizes were calculated to determine the practical significance of the observed differences between YRE and TCS students in academic achievement. According to Tallmadge (1977; cited in Wolf, 1986), the National Institute of Education's Joint Dissemination Review Panel considers an effect size of 0.33 (and in some cases as small as 0.25) to be of practical significance.

Descriptive statistics for pre- and post-reading NCE scores for the total sample of YRE and TCS students are shown in Table 5.1. The t test for related samples, using the adjusted 0.005 probability level derived from the Bonferroni procedure, yielded a statistically significant difference ($t = 6.22$, $p = 0.001$) in favor of the YRE group. The effect size was 0.33, which is generally considered to be of practical significance.

Descriptive statistics for pre- and post-math NCE scores for the total sample of YRE and TCS are shown in Table 5.1. The t test with the Bonferroni adjustment revealed a statistically significant difference ($t = 5.87$, $p = 0.001$) in favor of the YRE group. The effect size was 0.30, which is close to the point of practical significance.

Descriptive statistics for pre- and post-reading NCE scores for the at-risk sample of YRE and TCS students are shown in Table 5.2. The t test for related samples, using the adjusted 0.005 probability level derived from the Bonferroni procedure, yielded a statistically significant difference ($t = 4.87$, $p = 0.001$) in favor of the YRE group. The effect size was 0.67, which is of practical significance and of medium magnitude.

Descriptive statistics for pre- and post-math NCE scores for the at-

TABLE 5.1
Descriptive Statistics for Pre- and
Post-Achievement Scores for the Total Sample

	Reading NCE Scores		Mathematics NCE Scores	
Groups	Pre M (SD)	Post M (SD)	Pre M (SD)	Post M (SD)
Year-round Education (N = 311)	61.34 (18.41)	61.46 (18.37)	62.07 (17.66)	61.13 (18.54)
Traditional Calendar (N = 311)	61.37 (18.05)	55.99 (16.80)	62.47 (17.63)	56.19 (16.43)

risk sample of YRE and TCS are shown in Table 5.2. The difference between the mean scores was not statistically significant at the designated alpha level (t = 2.11, p = 0.04). The effect size was 0.29, which was close to the point of practical significance, but likely meaningless, as statistical significance at 0.005 was not observed.

Both descriptive and inferential statistics for the pre- and post-reading NCE scores for the total sample of YRE and TCS students at two, three, and four years of program implementation are shown in Table 5.3.

TABLE 5.2
Descriptive Statistics for Pre- and
Post-Achievement Scores for the At-Risk Students

	Reading NCE Scores		Mathematics NCE Scores	
Groups	Pre M (SD)	Post M (SD)	Pre M (SD)	Post M (SD)
Year-round Education (N = 43)	45.46 (17.97)	51.61 (16.54)	47.97 (16.59)	45.93 (17.55)
Traditional Calendar (N = 43)	45.25 (16.43)	41.77 (14.62)	48.35 (18.57)	42.19 (13.06)

TABLE 5.3
Pre- and Post-Reading Scores by Number
of Years of YRE Program Implementation

	Year-Round Education		Traditional Calendar			
Groups	Pre M (SD)	Post M (SD)	Pre M (SD)	Post M (SD)	T Value for Post Means	Effect Size
2 years (N = 72)	54.24 (18.55)	55.14 (15.94)	53.79 (17.65)	48.97 (14.38)	4.55**	.43
3 years (N = 199)	65.70 (17.07)	65.27 (17.95)	65.74 (16.97)	60.53 (15.77)	4.05**	.30
4 years (N = 37)	54.13 (16.10)	55.81 (18.49)	54.50 (16.52)	47.13 (16.84)	2.99*	.52

*p < 0.005
**p < 0.001

The *t* test for related samples yielded a statistically significant difference in favor of the YRE in all comparison years of implementation. Although the effect size analysis revealed increasing effectiveness of the YRE program in reading from the second to the fourth year of implementation, the effect of the third year was the smallest.

Both descriptive and inferential statistics for the pre- and post-math NCE scores for the total sample of YRE and TCS students at two, three, and four years of program implementation are shown in Table 5.4. The *t* test for related samples yielded a statistically significant difference in favor of the YRE in all comparison years of implementation. The results for math revealed decreasing effectiveness of the YRE program for the same time period. Similar to the reading results, the effect of the third year was the smallest.

A major finding of this study is that YRE students, whether the total sample or the at-risk subsample, performed substantially better on the post-test achievement measures (administered April 1993), even though the YRE and TCS students performed very similarly on the pre-test achievement measures (administered April 1992).

Inspection of the post-test differences between the YRE and TCS groups reveals that they were not due to pre-test–post-test gains by the YRE students, but rather to a decrease in performance by the TCS students. YRE scores for the total sample, for the most part, remained stable, as NCE mean scores should. YRE scores for the at-risk students resulted in a rather significant gain in reading and a slight loss in math-

TABLE 5.4
Pre- and Post-Math Scores by Number
of Years of YRE Program Implementation

Groups	Year-Round Education		Traditional Calendar		T Value for Post Means	Effect Size
	Pre M (SD)	Post M (SD)	Pre M (SD)	Post M (SD)		
2 years (N = 72)	54.46 (15.98)	54.23 (19.12)	55.05 (16.70)	46.70 (14.64)	4.24**	.51
3 years (N = 199)	66.16 (16.96)	65.02 (17.42)	66.86 (16.41)	61.07 (14.72)	4.53**	.27
4 years (N = 37)	55.44 (16.39)	55.15 (16.88)	54.19 (16.98)	49.12 (16.43)	3.32*	.37

*$p < 0.005$
**$p < 0.001$

ematics. The TCS achievement scores, on the other hand, dropped significantly in all instances.

The sustained academic performance of the YRE students may be a function of instructional time being utilized more efficiently. Unlike YRE classrooms, the TCS teachers spend five to six weeks in the fall in review, due to the lengthy summer break (Bradford, 1992).

In this study the highest effect size was found in reading for the at-risk students, even though they were most likely not deficient in the English language. This result supports the belief of YRE proponents that attending year-round schools can increase retention of knowledge for all students (Mutchler, 1993), including those who are disadvantaged (Morse, 1992). The problem of how to deliver instruction to at-risk students has been of concern to educational administrators for many years. The performance of students who have experienced little academic success and are at risk of dropping out of school may be increased by more continuous and sequential instructional support, especially in reading.

It is possible that the larger class sizes for TCS students account for their lower performance relative to YRE students. Although some research has indicated that class size alone does not significantly impact achievement (Slavin, 1990), other results do indicate a direct relationship between class size and achievement (Glass & Smith, 1978). Numerous studies suggest that a smaller class size of approximately fifteen is more conducive to student learning (Odden, 1990; Achilles et al., 1994; Nye et al., 1993; Mitchell & Beach, 1990). Yet in nine of the ten schools the YRE class sizes were above this cutoff point.

In both reading and math, statistically significant differences were found at all years of YRE program implementation. In other words, regardless of the length of program implementation, the YRE classes outperformed the TCS classes. The fact that mean NCE scores were higher in the third year for both YRE and TCS students could be attributed to the fact that three of the five third-year programs were in high SES schools.

Effect sizes ranged from 0.27 to 0.52. Although the NCE scores were higher in the third year, the effect size analysis found YRE to be less effective in the third year of implementation. This finding mirrors the results from previous research (Bechtel, 1991) in which YRE schools in the first and second years of implementation demonstrated greater gains in academic performance than the TCS schools, but in the third year the YRE schools had a weaker academic performance than the TCS schools. A study by Fardig (1992) also found that scores increased after the first year of YRE program implementation and then leveled off again to pre-YRE levels. In this study the fact that the effect sizes rise again, however, in the fourth year suggest that the effect of the YRE program may be sustaining. In fact, it has been suggested that achievement effects may be not be seen from a new program until the fourth year of program implementation (Shephard & Baker, 1977).

As this study indicates a learning loss sustained by the TCS students from April 1992 to April 1993, it is recommended that future research focus on YRE and TCS cohort analyses in order to determine if there is a cumulative achievement loss over a period of years in the traditional calendar school or, alternatively, a cumulative achievement gain over a period of years in year-round education.

A limitation of the present study is that the students, as well as the teachers, were self-selected for the YRE program. Therefore, they may not be representative of the population. As most single-track YRE programs are voluntarily implemented by school districts, it is recommended that future research should focus on multi-track programs, where programs are generally mandated.

The relationship between time spent in school and achievement may be more complex than it appears and can be related to more variables than school schedule alone. Research such as this, however, suggests that time can be utilized more effectively and should be spent in the successful completion of learning tasks, where instructional time is not interrupted by lengthy intervals. It may be that a single-track year-round education program is a particularly effective intervention, in particular for the at-risk student in reading, because it sustains student achievement through spaced learning and remedies the retention loss that occurs over the summer in the traditional calendar school.

REFERENCES

Achilles, C., Kiser-Kling, K., Aust, A., & Owen, J. (1994). *Success starts small.* Final Report. Greensboro, NC: University of North Carolina.

Bechtel, R. (1991). A study of academic growth in third grade students and its relationship to year-round education. (Doctoral Dissertation, Pepperdine University, 1991). *Dissertation Abstracts International, 52,* 2404.

Bradford, J. (1992). *Year-round education: A national perspective.* Paper presented at the National Commission on Time and Learning, Mufreesboro, TN.

Brekke, N. (1992a). *What YRE can do to enhance academic achievement and to enrich the lives of students that the traditional calendar cannot do.* ERIC Document Reproduction Service No. ED 352 223. Oxnard, CA: Oxnard School District.

Brekke, N. (1992b). Year-round schools: An efficient and effective use of resources. *School Business Affairs, 27–37.*

CTB-McGraw Hill. (1976). *Technical paper No. 2, interpreting NCE's.* Mountain View, CA: Research Management Corporation.

Fardig, D. (1992). *Year round education: Program evaluation report.* Program Evaluation Office Technology and Media Services. ERIC Document Reproduction Service No. ED 344 310.

Gándara, P., & Fish, J. (1994). Year-round schooling as an avenue to major structural reform. *Educational Evaluation and Policy Analysis, 16* (1), 67–85.

Glass, G., & Hopkins, K. (1984). *Statistical methods in education and pscyhology.* (2nd ed.) Boston: Allyn & Bacon.

Glass, G., & Smith, M. (1978). *Meta-analysis of research on the relationship of class size and instruction project.* San Francisco: CA: Far West Laboratory for Educational Research and Development.

Goren, P., & Carriedo, R. (1986). *Policy analysis on the implementation of an expanded multi-track year-round school program.* San Diego, CA: San Diego City Schools, Planning, Research and Evaluation Division.

Hall, G., & Hord, S. (1987). *Change in schools.* Albany: State University of New York Press.

Hayes, D., & Grether, J. (1969). *The school year vacations: When do students learn?* Revision of a paper presented at the Eastern Sociological Association Convention, New York.

Hazelton, J., Blakely, C., & Denton, J. (1992). *Cost effectiveness of alternative year schooling.* College Station: Texas A&M University, Center for Business and Economic Analysis.

Hoover, H., & Hieronymus, A. (1993). *NAPT conversion tables with summary statistics, grades 3–11, form 2, 1993.* Chicago IL: Riverside.

Kneese, C. (1996). Review of research on student learning in year-round education. *Journal of Research and Development in Education, 29* (2), 60–72.

Levin, H. (1987). Accelerated schools for disadvantaged students. *Educational Leadership, 44* (6), 19–21.

Mitchell, D., & Beach, S. (1990). How changing class size affects classrooms and students. *Policy Briefs, No. 12.* San Francisco: Far West Laboratory for Educational Research and Development.

Morse, S. (1992). The value of remembering. *Thrust for Educational Leadership, 21,* 35–37.

Mutchler, S. (1993). Year round education. *Insights on Education Policy and Practice, 2,* 1–5. Austin, TX: Southwest Educational Development Laboratory.

National Association for Year Round Education. (1993). *Twentieth reference directory of year-round education programs for the 1994 school year.* San Diego, CA: National Association for Year Round Education.

Norm-Referenced Assessment Program for Texas. (1993). *Overview and content outline.* Chicago, IL: Riverside.

Nye, B., Achilles, C., Zaharias, J., & Fulton, B. (April). *Class-size research: From experiment to field study to policy application.* Paper presented at the annual meeting of the American Educational Research Association, Atlanta, GA.

Odden, A. (1990). Class size and student achievement: Research-based policy alternatives. *Educational Evaluation and Policy Analysis, 12,* (2). 213–227.

Pallas, A., Natriello, G., & McDill, E. (1989). The changing nature of the disadvanted population: Current dimension and future trends. (Report No. 36). Baltimore, MD: Center for Research on Elementary and Middle Schools. (ERIC Document Reproduction Service No. 320655).

Pelavin, S. (1977). *A detailed study of a year-round school focusing on migrant and other disadvantaged children.* Menlo Park, CA: Stanford Research Institute.

Pelavin, S., & David, J. (1977). *Research on the effectiveness of compensatory education programs: A reanalysis of data.* ERIC Document Reproduction Service No. ED 147 386.

Quinlan, C., George, C., & Emmett, T. (1987). *Year-round education: Year-round opportunities. A study of year round education in California.* Sacramento CA: California State Department of Education.

Shepard, M., & Baker, K. (1977). *Year round schools.* Lexington: D. C. Heath.

Slavin, R. (1990). Class size and student achievement. Is smaller better? *Contemporary Education, 62* (1), 6–12.

Stallings, J. (1980). Allocated academic learning time revisted or Beyond time on task. *Educational Researcher, 9* (11), 11–16.

Task Force on Education and Economic Growth. (1983). *Action for excellence.* Denver, CO: Education Commission of the States.

Wolf, F. (1986). Meta-analysis: Quantitative methods for research synthesis. London: Sage Publications.

CHAPTER 6

Time: A Barrier to and Impetus for Reform. One District's Journey

Judy Fish

It takes all the running you can do to keep in the same place.
—The Red Queen, Through the Looking Glass

This is the story of one district's attempt to deal with the issue of rapid growth in the student population by manipulating time. We initiated calendar and curricular reforms as fast as we could to keep pace with the bulging student population and the ensuing housing and programmatic needs, and now, after a decade of running, we find ourselves in the Red Queen's predicament of being "in the same place" as we started. Initially, time was so successfully restructured that not only was the problem of accommodating growth accomplished, but also a chain reaction of reforms was set in motion, leading to improved student learning, changes in teachers' job structure, and community "buy-in" to the new way of organizing the school year. The changes have been institutionalized to such an extent that we have come full circle. In an ironic twist, restructured time has replaced the traditional use of time as a barrier to reform. Let me explain.

The story is told by the current assistant superintendent of educational services who, at the time of the reform effort, was the principal of the school initially affected by the changes. The voices of other players are woven throughout the narrative. Specifically, the stories of the central administration, teachers, students and parents impacted by the changes will be heard.

In most cases of systemic reform, educators respond to a public demand—often politically motivated—that education address specific areas. The pressure upon educators comes initially, from outside the system. The extent to which mandated reforms stick or have even a chance of being implemented varies greatly.

Much has been written about this issue of why some reforms "take" and others do not. (Fullan, 1993; Kirst, 1984; Wise, 1976). Kirst (1984) cites three factors that raise the odds that a particular educational reform will be institutionalized: (1) whether the reform involves structural or organizational change; (2) the ease of monitoring the change; (3) the emergence of a constituency or lobby for the retention of the reform. All three of Kirst's requirements were met initially. A specific calendar change involving a definite restructuring of learning blocks was implemented. In the early years, once the calendar change was agreed upon, monitoring it was not an issue. Also, initially the retention of the calendar was in the best interests of all constituents. In this district the pressure to change came from outside the system in the form of an influx of students and a state facilities budget crisis, but the need to change was felt personally by all the constituents.

Each of these constituents looks at the issue of time and reform through a different lens. In general, the superintendent and business manager use a wide-angle lens that deals with mandates, legislation, cost-effectiveness, and a sensitivity to balancing the various interests of the other groups. Time becomes the variable used to attend to what is required and efficient, yet popular. The principal's lens focuses on the school's scenery—maintaining the overall health of the school and meeting specific needs of students, teachers, parents, and district constraints. Time becomes the variable to balance what is feasible with what is effective in meeting the needs of the other constituents. The teacher uses a zoom lens with the dual purpose of maximizing student success and job satisfaction. Parents, wanting the best possible learning environment for their children, use a close-up lens. To the extent that reform efforts meet these varied goals, the potential for consensus increases.

In this story, although the players affected by the changes had different—albeit sometimes overlapping—agendas, because the manipulation of time met their agendas, the reforms were implemented with great success. Time was the impetus for reform. But when the situations evolved such that the implemented reforms no longer served the various agendas that had changed, time became a barrier to reform.

One significant lens through which the reform efforts were beamed to the larger community was operated by the local newspaper. The ultimate success or failure of the reforms was to some extent dependent on the newspaper's focus on the positive aspects of the restructuring of time. The headings for the various chapters of the story are taken from headlines from the Antelope Valley Press (1988–97).

TRADITIONAL USE OF TIME AS A
BARRIER TO REFORM: THE PROBLEM

"Palmdale: Fastest Growing Community
in the State of California"

To understand the Palmdale School District's experiment in reorganizing time, it is necessary first to discuss the changing dynamics of the larger community. Palmdale is the third fastest-growing community in the nation. The current population of 111,980 represents a growth rate over the past 12 years of 769 percent. It is one of several distinct communities in the Antelope Valley located 70 miles northeast of Los Angeles over the San Gabriel Mountains in the Mojave High Desert. The overall population of the Antelope Valley is 350,000; 34 percent are commuters to the Los Angeles Basin (Table 6.1). The rapid growth rate over the past 12 years is the result of families searching for affordable housing and better living conditions—less smog, less crime, less congestion. Unfortunately, many have brought the problems of the Los Angeles basin with them. The population explosion has been so dramatic that government agencies have had a difficult time meeting the increased service demand. A disproportionately high rate of unemployment, the national record for foreclosures, an increase in ethnically and linguistically diverse populations, rising racial violence, and escalating gang and drug problems have compounded the geographic isolation and created a tense, fragmented community.

"Year-Round Schools: Overcrowding Option"

The fast growth rate and changing demographics of the community likewise have impacted the schools in Palmdale, a K–8 district with an enrollment approaching 20,000. Currently the district has 22 sites spread over 70 square miles with 9 more scheduled for construction over the next 10 years. In 1985 there were 8 schools with a total population of 5,050 students. Thirteen schools have been built in the past 12 years, and the average student population per school has increased from 650 to 1,100 during the past decade (Table 6.2). As the population has grown, the task of continuing to house students has become increasingly difficult and complex. Qualifying for state buildings or state funds to build schools has required a major effort, as the rules for priority status change frequently. Additional trailers and state relocatables have been added, infrastructures

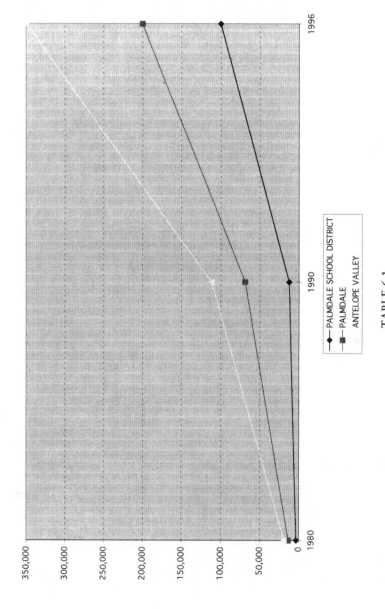

TABLE 6.1
District Population Growth, 1980–1996

Legend:
- PALMDALE SCHOOL DISTRICT
- PALMDALE
- ANTELOPE VALLEY

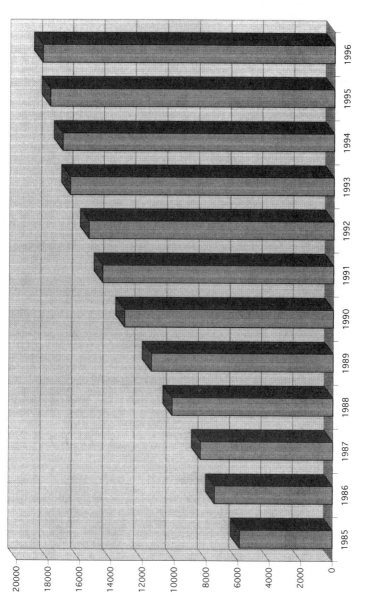

TABLE 6.2
Palmdale School District Growth, 1985 to 1996

changed to accommodate more electrical hookups, developer fees charged, taxes levied by the formation of a Mello-Roos district, state bonds passed—all in an attempt to keep pace with the population boom.

By 1988, in order to ensure continued access to state funds, the State Office of Local Assistance mandated that a district increase its capacity to house 20 percent more students than possible with a traditional calendar. New laws provided both incentives for transitioning to a multi-track year-round calendar in which student attendance rotates to accommodate more students, and penalties—in the form of loss of priority status for funding of new schools—for not converting to a multi-track system. (Gándara & Fish, 1994)

Paralleling the need to find new ways of manipulating time to increase student housing capacity was an urgency to address the changing needs of an increasingly at-risk population. Over the same time period that the population exploded, the district experienced a rapidly changing diverse population. Between 1989 and 1996, the percent of Caucasians declined from 66 percent to 42 percent. The Hispanic and African American population doubled. At the current rate of growth, the single largest ethnic group served by Palmdale School District will be Hispanic within a very short period of time. Within that group fully 40 percent are identified as English Language Learners (Table 6.3).

"Palmdale School District Wins Friends with Innovative Programs"

Palmdale School District has a long-standing reputation for embracing challenges and exploring innovations to provide the best possible learn-

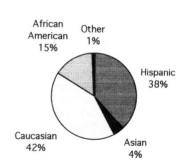

District Ethnicity, 1989

African American 7% Other 1% Hispanic 22% Asian 4% Caucasian 66%

District Ethnicity, 1996

African American 15% Other 1% Hispanic 38% Asian 4% Caucasian 42%

TABLE 6.3
Ethnic Breakdown, 1989–1996

Source: Title VII Grant Proposal, 1997.

ing environment for students. The board of trustees encourages "break-the-mold" thinking in the pursuit of programs deemed beneficial to the academic and social well-being of the children.

In looking to restructuring time to accommodate growth, the over-arching goal of the board and central administration was to accomplish this while not only maintaining the high-quality instructional programs for which the district was noted, but also maximizing the learning potential of *all* students, especially those deemed at-risk such as students served by Title I, Gifted and Talented, and Bilingual Programs. And, of course, they recognized the need to secure the approval of the parent and teacher constituencies. The major impetus for changing the calendar was a facilities issue —how to house more students using the space available that was already at-capacity. However, the task was approached with multiple goals in mind.

The superintendent recognized that buy-in from the teachers, parents, and the greater community was possible only if the student housing prob-lem was looked at in terms that would also enhance instruction and learn-ing and meet their personal family-oriented needs. Palmdale is a conser-vative community with a strong commitment to parental involvement in the education of their children and traditional family values. Parents have strong opinions on what constitutes schooling—what children learn, how they learn, and when they learn. Any manipulation of time would have to involve parents in the decision-making process. Furthermore, to get total buy-in, the district would have to look at what impact changing the cal-endar would have on the broader community—service organizations, reli-gious groups, parks and recreation, summer camps, baby sitting needs. Not to be overlooked was the role the media could play in facilitating the changes. Over the years the local newspaper support has varied greatly, depending on which way the political wind has blown. It was in the con-text of these issues that the district embarked on a journey to reorganize the use of time. That journey, continuing to this day, has met with vary-ing degrees of success, depending on through whose lens success is viewed.

RESTRUCTURING OF TIME AS AN
IMPETUS FOR REFORM: THE SOLUTION

"Year-Round School Proposal Holds Considerable Merit"

In 1986–87 there were approximately 350 schools nationwide with some form of year-round education program (YRE). In 1996–97 there were 2,510 schools using a year-round calendar. Forty-five percent of the schools on a year-round calendar use a multi-track calendar (National Association for Year-Round Education, 1996; Table 6.4).

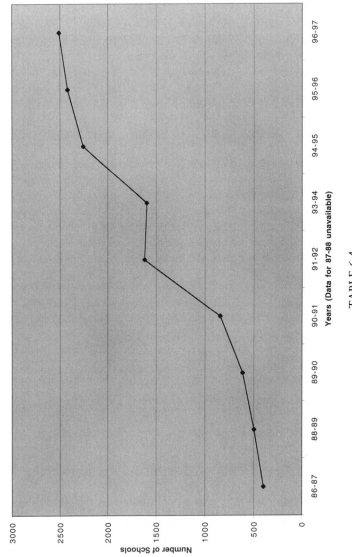

TABLE 6.4
Growth in Year-Round Schooling, U.S., 1986–1997

Source: Twenty-Third Reference Directory of Year-Round Education Programs for the 1996–97 School Year.

A brief explanation of what is meant by a multi-track year-round calendar may be necessary for the novice. Year-round education reorganizes the school year by breaking up the traditional summer vacation into shorter, more frequent vacations or intersessions spread throughout the year. In this way, the learning is more continuous and summer learning loss is minimized while extended learning opportunities are maximized. Table 6.5 summarizes the advantages of a year-round calendar over a traditional calendar, recognized by proponents of year-round schools.

Multi-track year-round education has as its overarching goal maximizing the use of space and fiscal efficiency while maintaining the goals of expanding time for learning and retention of learning. The student population is divided into several groups or tracks. The instructional and vacation periods of each group are staggered such that some students are always in session while one group is always on vacation or intersession. The whole year is utilized and all facilities are occupied year-round.

For example, the particular multi-track calendar used in Palmdale has five calendar tracks. Four groups of students are in session or "on track" at one time, while the fifth group is on vacation. Usually the teacher and students within a particular class are on the same track and

TABLE 6.5
What YRE Can Do (That a Traditional Calendar Cannot)

- YRE enhances the retention of learning by reducing the traditional three-month summer vacation to shorter vacation periods
- YRE provides intersessions for remediation and/or enrichment
- YRE provides winter vacations/intersessions for those students needing a significant pause between semesters
- YRE provides quality substitute teachers and quality teachers for school/intersession programs throughout the year
- YRE reduces teacher and student burnout

- YRE provides continuing, year-long opportunities for staff development
- YRE provides students on intersession the opportunity to volunteer in various capacities at school and in the community
- YRE provides high school students the opportunity for year-round employment
- YRE can extend and enrich opportunities for co-curricular and extracurricular activities
- YRE provides students and their families with multiple vacation options during the school year

---

Source: National Association for Year-Round Education, Conference Brochure, February 1997.

rotate on and off together, although the type of year-round program Palmdale began with varied from this. More will be said about the difference later. Groups or tracks rotate so that each group attends school approximately sixty days followed by a fifteen-day vacation. This cycle repeats three times, giving all students a total of 180 days of school and forty-five days of intersession. In addition, all students and staff have a two-week winter break, one-week spring break, and three weeks off in the summer. This particular multi-track calendar increases housing capacity by 25 percent. Students and teachers change to a different classroom when returning from their intersession so the rooms are always occupied and thus can accommodate an additional fourth over the original number of students. Time and space are manipulated to be used most efficiently. This plan is called 60/15 to correspond to the days in session versus days on vacation within a trimester (Table 6.6). Other multi-track calendars have the potential to increase capacity by as much as 50 percent. Each has its advantages and drawbacks academically, fiscally, and in terms of use of facilities. But all involve a reorganizing of time and space to better meet the needs of the district or community.

Although research findings on the academic merits of multi-track or single-track year-round education are inconsistent, most studies indicate that transitioning to year-round education has not resulted in a loss of learning as measured by achievement on standardized tests (Ballinger, Kirschenbaum, & Poimbeauf, 1987; O'Neal, 1991; Six, 1993; Alcorn, 1992). Many studies suggest increased learning for some at-risk populations, in particular English Language Learners (Ballinger, Kirschenbaum, & Poimbeauf, 1987; Gándara & Fish, 1994). Advocates of year-round education cite shorter vacation breaks as resulting in greater retention of learning and the potential for extending the opportunities for remediation or enrichment during intersession as possible reasons for improved student learning. A recent meta-analysis of thirty-nine studies revealed that achievement test scores decline over the traditional summer vacation (Cooper et al., 1996). Summer loss equaled approximately one month on a grade-level equivalent scale and impacted math more negatively than reading.

Associating changes in test scores with year-round education is problematic. There are too many other variables that affect student achievement. A review of the literature on the effects of reducing class size on student achievement suggests that merely lowering the number of students will not result necessarily in improved learning. The way we teach must also change (Robinson, 1990). A similar caution is in order in explaining the impact of year-round education on student learning. If all that changes is the structure of the year, the potential for improving learning has not been maximized. The way reorganized time is used is

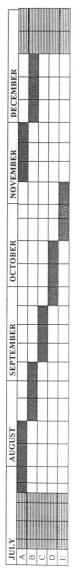

	JULY	AUGUST	SEPTEMBER	OCTOBER	NOVEMBER	DECEMBER
A						
B						
C						
D						
E						

	JANUARY	FEBRUARY	MARCH	APRIL	MAY	JUNE
A						
B						
C						
D						
E						

	School in Session
	Off Track
	Holiday / Students and Staff

ADVANTAGES

All tracks receive a summer break of approximately three weeks

School can be "shut down" for approximately six weeks

Few changes for rotating teachers

180 days of instruction available for all terms

The same holidays and winter break currently provided on the traditional calendar are retained

Space on the calendar for pupil free-days and/or potential extension of the school year--beyond 180 days is available

More opportunity for seasonal cleaning and maintenance when compared to all other year-round calendars

Increased opportunity for enrollment in remediation and enrichment courses

DISADVANTAGES

Reduced increase in capacity when compared to four-track

Five-track calendars make organization more difficult in small elementary schools when compared to three- or four-track calendars

TABLE 6.6

Palmdale School District, 60/15 Five-Track Calendar Model

critical. To the extent that studies neither differentiate among the kind of year-round education programs nor examine how time is manipulated to academic advantage, the results of such studies will continue to be inconsistent.

School in Palmdale Launches First Year-Round Program: Predicted as Trend-Setter for the Antelope Valley"

It was within this frame of reference that Palmdale School District officials, in looking for solutions to overcrowding through the adoption of a multi-track year-round calendar, recognized the added opportunity for instructional reform. In 1988, the California State Department of Education distributed a call for proposals to implement pilot programs using a multi-track year-round model called the Orchard Plan (discussed in more detail in Chapter 4). The plan, named after the school in Orem, Utah, where it originated, contained elements that matched Palmdale School District's goals. These were to increase student housing capacity by at least 20 percent, qualify for state funding for new schools, and address improving student learning and extending learning opportunities for at-risk students with support from teachers, parents, and community leaders. Parents, teachers, and support staff had to volunteer to take part in the program and be involved in the planning process—a requirement critical to the successful implementation of any change as drastic as restructuring the school year. It helped that the proposed plan also had the stamp of approval from the California Department of Education.

Cactus School, an alternative school of choice within the district, submitted a proposal and was selected as one of four schools throughout the state to pilot the Orchard Plan. Planning began in 1988–89. Funding of $180,000 was spread over the planning year and first two years of implementation. Table 6.7 summarizes the key features of the Orchard Plan. The basic calendar structure follows the 60/15 calendar described earlier. However, unlike the 60/15 calendar and other YRE programs where teachers and their students attend school on the same calendar track, Orchard Plan teachers work an extended year. Students from each of the five tracks or groups are assigned to each teacher. The students rotate on and off track for their intersessions or vacations but teachers remain. Teachers have a fifty-minute planning period each day, since team teaching and collaborative planning are critical components.

Another critical requirement of the plan called for categorical funds to be redistributed to support innovative intersession programs targeted for at-risk students. These programs were to provide alternatives to the

WHAT IS THE ORCHARD PLAN?

The Orchard Plan (AB 1650) is a type of year round program in which school is in session for 11 months each year. Students are placed on one of five rotation tracks or calendars, and attend school for 60 days followed by 15 days of vacation (inter-session). This cycle (60-15) repeats three times. All students and staff are on vacation in July, two weeks in the winter, and one week in the spring.

HOW DOES THE ORCHARD PLAN DIFFER FROM OTHER YEAR ROUND PROGRAMS?

Teachers never rotate or rove; no storage cabinets needed
Unlike other year round programs where the students and their teachers are on the same track and go on vacation at the same time, the Orchard Plan teachers work an extended year. Students from each of the five tracks are assigned to each teacher. Thus, students rotate on and off track but teachers remain. There are four tracks in session at any given time.

Class size reduced
Statewide, the average class/roster size is 31 students. While Orchard teachers have 35 students on their class roster, one track (7 students) is always on intersession (vacation). Therefore, Orchard class size is 28.

Statewide average
traditional class size   31

Orchard class size
(four tracks in session at one time)   28

Curriculum planning and instructional delivery clearly defined
The curriculum is planned in advance in three/six/nine week units so that there is closure as track configurations change within the classroom every three weeks. Thus, outcomes are clearly defined and the instructional delivery is well paced.

Teachers collaborate
Teams of teachers work cooperatively to develop and deliver the curriculum. All teachers are on site all year, allowing for greater articulation between/among staff.

Student leadership/friendship opportunities increased
Teachers report that there are more opportunities for new friendships and new classroom leaders as some students rotate on and off track every three weeks. There is renewed student enthusiasm as new units begin.

Special needs students on all tracks
Since each class has students from all tracks, the potential for a special needs segregation to one track is eliminated.

Intersession opportunities expanded
Since each class has students from all tracks, students "off" track can be invited back for extra help or for special events (in addition to intersession offerings). Pull-out programs during regular session can be reduced.

Parent's requests more easily accommodated
Placing family members on the same track, even after the year has begun, is easier with Orchard program because each teacher has students from all tracks. Class sizes are easier to balance.

Teachers make more money
Orchard teachers work approximately 39 days more than other teachers. This increases their salary by about 20 percent and eliminates the need for summer employment.

Savings in teacher benefits realized
Twenty percent fewer teachers are required since teachers work an extended year. Savings are mainly in reduced benefit costs since teachers are paid for their extra days.

Number of teachers needed reduced
In growing districts, recruitment costs and efforts are cut, since 20 percent fewer teachers are needed in Orchard schools.

TABLE 6.7
Orchard Plan Features

traditional pull-out support special needs students tend to receive that disrupts the regular flow of the core instruction for those students with the greatest need for access and continuity.

"Parents Protest Possible Closing of Special School"

Why was this major plan to restructure time initially carried out so successfully when what we know about complex change is that it rarely happens smoothly and seldom as planned (Fullan, 1993; Spillane, 1998)? An understanding of the history of Cactus School will help explain the successful implementation of the program as expressed so enthusiastically in the front-page headlines of the Antelope Valley Daily News, "Parents Embrace Year Round Plan—As Other Districts Face Protests."

Founded on the principles of mastery learning and outcome-based education in 1983, Cactus School grew from a small program of 90 students to a K–8 school of 1,300. In 1988, Cactus was a successful alternative school of 550 K–6 students located in an old airport facility with four large rooms each capable of holding two to three classes. The teachers, who volunteered to teach at Cactus, embraced innovations, worked collaboratively in both planning and teaching, and were dedicated to the school. Parents who elected to send their children to Cactus were required to volunteer thirty hours each year. They took an active interest in the school and their child's progress. Quick to praise and always willing to help, they were comfortable voicing concerns too.

At the time the district was exploring potential multi-track year-round programs, strong consideration was also being given to disbanding Cactus School for political, financial, and legal reasons. The airport facility did not conform to the state field act, which required certain earthquake safety features to be approved for student use. It was expensive to continue leasing the site from the airport and transportation costs were high since the students came from all areas of the community. It was felt that the original goal of infusing the basic tenets of the school throughout the district had been met. Other school communities felt that Cactus had become an elite school of choice for middle-class white children. Politically it was difficult to justify Cactus's continued existence.

The night the board of trustees was to vote on the future of Cactus School parents and staff packed the board room and spilled out into the halls. It was obvious from the many parent testimonials that they loved their school and its innovative programs. After much heated discussion that lasted late into the night, the board tabled the decision for further consideration. As a solution to several issues, the superintendent proposed that Cactus pilot the first year-round school in the district, open to all families in the community. The day was saved for the district and the school. It was a win-win situation.

In order to fulfill the promise of opening the pilot project to all families, a team of staff and parents went from school to school holding evening informational meetings. At that time there were twelve schools in the district. The school opened for the first year-round, multi-track program in 1989, filled to capacity with 950 students and with a waiting list of over 500.

This was not necessarily a vote of confidence in year-round education but a compromise arrived at by all constituents to meet the varied goals. The district's administration needed both to resolve a sensitive issue surrounding the continued existence of a school of choice with no major difference in focus from other schools, and to begin the task of accommodating a bulging student population. Parents and teachers at Cactus School wanted their school to continue at almost any cost. Other schools were willing to support the effort because they were not the "guinea-pig" for year-round programs. The newspaper, thriving on the initial story of the controversy of Cactus's potential closing, carried the story forth "with gusto." It helped that Palmdale School District was the lone district among ten neighboring districts with similar growth problems that was willing to change to a year-round calendar.

The first year-round program succeeded beyond the district's wildest dreams. At the end of the first year, 96 percent of parents responding to a survey expressed satisfaction or extreme satisfaction with the program. One hundred percent of the teachers returned the second year. Waiting lists for the second year were so long that the board voted unanimously to convert two more traditional schools to the Orchard Plan in 1990–91. Newspaper headlines and editorials praised the district for "being on the leading edge" in piloting "this educational innovation" (*Antelope Valley Press*, April 30, 1990).

At the end of the third year, although there were no significant differences for either reading or math gain scores for matched samples of students between Cactus School and a comparable school, there was a considerable increase in reading scores bordering on significant ($p = 0.06$). Math scores increased to a lesser degree ($p = 0.10$). Title I students targeted to receive fifty hours of remediation during intersessions showed significant gains in reading scores ($p = 0.007$) (Gándara & Fish, 1994).

INSTITUTIONALIZING AND EXPANDING
RESTRUCTURED TIME: BUILDING ON SUCCESS

"Palmdale to Expand Year-Round Classes:
Waiting Lines Form at Dawn"

During the transition to year-round education at Cactus and two additional schools, the student population continued to grow at the rate of

1,000 to 1,500 students per year. The community had accepted the calendar change at three schools of choice, but would they accept the
inevitable—all schools mandated to change to a year-round calendar? In
a survey sent to all parents in the community, 47 percent of the 32 percent who returned the survey indicated they would send their children
to a year-round school. In 1991–92, the district put this to the test. Six
more schools transferred to the more traditional 60/15 year round program. In 1992–93 the remaining schools adopted the 60/15 year-round
calendar.

Perhaps the largest and most lasting impact reorganizing the calendar has had on the community at large and within the school system is
with intersession programs. The three-week time frames with one-fifth
of the student population available for additional learning opportunities
lends itself to units of study focusing on a range of offerings from remediation to enrichment. One of the major components of the Orchard
pilot proposal was that there be extended learning opportunities available through the reallocation of state and categorical funds to support
intersession rather than pull-out programs. The follow-up study to the
state pilot program in three statewide schools indicated that all three
schools were able to offer at least fifty hours of additional instruction to
at-risk students. However, getting these students to return for classes
and finding space to accommodate additional classes—given that
multi-track year-round programs exist to compensate for overcrowding—was difficult. Initially success with this component was limited in
Palmdale (Gándara & Fish, 1994). As more schools changed to the year-
round schedule, the commitment to intersession programs varied from
site to site, depending on interest, space, funds, and staff availability.

With time, many schools have overcome the problem of where to
find space for intersession activities by reaching out to the community.
Initially meetings were held to familiarize youth-related and civic organizations with the new calendar and with its potential to benefit youth
programs. Often community members were invited to propose and
teach intersession courses. Slow to develop at first, intersession opportunities have mushroomed, limited only by the imagination and
resources available. Partnerships have been formed with the local Performing Arts Center to use their facilities during the day. Parks and
recreation classes are offered year-round. Religious and other youth
organizations have adjusted their summer camp programs. Outdoor science camp, which formerly took students off campus during their regular year for a week, is often held during intersession. The sheriff department asked for identification cards so that students on intersession can
be identified as on vacation rather than as truant. Flyers, cleared
through the district, often announce these programs, including interses-

sion celebration dances for the older students. The year-round calendar has replaced the traditional calendar as the norm, the expected, the basic time structure around which all youth-related activities in the community are planned.

In addition to regular intersession activities, schools have branched out to provide before- and after-school reading and math remediation classes, homework clinics, clubs, and computer classes. The longer the calendar is in use, the more creative ways the schools and the community have discovered to enhance and extend the learning time. Breaking with the traditional structure of time appears to have freed minds to explore new ways to ensure the system is not a slave to time but that time works for learning. What began as a voluntary program as an option to relieve overcrowding and save a school from extinction spread as a mandate to neighborhood schools and finally became institutionalized as community service organizations adjusted their programs and schedules to adapt to the new calendar.

Up to this point the story has been fairly straightforward. By the end of a four-year phase-in of the new calendar structure, year-round education was firmly entrenched in the community. All three of Kirst's criteria for lasting reform were in place. Changing a calendar cycle is a major organizational change and once implemented throughout the district one that proved difficult to adjust as the continuing tale shall show. The new calendar was easy to monitor; in fact, each year, once designed to accommodate a new cycle of holidays and intersessions could *not* be changed. There was no need to lobby for the retention of the calendar beyond the initial years. Necessity had truly been the mother of invention and although the constituents may have had varying degrees of enthusiasm—or lack thereof—for the calendar, everyone recognized that is was necessary to alleviate overcrowding.

The story now becomes more complex. As the years went by, the implemented reforms perceived to be securely in place began to conflict with shifting agendas. The various constituents needed to refocus their lenses to continue to meet their goals. The board and superintendent looking through their wide-angle lens saw that the student population was continuing to grow at such a rapid pace that housing students was going to be a problem again. However, because—at least in its structural manifestation—the reform effort had become institutionalized, the community thwarted attempts to make adjustments to the calendar to accommodate continuing student growth. Also, underlying the structural change of the calendar were reforms associated with student achievement. As indicated above in the discussion of the slow evolution of intersession programs, these changes were more difficult to secure. With time, the initial enthusiasm for curricular and instruction reforms that had been an integral part of the Orchard design waned. Teachers working the extended year calendar complained that there was little time for staff development and began to feel the need for a break from teaching 219 days a year. Viewing the situation through their zoom lens, in order to maintain job satisfaction, teachers looked to minimize burnout while continuing to maximize salary. Teachers at 60/15 schools, while embracing the frequent breaks spread through the year, dreaded the classroom rotation necessary when returning from scheduled breaks. They felt time was wasted with many start-up and winding-down periods.

Administrators at the schools accustomed to a summer down time for reports, vacation, and curriculum development, began to lobby for assistant principals as the feasibility of meeting the needs of parents, staff, and students became insurmountable. Traditionally, only the intermediate schools had qualified for help. Now, with schools of 800 to 1,300 students, the task of managing the school without help was becoming impossible. Central office administrators likewise felt burnout as one cycle in the annual ritual of budget, attendance accounting, reports, enrollment, and scheduling was still in full force at the same time as the next year was gearing up to begin.

Parents and some teachers at the original Orchard School, Cactus, became restless and dissatisfied with what they viewed as a watered-down version of the original program. Rumors spread that some teachers were not teaming to deliver the curriculum to all students in a more individualized fashion. Some parents felt that teachers played "catch-up" with students returning to the classroom after three-week breaks.

Local capacity to implement change has been recognized widely as a critical element in meaningful reform (Elmore & McLaughlin, 1988; Spillane & Thompson, 1997). The ability of classroom teachers to change their instructional practices is dependent on their knowledge of the subject matter, knowledge of teaching and learning, and commitment to change (Shulman, 1987). Initially teachers received intensive training in curriculum design and delivery. As time passed and more teachers transferred or were hired to teach at Orchard schools, the training and the enthusiasm for implementing the program lessened.

Spillane and Thompson (1997) argue further that the capacity of the local educational agency (LEA) to support the reform effort hinges to a large degree on the LEA leadership's ability to "learn new ideas from external policy and professional sources and to help others within the district learn these ideas." The focus shifted from the Orchard design to the implementation of the year-round calendar in all schools. Thus, the initial guidance and support from central administration weakened.

Also, new principals lacked the training for the Orchard design and had no sense of the history of why changes had occurred.

Eisner (1994) maintains that the ideology or belief system of those within the educational institution—whether at the policy or practitioners' level—affects what is taught (or not taught). Over time, with continued growth, new teachers *and* new administrators brought their agendas forward. The structure was in place but some sense of the original instructional purpose for change was minimized.

Kirst's second and third criteria for the institutionalization of the instructional reforms were no longer firmly in place. It was becoming increasingly difficult to monitor the instructional changes and conflicting interests threatened some elements of the reform.

"District to Open Last Innovative School:
Grant Focuses on Breakthrough in Learning"

Partially in response to the perception of some teachers and parents that the Orchard program was no longer being carried out as originally designed, partially as the logical next step in breaking from the constraints of time, Palmdale School District opened a new school of choice, the Palmdale Learning Plaza (PLP) in 1994. Designed originally as a "break-the-mold" charter style K–8 school, called a learning center, PLP was funded by a grant received from the Community Learning Center (CLC) project based in Minnesota. The CLC itself was one of eleven projects funded by the New American Schools Development Corporation (NASDC). Cutbacks in funding from NASDC resulted in partial funding for the CLC, and thus the PLP did not receive monetary support beyond the initial planning year.

Because of Palmdale School District's history of successful restructuring efforts and curricular innovations the creation of the PLP flowed naturally as the logical next step in exploring new ways to ensure relevant learning by breaking time and space barriers. It was billed as combining an array of innovative instructional strategies used throughout Palmdale's schools within a totally new structure incorporating the concepts of "community as campus," "teachers as learners," and "students as resources" (Palmdale Learning Plaza Brochure). Basic tenets of the project included site-based shared governance, flexible schedules for students and teachers, opportunities to expand learning beyond the school walls, application, project-based learning, and performance assessment (Table 6.8). It also served to placate those parents who were dissatisfied with the Orchard program. Many teachers and parents transferred to the Learning Plaza with renewed enthusiasm.

When an informational meeting was held to explain the new school

TABLE 6.8
Palmdale Learning Plaza

1. All participants are learners and facilitators—staff development is critical.
2. All learners will keep personal growth plans (ILPs or Individual Learner Plans).
3. All ages will work together.
4. All learners are resources and considered talented. Everyone's ideas are valued.
5. Standards and expectations are high.
6. The community is a rich learning environment.
7. Social services are integrated.
8. The Plaza and the community merge.
9. Lifelong learning is cherished.
10. All learners are innately eager, curious, and thirsty for learning.
11. Learning involves active engagement, exploration, and inquiry and has relevance.
12. Parents and the community are indispensable partners with their children.
13. We believe in celebrating all success—academic and personal.
14. We believe that staff must work collaboratively to ensure the success of our students and the overall welfare of our school.

of choice to the community, the board room and adjacent hallways were jammed. Enrollment for the first year was expected to be 300 to 400. The superintendent, however, had promised that all those who signed up that first night would be accommodated. Enrollment closed that night at 829. The school opened with 786 students.

*"At This School, A Is for Aeronautics: Innovative Class
    Teaches Math, Science as Two Classes Build Airplane"*
"High Tech Labs to Open in Mall"
"School to Open Desert Study Site; Students Serve as Desert Docents"
"Students Get Job Experience in A.V. Mall"

The Palmdale Learning Plaza is organized around plazas or themes such as the environment, business, aeronautics, the arts, and technology. Core subjects are taught through these themes in age clusters rather than grade levels. The kinds of projects students are involved in lend themselves to a flexible use of time. For example, the students in the aeronautics plaza have just completed and flown successfully a two-seater Kit Fox airplane that they built during the regular day, after hours, and on weekends, with guidance from the Experimental Aircraft Association. As a result of the community partnership formed to complete that project, the school is now immersed in a Cooperative Agreement (CAN) with NASA. Several teachers, working with engineers, are writing curriculum units that integrate math and science through aeronautic events to be delivered on the internet for other teachers and students.

Students in the environmental plaza have constructed a nature walk and desert tortoise habitat, funded by a state environmental grant for which the teachers successfully applied. Community docents from local museums are training primary age students to be docents. Through the business plaza students are connected with businesses in the mall and given opportunities to apply concepts learned in the classroom through work experience.

"Families Pick Which Off-Track Days They Want"

During the first year, parents and teachers chose an Orchard-style calendar. Classes were also offered on Saturday for remediation or enrichment units. There were two starting and ending times to provide flexible scheduling options for families. As the program evolved, teachers realized more time was needed for planning, curriculum development, refinement of programs, and additional parent/student/teacher conferencing. The Plaza truly was a learning environment that required collaboration and communication at all levels. The teachers recognized the limitations of the Orchard plan, which allowed for few nonstudent days for teachers. Working with a committee of parents, the teachers—not the administration—designed a new, more flexible calendar that built in one day a month for staff development and one day a month for conferencing.

Families select 180 school days and 20 vacation days from among 200 available days (see Table 6.7). In addition, everyone—staff and students—has the common vacations that the other schools have—three weeks in summer, two weeks in winter, and one week in spring! Thus, the number of students in daily attendance fluctuates. One day there may be as few as ten students in the class, another day as many as thirty-five. The individual schedules are predetermined at the beginning of the year. All students must attend the first week of the year for assessment and placement and one week in May for annual mandated testing. In grades 4 through 8, the maximum number of students on the class roster is thirty-five, while for kindergarten through third grade there are twenty-five students enrolled per class. The Plaza offers the only full-day kindergarten in the community. Ideally, the Plaza staff would prefer that students "make up" days missed for illness by attending school on days previously targeted for vacation, but in an ironic twist, one arm of the state Department of Education encourages perfect attendance while another arm bases funding on an average daily attendance of 97.5 percent. The Palmdale Learning Plaza completed its third year of using the flexible schedule. The state department requirements regarding student mandated attendance during regular attendance cycles prevented the continuation of this flexible calendar. Rather than returning to the original Orchard calendar, the school is piloting a five track calendar featuring four weeks on track followed by one week off.

The Plaza receives the same funds as all the other schools in the district but has jurisdiction over how those funds are spent. They receive their full entitlement but must pay all bills and salaries from their budget. A cost comparison for utilities indicates a considerable savings over the other eighteen schools in the district.

Plans are under way to design a permanent facility for the Plaza, which is currently housed in trailers and relocatable buildings on land adjacent to a permanent school. Teachers, support staff, and parents will have the opportunity to work with the architect on a "break-the-mold" learning environment. As was the case with restructuring time, flexibility will be a critical element in designing the campus and structures. How fitting that the two barriers to reform—time and space—are being tackled "head-on."

The Plaza already had one satellite campus—a 5,000 square foot storefront located at the Antelope Valley indoor mall. This space housed a state-of-the-art technology lab and, prior to its transfer to a hangar at the local airfield, the two-seater airplane was built there. During the evening hours, computer and English as a Second Language classes were held for parents and the general public. This satellite, however, was closed at the end of the 1997-98 school year due to a lack of mall space.

After four years in operation, the Palmdale Learning Plaza has the highest standardized achievement test scores in the district. Time has been the vehicle for accommodating instructional and curricular changes leading to improved student achievement once again. Through the creation of a new school, the goals of some constituents were met and once more time, which had become a barrier, became an impetus for reform.

"Planetarium Nears Completion"

The most recent innovative addition to the district is the development of the Planetarium, located fittingly on the Cactus campus where creativity in the use of time was born. The Planetarium facility has a 40-foot dome, seats 114 people, and houses a Spitz System 512 planetarium instrument and remote control console, special effects projectors, and rear and front screen slide projection system. With the plan to expand the use of the facility beyond the regular school day and to the high school district, community college, and adult groups, the original Palmdale Learning Plaza concept of "community as campus" will have to be expanded to include "campus as community." With its opening in August 1998 the Planetarium Theater has become a learning resource and cultural center that transcends space and time.

At this time, Palmdale School District, nine years after opening the first year-round program, has four schools on the 60/15 Orchard Plan, one school (PLP) with a unique calendar plan, and sixteen schools on a more traditional year-round 60/15 calendar. In addition, the Head Start Program with 1,500 students is on a modified Orchard calendar and an Alternative Education School of 160 students is on a flexible calendar combined with an independent study program. Internal to the 16 schools on the 60/15 calendar, approximately 25 percent of the teachers have "Rainbow" or Orchard-style classrooms where students come from all tracks and teachers work an extended year.

RESTRUCTURED TIME AS A BARRIER TO CHANGE: THE PROBLEM REVISITED

"Palmdale Schools at Capacity Again"

It is at this point in the journey that the quote with which the chapter began becomes most apt, "It takes all the running you can do to keep in the same place." The district just could not run fast enough to keep pace with the growth rate. Enrollment has continued to climb, albeit more slowly, but many of the 22 campuses are impacted once more. Several of the K–6 campuses and three K–8 sites exceed 1,300 students. Even "small" schools approach 1,000 students. Many schools were built to house approximately 700 students on a traditional calendar. Table 6.9 shows projected growth relative to housing capacity.

Several factors contribute to the current crisis—the second wave, if you will—that exists in Palmdale in housing students. Steady growth has rendered the current year-round calendars insufficient to accommodate continued growth. The California Department of Education building program has dried up. Districts cannot get in line to receive any more funds for building or renovating existing facilities unless they can pay for 50 percent of the cost from local funds. The district's general fund cannot support a drain on the budget of this magnitude. Ten more schools are projected to be required over the next twelve years at a cost of $8 million per school. For each site, $4 million would have to be

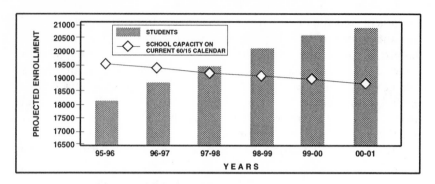

TABLE 6.9
Palmdale School District, Projected Growth Rate

Source: P.S.D. Information Bulletin, 1996.

raised locally through passage of a general obligation bond, which would increase taxes.

To complicate matters, legislation was passed in 1996 providing incentive funding to reduce class size in primary grades from 30:1 to 20:1 (Class Size Reduction Program of 1996, SB 1777 O'Connell). Thus the dilemma: How could a district, with a strong history of commitment to innovations to meet student needs, not take part in a program with such potential to impact student learning? On the other hand, how could a district that already exceeded capacity and that had already reorganized time and space to maximize capacity accommodate 112 additional classes? (Every two existing primary grade classes would produce the need for an additional one.)

*"Information Meeting Held as Palmdale School District
Faces Overcrowding. New Calendars Anger Parents"*

The board and superintendent, recognizing the conflict between their goals—to house students and maintain high-quality programs, and those of the parents—to maintain the new status quo, faced the issue "head-on." As in the past, the district went to the parents of each school in open meetings to discuss the problem. A student housing committee comprising parents, teachers, school staff, administrators, and community members explored new calendar options that had the potential to increase student capacity by 30 to 40 percent over traditional calendars. These options were presented in informational meetings similar to those of nearly a decade ago. At these "town hall" meetings, parents expressed grave concerns with changing the calendar. The district had done a good job of convincing the community that the Orchard plan and the 60/15 calendar were good for students and families. They liked the short breaks, the extended learning opportunities, the improved test scores, and the common breaks at winter, summer, and spring. The new calendars would reduce the number of student days from 175 to 160, lengthen the breaks, lengthen each day by 17 minutes, and eliminate common vacation periods (Table 6.10 and 6.11).

District Fails to Pass Local Bond—Stealth Tactics Used"
"Palmdale to Try to Pass Bond Again"

The parents suggested we try to pass a local general obligation bond to raise the money to fund 50 percent of each new school. In June 1996 and again in March 1997 the district attempted to pass a general obligation bond. Many parents who had attended the recent meetings made good on their promise to help. The district published a newsletter and fact sheet detailing the issues and options. Both bonds failed to receive the two-thirds majority needed to pass even though the taxes would not have amounted to more than 27 dollars per year per household. The first attempt failed by 112 votes! The second by a large margin. The public was adamant—*no more taxes*! Editorials and front-page headlines expressed grave concern about the possibility of more taxes. Whereas once the local paper had championed the district's restructuring efforts, now the editors accused the district of trying to pass a bond using "stealth tactics." The community viewed the bond measure through the lens of the press and said "no." The issue became a political one. No one had the solution but all those opposed felt the state government should totally fund the new schools. The paper accused the district of "manip-ulating the public" to try to pass the bond.

In a final effort to ensure that class size reduction could take place, in spite of the failure to pass a local bond, additional trailers were pur-chased for some schools and necessary electrical hook-ups provided. In schools built since 1988 that had moveable interior walls, the district worked with the architects to reorganize space to create three additional classrooms per school.

And now, in 1999, the district enters phase 3 of the journey—end-ing unknown. Up to this point, housing students has been coupled with the goal of providing the best possible instructional program and learn-ing environment for students. We have managed to stay on the cutting edge of curricular and programmatic innovation. Three potential calen-dar options—variations on the 60/15 multi-track model—have been given serious consideration. At this moment in time, however, these cal-endar options are on hold because none of the constituents is willing to

	JULY	AUGUST	SEPTEMBER	OCTOBER	NOVEMBER	DECEMBER
A						
B						
C						

	JANUARY	FEBRUARY	MARCH	APRIL	MAY	JUNE
A						
B						
C						

School in Session
Off Track
Holiday / Students and Staff

ADVANTAGES
Increases capacity by 50%
Long instructional blocks
Time and space for intersession is increased
Accommodates small school
Fewer changes for rotating or roving teachers

DISADVANTAGES
Longer academic day
One week off for winter vacation
163 days of instruction instead of 180
Long intersession block

TABLE 6.10
Palmdale School District, Concept 6 Calendar Model

JULY	AUGUST	SEPTEMBER	OCTOBER	NOVEMBER	DECEMBER
A					
B					
C					

JANUARY	FEBRUARY	MARCH	APRIL	MAY	JUNE
A					
B					
C					

School in Session
Off Track
Holiday / Students and Staff

ADVANTAGES
Increases capacity by 50%
Space for intersession is increased
Accommodates small school

DISADVANTAGES
163 days of instruction instead of 180
Longer academic day
One week off for winter vacation
Short instructional blocks

TABLE 6.11
Palmdale School District, Modified Concept 6 Three-Track Calendar Model

take the plunge and make further changes. The district's long-term debt has been restructured to allow for the building of two additional schools.

Meanwhile, in yet another ironic twist, the State Superintendent Delaine Eastin, in an effort to mandate educational reforms such as universal preschool, mandatory summer school, and a longer school year, initially wanted the bond to target those multi-track districts that develop a phase-out plan to eliminate year-round multi- track programs. Only those districts that have been growing rapidly over the past decade, and were required to switch to a year-round schedule to qualify for building funds, can fully appreciate the irony of this "about-face" requirement!

And here in Palmdale School District, as this book goes to press we head into a board election in November 1999. This time, the lens of the board is focused primarily on reelection and garnering the support of parents and staff. To keep the parents content, the current year-round calendar is essential. To keep the teachers happy, the extended year contract with its increased salary is critical. But the number one priority of board members is to improve student learning. Thus, some form of the instructional reforms, especially those having to do with extended learning opportunities through intersession programs, will prevail.

This story provides an example of the potential long-term effects of reforms involving restructuring time. It also demonstrates how time as a vehicle for reform can sometimes become a roadblock for reform. When asked by the White Rabbit "Where shall I begin . . . ," the King responded, "Begin at the beginning and go on 'til you come to the end; then stop" (*Alice in Wonderland*). Sometimes, however, the end is just another beginning.

REFERENCES

Alcorn, R. D. (1992). Test scores: Can year-round schools raise them? *Thrust for Educational Leadership, 21* (6).

Ballinger, C. E., Kirschenbaum, N., & Poimbeauf, R. P. (1987). *The year-round school: Where learning never stops.* Bloomington, Ind.: Phi Delta Kappan Educational Foundation.

Cooper, H., Nye, B., Charlton, K., Lindsay, J., & Greathouse, S. (1996). The effects of summer vacation on achievement test scores: A narrative and meta-analytic review. *Review of Educational Research, 66* (3), 227–268.

Eisner, E. W. (1994). *The educational imagination* (3rd ed.). New York: Macmillan.

Elmore, R. F., & McLaughlin, M. W. (1988). *Steady work: Policy and the reform of American education.* Santa Monica, CA: RAND.

Fullan, M. G. (1993). *Change forces: Probing the depths of educational reform.* New York: Folmer.

Gándara, P., & Fish, J. (1994). Year-round schooling as an avenue to major structural reform. *Educational Evaluation and Policy Analysis, 16* (1), 67–85.

Kirst, M. (1984). *Who controls the schools?* Palo Alto, CA: Stanford Alumni Assoc.

National Association for Year-Round Education Staff. (1996). *Twenty-third reference director of year-round education programs for the 1996–97 school year.* San Diego: National Association for Year-Round Education.

O'Neal, S. (1991). *Year-round education: The second year, 1990–91.* Albuquerque, Albuquerque Public Schools, Planning, Research and Accountability.

Robinson, G. E. (1990). Synthesis of research of the effects of class size. *Educational Leadership, 47,* 80–90.

Shulman, L. (1987). Knowledge and teaching: Foundations of the new reform. *Harvard Educational Review, 57,* 1–22.

Six, L. A. (1993). Review of recent studies relating to the achievement of students enrolled in year-round education programs. *National Association of Year-Round Education.*

Spillane, J. P. (1998). State policy and the non-monolithic nature of the local school district: Organizational and professional considerations. *American Educational Research Journal, 35* (1), 33–63.

Spillane, J. P., & Thompson, C. L. (1997). Restructuring conceptions of local capacity: The local educational agency's capacity for ambitious instructional reform. *Educational Evaluation and Policy Analysis, 19* (2), 185–203.

PART III

Time as Process
in School Reform

CHAPTER 7

Teachers' Use of Time
in a Period of Change

Allan Pitman
and Thomas Romberg

For the past quarter century, mathematics teachers have been under great pressure to make substantive changes both in the content of what they teach and in their pedagogical practices. For many, such changes represent a reconceptualization of what constitutes the discipline of mathematics itself. Standards documents such as those produced during the past decade by the National Council of Teachers of Mathematics (1989, 1991, 1995) present a vision of school mathematics that assumes that all students should learn more and somewhat different mathematics in a discourse community. New curriculum materials, which reflect this vision, are currently being published, and teachers are being encouraged to use the materials to implement school mathematics reform. How teachers deal with reform (and the reform curricula and materials) will be governed in large part by their previous conceptions of mathematics, by the value they attach to the changes, and by the time (and resources) that they can—or will—devote to making those changes. One way to document how teachers actually implement change is to examine how time is used in their classrooms.

The study of teachers' change in practices and their relation to time usage has a history spanning at least since the early 1970s, when Rogers and Shoemaker (1971) argued that the time to take-up of an educational innovation was distributed approximately normally across a population of teachers. A basic weakness of this approach was the implicit assumption that all teachers were taking up the same innovation, without significant adaptation. The time-on-task research of the early 1980s began to provide some insight into the ways in which teachers used time in the classroom, but failed to take account of the sequencing of activity in the classroom.

The studies reported in this chapter aim to redress these weaknesses by seeking insight into the understandings that teachers bring to the implementation of an innovation which is, in itself, the subject of a complex series of negotiated understandings. Thus, the form in which a teacher will change her or his practice (and the time devoted to making the change) is contingent upon the value attached to the new material or method, and the understanding of how it conflicts with prior understandings and beliefs. What emerges is the view that, despite structures that aim to impose the ways in which teachers structure their classroom time, teachers exercise a great deal of agency through their interpretations, adaptations, and valuing of a particular innovation.

Although this chapter will focus on teachers' use of time as they implement new curriculum materials within the classroom, any consideration of teachers' use of time must go beyond simple organizational aspects or whether a given teacher is employing certain materials or curricula. Such consideration must also explore teachers' interpretations of the curricular materials, their professional backgrounds, their school contexts, and their own conceptions of mathematics.

THE "RHYTHM OF INSTRUCTION"

A teacher's day is regulated by the clock: The school timetable traditionally imposes a rigid division of the time available for instruction in the various parts of the curriculum and the time available to particular groups of students. Again, traditionally, the sequencing of activities in classrooms—in particular, mathematics classrooms—is predictable. For example, in Weller's (1991) study of traditional mathematics classrooms, he found a common daily pattern of instruction: "a repeating pattern of instruction . . . which consisted of three distinctive segments: a review, presentation, and study/assistance period. This 'rhythm of instruction' was not unplanned or coincidental" (p. 128). That teachers of mathematics see their subject as more codified and routine in form than teachers in English or social studies has been noted by other authors (e.g., Jackson, 1986; Rowan, Raudenbush, & Cheong, 1993; Stodolsky, 1988). Indeed, given the "routine work" of traditional school mathematics, mechanistic forms of organizational management would be considered appropriate (Perrow, 1967).

In contrast, the reform approach to teaching mathematics and new reform curricula assume that the allocation of time for specific activities will often be quite different from traditional sequencing. The reform curricula show, "on the whole, a substantial departure from teachers' prior experience, established beliefs, and present practice. Indeed, they hold out an image of conditions of learning for children that their teachers have themselves rarely experienced" (Little, 1993, p. 130). Burrill (quoted in de Lange, Burrill, Romberg, & van Reeuwijk, 1993) reflected on this challenge:

> The surprise came when we tried to teach the first lesson. There was little to "teach"; rather, the students had to read the map, read the keys, read the questions, determine what they were being asked to do, decide which piece of information from the map could be used to help them do this, and finally, decide what mathematics skills they needed, if any, in answering the question. There was no way the teacher could set the stage by demonstrating two examples (one of each kind), or by assigning five "seat work" problems and then turning students loose on their homework with a model firmly (for the moment) in place. (p. 154)

Such departures from traditional practices are new to mathematics teachers. It would, however, be false to draw the conclusion that teachers, when confronted with new material, do not have a powerful say in how they use their time professionally. Even though school systems are organized in a multitude of ways (from highly centralized structures, which provide great detail about expectations of outcomes and content delivery, to school-based organizations, which formally leave many curricular and pedagogical decisions to teachers), the decisions about the allocation of time across content and the organization of time within a given class is firmly in the individual teacher's hands. The contention of this chapter is that the way teachers use time is a good indicator of their ability to shift from mechanistic instructional routines to nonroutine (reform) teaching of mathematics.

FACTORS THAT INFLUENCE TEACHERS' USE OF TIME: A LOOK AT FOUR STUDIES DEALING WITH CURRICULAR CHANGE

Although the four studies we examine briefly in this section dealt with the impact of externally conceptualized curricular change (like that envisioned by the current school mathematics reform movement) on teachers (e.g., their beliefs, practices, etc.), we use the summaries to look briefly at factors that influence teachers' use of time.

Science Teachers in Hong Kong

In this study, Pitman (1979) looked at the reactions of Hong Kong high school science teachers to a new curriculum. In the mid-1970s, the Hong

Kong Ministry of Education introduced the Nuffield integrated science curriculum to the colony's schools on a voluntary basis, with a small financial incentive offered to schools that implemented the program. Implementation of the program could occur at one of two levels: Either entire schools implemented the program (and were monitored) or individual teachers implemented the program (in its entirety or in part). The focus of the study was on what the teachers understood the change to be in relation to their previous practices. Berlyne's (1965) categories of response to change (disequalization, suppression, conciliation, and swamping) were used to examine the situation of teachers confronted with pressure to introduce a substantive change in practice.

In this study we found that teachers uncritical of ideas initiated by experts and authorities tended to favor the change and see it as substantive. Those tending to suppress the problem of changing their practice and who were not supportive of integrated science tended to make adaptations to their practice, but not along the lines suggested. We also noted that some did not see the introduction of integrated science as significantly different from what they were already doing, even though, in reality, the curriculum required a fundamental shift in practice if change other than at a superficial level was to occur. Of particular interest was the observation that the perceived familiarity of the teachers with the innovation was not related to how they dealt with the change (by disequalization, suppression, conciliation, or swamping). Further, their contact with resource people (in this case, science inspectors) did not affect their acceptance or rejection of the program, but did tend to reduce the tendency to conciliate it with their past practices.

Although use of time was not directly examined in this study, we are confident, in retrospect, that differences in how teachers used time in their classrooms would (again) reflect Berlyne's (1965) categories of response: that the amount of effort and time a teacher will devote to transforming practice is determined at least in part by the degree to which an innovation is valued, how it is valued, and the extent to which it is interpreted as representing a significant change.

Individually Guided Instruction (IGE)

In their study of schools reported to be exemplary in their implementation of a reform mathematics program, Individually Guided Instruction (IGE), Popkewitz, Tabachnik, and Wehlage (1982, 1985) found significant differences from the expectations and assumptions of the program's developers. They noted that in implementing reform, schools (and school districts) "exhibit remarkable resilience; innovations are first incorporated into existing patterns of behavior and belief, then used to legitimize ongoing patterns of educational conduct, while being identified in slogans . . . [that] suggest reform" (Popkewitz, Tabachnik, & Wehlage, 1985, p. 138). In the schools they studied, the authors identified three patterns of schooling, each of which had a distinctive influence on both the actual implementation of the program and the ways in which teachers within a given institutional configuration responded to the planned change.

Technical schooling. In the three schools in this study with this pattern, the instructional emphasis was on management and efficient processing of students. Teachers devoted their time to class preparation, record keeping, and keeping students "looking busy" (Popkewitz, Tabachnik, & Wehlage, 1985, p.141). This social control demanded standardization of knowledge, with mathematical concepts sequenced and discrete. What characterized the curriculum implementation in these schools was the reduction of the curriculum to what could be measured objectively: The procedures and tools of the curriculum became its substance; serendipity in teacher–student interaction was excluded from the classroom; and the coherence of implementation came from teacher identification with the IGE slogans of reform.

Constructive schooling. In the one school in the study with this pattern, teachers focused on children's intellectual and social development. In the context of the classroom, this meant time spent on discovery, exploration of concepts, and integration of knowledge and skills, with emphasis as well on creativity/aesthetic pursuits. This constructivist approach encouraged individual (student) responsibility and initiative in learning, allowed great teacher autonomy (which led to much individual interpretation of the curriculum), and sometimes created conditions for teacher burnout (Popkewitz, Tabachnik, & Wehlage, 1982, p. 95). At this school, teachers appeared to adopt the main elements of the reform curriculum, but IGE procedures and technologies were adopted only if they enhanced the institutional pattern. Unit meetings were, in fact, discussions of curriculum issues; IGE record-keeping procedures were used only when there were (already in place) district mininum objectives. Again, teachers' use of time reflected the ethos of the institution.

Illusory schooling. In the two schools in the study with this pattern, teachers (and administrators) believed in the effect of the outside communities (in both cases, termed "difficult" by the staffs) to influence schooling and were, therefore, pessimistic about children's ability to learn. Despite much use of the language of reform, instruction followed outlined sequences (taken from whatever textbook then in use), and "the routines of school work [were] often without content" (Popkewitz, Tabachnik, & Wehlage, 1985, p. 152). IGE was given "ceremonial" or public relations use: Signs proclaimed that these were IGE schools, IGE technologies provided information to parents about objectives and test scores, and so forth. Reform was secondary to controlling the student population, and teachers gave the majority of their time to "what was considered the necessary behaviors, self-control, and attitudes, rather than formal schoolwork" (p. 149).

Teachers Transforming Planned Change

In this study (Romberg & Pitman, 1990), we directly examined the ways in which teachers used their classroom time when working with highly structured teaching materials. We were able to identify strong variation in the total amount of time given a particular unit of work, the ways in which that time was divided up with respect to classroom organization, and the nature of the mathematical tasks to which time was devoted. Using a time-based graphical representation of observer records, interviews, and analysis of teaching materials, we gained insight into the modifications made and the reasons given for those modifications.

For example, one activity designed for grade 2 students presented children with a worksheet containing ten addition and subtraction sentences for completion. The intent was that the children would be involved in seat work without prior teacher demonstration of procedures for completing the sentences, thus generating cognitive conflict. This conflict would later be resolved through extended classroom discussion. We had estimated that the activity would require forty minutes of classroom time: about five minutes of large-group introduction, ten minutes of individual work (with some children possibly working in pairs), and twenty-five minutes of large-group work (discussion), and we expected a high level of pupil–teacher and pupil–pupil interaction. The six teachers observed devoted from fifteen minutes to fifty minutes over two days to the task. Groupings ranged from a fairly faithful presentation over thirty minutes, to small-group activity replacing the individual seat work, to the entire time being devoted to individual seat work.

The ways in which the teachers reapportioned the time devoted to this task reflected the substantive pedagogical changes that they made to the content of the activity. Some failed to allocate time for the generation of cognitive conflict, either because they failed to see its value pedagogically, or they avoided the potential management problems associated with generating frustration for students. As one teacher noted, "such discussion . . . is seen as bad teaching since teachers should tell students what to do"' (Romberg & Pitman, 1990, p. 223).

What emerged very clearly from this study was that, even under the confining conditions of having observers/developers sitting at the back of the room, these teachers made fundamental decisions about the allocation of their teaching time and about the character of that time. They made adaptations, based upon their beliefs about the interests of the children in their classes and about mathematics, in such ways that the notion of "teacher-proof" materials became nonsense. If the authors of such materials are to see relatively faithful implementation of their ideas, then a great deal of effort apparently must be devoted to making very explicit both the theoretical assumptions and arguments on which the innovation is based and the implications of the innovation for practice.

Teachers do have to make adaptations of innovations and decisions about whether to accept or reject innovations. With this professional role, however, there is responsibility: The freedom to make decisions is not license. As we have observed, many of the changes made by teachers, and reflected in their use of time, were reasonable, but some teachers, when they changed the amount of time and nature of the task to which that time was allocated, did change the meaning of the mathematical ideas intended to be developed by the task.

Mathematics in Context: *Impact on Teachers*

Romberg (1997) synthesized the findings from nine separate case studies and combined them with formative information gathered when the units for *Mathematics in Context*[1] were being pilot-tested and field-tested in classrooms. The studies focused on how teachers have coped with the transition from traditional forms of instruction in mathematics classrooms to a reform approach. Each is a case study and as such is a rich description of the experiences of teachers and students in specific mathematics classrooms. Each tells a slightly different story, but taken together they suggest common themes about the teacher's role in the reformed classroom and the difficulties in making the transition from traditional to reformed instruction. As Sarason (1971) in his examination of the culture of schools argued, "any attempt to introduce a change into the school involves [challenging] some existing regularity, behavioral or programmatic" (p. 3). In each case where units from *Mathematics in Context* (MiC) were taught, the traditional school culture and the common instructional routines for mathematics classes were challenged, with the most striking difference faced by teachers being the shift in the daily pattern of instruction.

Four observations can be drawn from these studies. First, authority in the traditional classroom resides, as Weller (1991) argued, with the textbook author. He found that "the expert knowledge of the teacher was deliberately subjugated to that of the textbook. As a result of that process, the teacher was able to camouflage his role as authoritarian, thus eliminating student challenges of authority" (p. 133). In fact, the traditional use of the term "they" as the authority for what, how, and why something is to be done echoes what Provenzo, McCloskey, Kottkamp, and Cohn (1989) found: "The use of 'they' by the teacher allows her to express her feelings concerning the forces that are influencing and shaping her day-to-day work, without having to specify their actual source and origin" (p. 563). By contrast, in the field-testing of *Mathematics in Context*, teachers did not fall back on the use of the term "they" in the same manner. This may have been because the student booklets contained tasks for students to read and make sense of under the guidance of the teacher. This approach to instructional authority changed the work environment for both teachers and students from well-rehearsed routines to a variety of nonroutine activities and forced some teachers to reconsider how they interacted with their students.

Second, for most teachers in these studies, the adjustments in what they and their students were expected regularly to do was unsettling. This was clearly reflected in teachers' use of time in their classrooms. For example, when reflecting on the work of the two teachers in her study, Clarke (1995) noted that the teachers struggled with how much to tell the students:

> Both too little and too much structure seemed to limit the students' thinking. For example, with the initial presentation of problems there was a need to clarify, but at the same time not [a need] to present complete explanations. The challenge was to present a problem in such a way that the students could make a start, while not limiting their thinking by overexplanation. (p. 159)

In fact, in most classes teachers occasionally had to admit they did not know how to approach a problem and thus had to work on the tasks with the students as equals. Thus, the allocation of time to instructional activities was not always controlled by the teacher, but rather negotiated with the students.

Third, in traditional classrooms, the way a small number of adults (teachers and others) are able to organize and control a large number of students is seen as a problem of management. In this sense, the traditional teacher is primarily a manager of resources and personnel, and his or her use of time is focused on getting students to complete pages or to do sets of exercises. One common management approach has been to reduce the intellectual struggle for students. For example, Clarke (1995) found that one teacher in her study found the conflict between her view of student comfort and their cognitive struggles disturbing:

> The emotional well-being of the students was very important to this teacher, and she worked very hard at making the classroom environ-

ment comfortable and successful. . . . Students were not generally encouraged to struggle and it is this very struggle, the grappling with mathematical ideas, that reform encourages. This represented a contradiction between the practices this teacher believed allowed students to be comfortable and successful and the intended purpose of the unit. (pp. 160–161)

Finally, coverage of topics became a concern for most teachers. Traditionally, mathematics at a particular grade includes a number of topics, and the teacher is expected to allocate time so that all the topics are covered in the year. Because *Mathematics in Context* is organized around instructional units that integrate mathematical topics, teachers were often uncomfortable that traditional topics were not being addressed and unsure how they were to allocate time to particular units.

REFLECTIONS ON THE IMPACT OF CURRICULAR CHANGE ON TEACHERS

The four studies in the previous section demonstrate that expecting teachers to change their practices when confronted with demands to teach a new, and radically different, mathematics curriculum is problematic. Our analysis indicated that the gap between intended reform practices and those that are actually implemented is in part due to the fact that curricular change comes to the teacher in a highly mediated form. The negotiations, both conscious and tacit, that lead to the transmission and interpretation of an educational innovation must, by their very nature, also lead to the distortion of the original concept (Pitman, 1981).

Implementation: A Four-Step Process

In Figure 7.1, we argue that the time line for the implementation of new curricular materials follows a four-step negotiation process: product development, product projection by mediators, product interpretation by teachers, and product implementation in classrooms. Between each step, negotiations about the meaning of terms, the importance of details, and so forth, are carried out. Also, at each step there are negotiations with academic and administrative critics to sanction and legitimate the proposed changes. The model suggests that the implementation of a curricular innovation is dependent upon this series of negotiations, each likely to widen the gap between the image idealizations held by academic and administrative critics and the image transmitted toward implementation.

This divergence is grounded in the different motivations underlying the presentation of information. A curriculum developer, for example, is motivated by concerns about academic sanctioning (e.g., Do the materi-

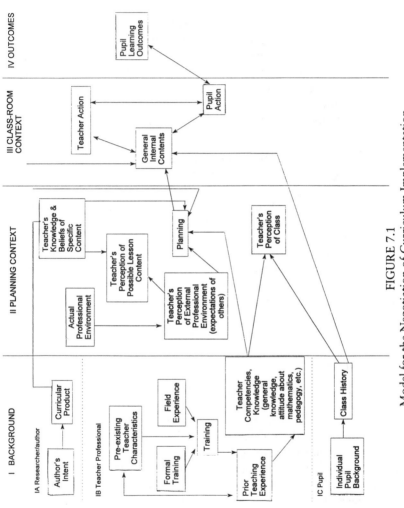

FIGURE 7.1

Model for the Negotiation of Curriculum Implementation

als meet the NCTM *Standards?*), funding maintenance, and the pragmatics of finding/working with the school supervisors or mathematics educators who are to act as mediators with teachers. Such concerns, however, might well lead to the clouding of some issues in the search for commonality of interest. The individual teacher, however, will base his or her own interpretation on the information received not (in general) from the developers, but from the mediators. The information provided by mediators and the interpretations of that information by school staffs can lead to implementations quite different from those intended. For example, the weak incentives given science teachers in Hong Kong (Pitman, 1979), along with lax negotiations, clearly led these teachers to various interpretations of the value of the material and, in turn, to a variety of implementations. A similar pattern was evident in the IGE schools (Popkewitz, Tabachnik, & Wehlage, 1985).

Although the gap between product idealization as viewed by the developers and actual product implementation was documented in terms of the discrepancy between expected and actual "use of time" only in the planned change study (Romberg & Pitman, 1990), all of the other studies showed similar gaps in realization. Because the work of both teachers and students in the step from product interpretation and product implementation in the model involves planning, teachers' use of time can be a useful empirical means by which to examine product implementation.

Factors Affecting Teachers' Implementation

In planning and implementing a unit of work, a teacher does not act in a historical vacuum. Affecting a teacher's planning and eventual implementation of the work are both a number of variables associated with that teacher's professional background (e.g., training, competencies, and experience; see Figure 7.2) and the context in which the planning and implementation take place.

As Goodson (1991) noted, in the working day of most teachers, there is minimal time set aside for reflection on practice or for professional activities other than active teaching, administration, preparation, and contemporaneous assessment of student work. For most teachers, the "work" of teaching does not stop at the building door: Correction of student work, preparation of resources, and engagement in extracurricular activities such as sports coaching are a regular part of life. Given that there is little time for reflection on practice while a teacher is "at work," is there, in fact, time for such reflection outside it?

Much analysis of teacher work tends to decontextualize that work from the pressures and constraints of family, other interests, and community commitments. In his analysis, Goodson (1991) made it clear that

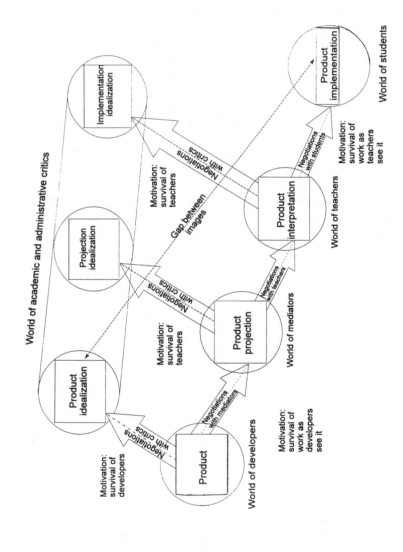

FIGURE 7.2
Conceptual Model Relating Lesson Content, Teacher Actions, and Pupil Action

any demands for changing the work of teachers must take into account the rest of the life world of that person, that, in fact, the total life pattern of a teacher is directly implicated in the way that person interacts with the work of schooling. He argued that individual teachers see their work from the perspective of their stage of life: A neophyte teacher is likely to see the work as a central concern, particularly if the teacher is single; a teacher who is also a parent will not necessarily allocate the same privileged place to his or her work; a teacher within five or six years of retirement, although still a dedicated practitioner, may not feel as positively responsive to pressures to change his or her practice. Within Goodson's broader view, the arguments of Huberman, Wieland, and Thompson (in press) provide a useful overview of U.S. attempts to describe teachers' career cycles. The terms various researchers have chosen to characterize the stages of occupational life suggest that the time and effort devoted to reconceptualizing an individual's practice is highly contingent upon where that individual is within these cycles. Any analysis of teachers' use of time in classrooms, therefore, must also consider both time spent outside the classroom and the stage of life of the particular teacher.

Both Romberg and Pitman (1990) and Romberg (1997) noted the importance (in implementation of reform) of the teacher's knowledge and beliefs regarding the content. In a subject such as mathematics, teachers hold a diversity of conceptions as to just what constitutes the subject and what it means to "do mathematics." Equally important is the teacher's perception of just what the reform means: If no substantive change is perceived, then only symbolic and terminological changes are likely to occur with little time devoted to a transition in practice. If, on the other hand, the change is perceived as redefining subject matter (content) and/or requiring major change in pedagogical methods or styles, that change can be perceived as challenging the teacher's self-assessment of his or her competencies and demanding of substantial time devoted to concentrated conceptual and practical effort.

The Connection Between Mathematical Content and Practice

The connection between content and pedagogy, especially when (as now) there is pressure to reform both, is important on two grounds. First, the teachers for whom the reform is intended do not all hold the same view of their subject discipline, and, second, a shift in the former is also likely to lead to changes in the latter. Romberg and Middleton (1994), for example, identified four distinct groups among the high school mathematics teachers who were involved to varying degrees in the Ford Foundation's Urban Mathematics Collaboratives Project: traditional, reform, nondiscriminating, and transition. Whereas "traditional" teachers characterized mathematics as scientific, logical, factual, and requiring effort on the part of the student, "reform" teachers saw mathematics as a dynamic, logical system, formed by thinking about processes. The views of the two other groups, those who did not discriminate or were eclectic in their view of mathematics and those who seemed to be in transition between traditional and reform positions, fell between these two "opposite" beliefs (Webb & Romberg, 1990, p. 90).

The link between content and pedagogy is also addressed by Richert (1994): "Knowing mathematics and teaching mathematics are two different things. . . . It is fairly safe to hypothesize that a reexamination of one's conceptions of mathematics . . . would result in a rethinking of one's teaching of mathematics as well" (p. 151). A central consequence of this is that a teacher, successful in dealing with curricular content, pedagogical techniques, and organizational control, must see pressure to change practice as a very real problem. For a teacher who is successful within the frame of his or her own reference, a change of substance challenges key concepts both of work and of self. To view the way a teacher deals with such change as linear—able to be represented as a time line for successful take-up or rejection—is simplistic. Pressure to change either content or practice creates conflicts in a teacher's conceptual framework about the work of teaching. Any planning of what is to occur subsequently in the classroom is thus embedded in the need to resolve this conflict. It is within this context that teachers make the decisions that constitute change. We have argued elsewhere that this is the case, even with the introduction of highly structured materials (Romberg & Pitman, 1990).

Change in practice and content (which means change in teachers' perceptions of their professional environment as well as in the demands of the teaching materials to be used when lesson planning occurs) can prove difficult for the individual teacher to reconcile with her or his (pre-reform) understandings of mathematical content, pedagogical beliefs, and knowledge of the nature of the students in class. Within the context of this conflict, teachers, both before and during their work in the classroom, make decisions that include, modify, or exclude content. Their decisions about their use of time, both in the classroom and in class preparation, also reflect that conflict. Any study of school mathematics reform in the classroom must be aware of how teachers' decisions and perspectives on reform are reflected in their use of time.

SUMMARY

As we evaluate the major reform in school mathematics now under way for over a decade in the United States (as in many other countries), it is clear that the contexts into which such change is introduced lead to a diversity of adaptations and transformations. Many of these arise as a direct consequence of how teachers choose to commit the time resources at their command. The decisions teachers make about their use of time are governed not only by the intrinsic qualities (mathematical, pedagogical, and curricular) of the emerging programs, but also by teachers' belief systems (e.g., about content, the abilities of their students, their own best interests), the institutional beliefs associated with the schools in which they work, and their life stages, both professionally and privately. The values they place on reform, both with respect to its intrinsic worth and to their personal motivation to invest time and effort (and to deal with probable discomfort) derive from this context.

Rather than looking at the reformation of the teaching of school mathematics as something monolithic, it is perhaps more appropriate to think of reform much as Schon (1971) characterized political movements: as having shifting centers, carrying no stable, centrally established message, and being survival-prone. By starting an analysis from this contrary perspective, the different "objective" interests and beliefs of those involved at all levels can be acknowledged while, at the same time, ways in which the key ideas are able to survive the inevitable transformations can be identified.

Finally, teachers' use of time should be considered an important empirical indicator. Variations in teachers' use of time can provide investigators with valuable information about the change process, the negotiations that have occurred, and teachers' valuation of such changes. This insight can only be obtained, however, if the information collected goes well beyond the broad consideration of issues such as claimed take-up of a reform or the gross amount of time devoted to particular pedagogical strategies, to the study of individuals and their interpretations of their classroom environments.

NOTE

1. Mathematics in Context is a middle school curriculum developed under the auspices of the National Science Foundation (National Center for Research in Mathematical Sciences Education & Freudenthal Institute, 1996–97).

REFERENCES

Berlyne, D. E. (1965). *Structure and direction in thinking*. New York: Wiley.
Clarke, B. (1995). *Expecting the unexpected: Critical incidents in the mathematics classroom*. Unpublished doctoral dissertation, University of Wisconsin–Madison.

de Lange, J., Burrill, G., Romberg, T., & van Reeuwijk, M. (1993). *Learning and testing mathematics in context.* Pleasantville, NY: Wings for Learning.

Goodson, I. (1991). Teachers' lives and educational research. In I. Goodson (Ed.), *Biography, identity, and schooling: Episodes in educational research* (pp. 137–149). Philadelphia: Falmer.

Huberman, M., Wieland, S., & Thompson, C. (in press). A life-history perspective on the teaching career. In B. Biddle, T. Good, & I. Goodson (Eds.), *International handbook on teachers and teaching.* Dordrecht, The Netherlands: Kluwer.

Jackson, P. W. (1986). *The practice of teaching.* New York: Teachers College Press.

Little, J. (1993). Teachers' professional development in a climate of educational reform. *Educational Evaluation and Policy Analysis, 15* (2), 129–151.

National Center for Research in Mathematical Sciences Education & Freudenthal Institute. (1996–97). *Mathematics in context: A guided curriculum for grades 5–8.* Chicago: Encyclopedia Britannica Educational Corporation.

National Council of Teachers of Mathematics. (1989). *Curriculum and evaluation standards for school mathematics.* Reston, VA: Author.

National Council of Teachers of Mathematics. (1991). *Professional teaching standards.* Reston, VA: Author.

National Council of Teachers of Mathematics. (1995). *Assessment standards for school mathematics.* Reston, VA: Author.

Perrow, C. (1967). A framework for the comparative analysis of organizations. *American Sociological Review, 79,* 686–704.

Pitman, A. (1979). *Conceptual conflict and innovation in education.* Unpublished master's thesis, La Trobe University, Melbourne, Australia.

Pitman, A. (1981). The necessary distortion of disseminated innovations. *Journal of Curriculum Studies, 13* (3), 253–256.

Popkewitz, T. S., Tabachnik, R., & Wehlage, G. (1982). *The myth of educational reform: A study of school responses to a program of change.* Madison: University of Wisconsin Press.

Popkewitz, T. S., Tabachnik, R., & Wehlage, G. (1985). The field study of six IGE schools. In T. A. Romberg (Ed.), *Toward effective schooling: The IGE experience* (pp. 131–157). Lantham; MD: University Press of America.

Provenzo, E. F., McCloskey, G. N., Kottkamp, R. B., & Cohn, M. M. (1989). *Metaphors and meaning in the language of teachers.* New York: Teachers College Press.

Richert, A. (1994). Knowledge growth and professional commitment: The effect of the Urban Mathematics Collaborative on two San Francisco teachers. In N. L. Webb & T. A. Romberg (Eds.), *Reforming mathematics education in America's cities: The Urban Mathematics Collaborative Project* (pp. 151–172). New York: Teachers College Press.

Rogers, E. M., & Shoemaker, F. F. (1971). Communication of innovations, Second edition. New York: Free Press.

Romberg, T. A. (1997). *Mathematics in Context*: Impact on teachers. In E. Fennema & B. S. Nelson (Eds.), *Mathematics teachers in transition* (pp. 357–380). Mahwah, NJ: Erlbaum.

Romberg, T. A., & Middleton, J.A. (1994). Conceptions of mathematics and mathematics education held by teachers. In N. L. Webb & T. A. Romberg (Eds.), *Reforming mathematics education in America's cities.: The Urban Mathematics Collaborative Project* (pp. 83–104). New York: Teachers College Press.

Romberg, T. A., & Pitman, A. (1990). Curricular materials and pedagogical reform: Teachers' perspectives and use of time in the teaching of mathematics. In R. Bromme & M. Ben-Peretz (Eds.), *The nature of time in schools: Theoretical concepts and practitioner perceptions* (p. 189). New York: Teachers College Press.

Rowan, B., Raudenbush, S. W., & Cheong, Y. F. (1993). Teaching as a non-routine task: Implications for the management of schools. *Education Administration Quarterly, 29* (4), 479–500.

Sarason, S. B. (1971). *The culture of the school and the problem of change.* Boston: Allyn & Bacon.

Schon, D. A. (1971). *Beyond the stable state: Public and private learning in a changing society.* London: Temple Smith.

Stodolsky, S. (1988). *The subject matters: Classroom activity in math and social studies.* Chicago: University of Chicago Press.

Webb, N. L., & Romberg, T. A. (Eds.). (1990). *Reforming mathematics education in America's cities: The Urban Mathematics Collaborative Project.* New York: Teachers College Press.

Weller, M. (1991). *Marketing the curriculum: Core vs. non-core subjects in one junior high school.* Unpublished doctoral dissertation, University of Wisconsin–Madison.

CHAPTER 8

Representing Time and Studying School Change: Lessons from a Collaborative Field Study[1]

Jon Wagner

In popular and folkloric discourse, we hear that time will tell, that it flies, passes, slows down, and measures; that it can be spent, or waits, that it can be stitched, and that it heals. But what do we hear that time does within processes of school change?

Some provisional answers to this question have emerged for me through a collaborative action research project entitled "Learning from Restructuring" (LFR). During the first four years of this project, Sandra Murphy and I—and several other colleagues from UC Davis and CSU Fresno—worked with fifteen schoolteachers and administrators to construct detailed accounts of changes occurring in their schools. Within these accounts, school practitioners articulated a rich array of relationships between time and the social life of their schools, relationships that have implications both for studying school change and for guiding it.

The practitioner accounts of school change developed through the LFR project were informed by other project data, including transcribed interviews, field notes, official and unofficial school documents, and examples of student work. But the accounts themselves were fashioned largely by school members in multisession oral presentations to other LFR participants. For their part, other LFR members did not just sit and listen. As interested peers, they interrupted change accounts presented by members of individual LFR schools to present confirming or contradictory evidence of their own, to ask for more detail, or to propose questions for further investigation—all with exceptional good will.

LFR data collection activities did not focus explicitly on issues of time and school change. Our attention was on other matters: changing models and strategies of assessment, regrouping practices within and across schools, the mobilization of teachers and community members around new school programs, and so on. But time was no stranger to these discussions, nor could much of what we said and heard make sense without shared understandings of time and school change.

Shared understandings of this sort are not easy to come by, as time can mean quite different things to different people—or to the same people in different situations. Indeed, the anthropologist Edward Hall (1983) argues that contrasting time orientations are a key source of miscommunication and misunderstanding between members of different cultural groups.[2] In a recent extension of Hall's work, Andrew Hargreaves (1994) has argued that school change issues are shaped in part by conflicts between the different time orientations of teachers and administrators (1994, p. 113):

> What we are witnessing in much current educational reform and associated changes in teachers' work is such impositions of modernistic, administrative time perspectives, with all their practical implications, on the working lives of teachers. We are, in effect, witnessing the growing administrative colonization of teachers' time and space, where monochronic, technical-rational time is becoming hegemonic time.

My approach departs from the work of Hall and Hargreaves in two key respects. First, rather than proposing a conception of "time itself" to use in analyzing social life, I look at social life to see how individuals are examining and using different conceptions of time. Second, my analysis does not identify particular time orientations with different groups of people. Instead, I argue that the same individuals, when faced with different challenges, may use different conceptions of time and do so in different settings, in the same setting, or even—as we will see—in the same sentence![3]

The starting point for my analysis is the discourse that school practitioners use in discussing and describing changes occurring in their schools. Within this discourse, school teachers and administrators refer to different dimensions of time to give shape and substance to social activities, or to articulate and "index" the pace and structure of these activities with other activities, events, and institutions. Taken together, these references help practitioners specify and characterize the complex social relationships among ideas, actions, actors, institutions, and events that constitute school change.

My examination of these matters is guided by these three questions:

In what different ways is time represented in practitioner accounts of school change? What implications do these have for understanding school change? And, what can we learn from these implications that might help us design more thoughtful strategies for studying and guiding school change? As a prelude to answering these questions, let me describe how the LFR project generated practitioner accounts of school change.

"LEARNING FROM RESTRUCTURING"

We began the Learning from Restructuring project in 1993 by working with four California high schools and two elementary schools. In 1994 we added six more schools—one elementary, two middle schools, and two high schools. Schools were identified as potential participants in LFR through informal networks of teachers and administrators, and by doctoral students from UC Davis and CSU Fresno, some of whom were also teachers and administrators. We invited schools to participate through letters and phone exchanges with a lead teacher or site administrator. The only incentive or "resource" we offered schools was the opportunity to work with us and with members of other LFR schools to understand better the restructuring efforts with which they were involved. All schools invited chose to participate, but one of the initial six schools withdrew at the end of the first eighteen months.

We selected LFR schools to represent the diversity of California's public school communities. Six schools are largely urban, five suburban, and one rural. Two high schools in the project are large, having over 2,500 students each, but others are much smaller, and one middle school has less than 150 students. Some school communities are politically liberal or progressive, others quite conservative. A majority of the students at two schools are primarily Anglo, but students at the others are ethnically diverse, and several schools enroll a majority of "minority" students.

We deliberately recruited schools that varied in their relationship to school reform efforts in general and to California's state-supported school restructuring initiative (SB 1274) in particular.[4] Six LFR schools were successful in obtaining SB 1274 funds to support their restructuring programs. Four others did not submit a 1274 proposal, and two submitted proposals that were not approved. Within these criteria, we also were able to recruit six schools that had teachers or administrators who were enrolled as graduate students in doctoral programs for which Murphy and I served as faculty members.[5]

From 1993 through 1995, we held five two-day LFR meetings, most of them organized around creating and reviewing school change accounts. Additional meetings were held in connection with interviews and field visits. We also crossed paths with LFR members at other meetings and conferences related to school change—including several statewide 1274 symposia and a statewide teacher research conference hosted annually by the CRESS Center, UC Davis. Contacts and exchanges with LFR schools also occurred in connection with other research projects conducted by Murphy and by me and through ongoing communication with the graduate students who worked as teachers or administrators at six of the schools.

LFR was developed as a collaborative action research project. Initially, Murphy and I defined our role primarily in terms of preparing accounts and analyses from data contributed by school members, then sharing with those same school members the accounts and analyses we had prepared. We defined research questions in dialogue with our K–12 partners. We then tried to identify data sources linked closely to specific questions and to design strategies for collecting and analyzing data to answer the research questions. As background for examining questions and data sources, we also sought to develop case histories of each school. For this purpose we interviewed key administrators and teachers and collected official and unofficial documents related to restructuring and reform efforts at each site.[6]

As we worked with K–12 colleagues to develop research questions and "school change portfolios," we also heard about changes taking place in their schools. Over the project's first twelve months, these accounts from LFR teachers and administrators increasingly captured our imagination and that of other project members. As we recognized their value in helping us understand school change, we moved these practitioner accounts toward the center of our study, and as we did, we also looked for ways to strengthen and extend them.

One result of this revised orientation was that LFR meetings became much more important than we had initially intended. We began to use these meetings to provide school members the time they needed to prepare detailed accounts of school change, to present these accounts, and to reflect on them.

As resources for *preparing* accounts, we organized two-way interviews between members from different schools; made available copies of school documents, interview transcripts, and field notes; and invited individuals to prepare written templates and outlines that could complement oral presentations of changes occurring at their school.

To encourage *reflection*, we encouraged project members from other schools to interrogate individual school change accounts as they were being presented. We also audiotaped and transcribed discussions at LFR meetings and shared some of the transcripts with other LFR members. In addition, we engaged the group as a whole in the analysis of LFR data sets. For example, at one LFR meeting, school members brought letters they had asked their students to write about changes under way at their schools; we spent a productive morning reading and examining these in conjunction with the change accounts of teachers and administrators. Finally, to develop trust and to stimulate retrospective evaluation among project members, we met with largely the same group of people over the course of several years.

Taken together, these features turned what we had proposed initially as "collaborative research" into an opportunity for inquiry-oriented "professional development" for participating teachers and administrators. As that transformation occurred, the project also generated research data that were richer by far than the "information" we sought initially from our "research subjects." This enriched data emerged primarily as a cumulative, multiyear series of school change accounts for each LFR school, within which different orientations toward time were very much evident.

REPRESENTING TIME IN PARTICIPANT
ACCOUNTS OF SCHOOL CHANGE

Within *change proposals and projects* at LFR schools, time was represented explicitly in three different forms: as a resource for individuals and groups to design and implement reforms; as a template for reorganizing existing school activities; and as a measure for extending or contracting "normal" expectations for how long it takes to complete academic and administrative tasks. These three considerations all refer to a kind of rational-bureaucratic time instantiated in the social organization of institutions and embedded in the logic of school planning and administration.

However, in their detailed *accounts of change actually under way*, members of LFR schools referred frequently to "turning points," "crises," and "moments of special opportunity." These references don't fit well within the rational-bureaucratic time orientations of reform proposals. They reflect instead the logic of living through change in schools and a sense of ongoing drama, uncertainty, and conflict about the substance and process of reform.

In their school change accounts, members of LFR schools also referred frequently to time as a "gap" between different instances of social life in schools, or as a source of fundamental disjunction among past, present, and future activities. Guiding social action *over* time presented school members with the challenge of overcoming these disjunctions, in response to which participants relied on several key "follow-up" strategies.

Contrasts among "proposal," "dramatic," and "disjunctive" time—and between other representations of time in LFR accounts—present challenges to the study of school change and to the design of planned change in schools. To suggest the scope of these challenges, let me illustrate these contrasts with some examples from LFR schools.

Time as a Development Resource in School Change Proposals

One of the most common features of restructuring in LFR schools—and, arguably, the feature valued most highly by teachers—was the increased availability of certain kinds of "extra" time for teachers: planning time, consulting time, time for training, time for networking or for coordinating programs, and, in some cases, time to become more familiar with their students.[7] In most LFR schools, "extra time" of this sort was created partly through rescheduling, partly through additional compensation to teachers, and partly through increased contributions of teachers' personal time. In terms of rescheduling, the most common arrangements involved some kind of "banking." As an elementary school principal described it:

> Part of the Accelerated school program was to have the school take stock and to bank time during the week. So that first year after our team came back from Accelerated schools, we met with our transportation people, because with 75 percent of our kids being bussed in, we're very tied to transportation. But we were able to work out with them a change in our schedule so we went to four days extended, and every Wednesday, shorten that day. So we built in time during the work day to start doing some planning.

"Banking" time provisions were noted by teachers from all but one of the twelve LFR schools. Another LFR teacher described how such arrangements worked at her high school:

> We're banking our time and we're throwing it into a Wednesday schedule that will allow us to dismiss early. Kids will still stay on campus, hopefully not killing each other between the time we dismiss and the time the buses come. What's supposed to happen in that time is that these people can meet, we can meet without going beyond the school day . . . we bank like seven minutes a day or something.

In some quarters, changes of this sort in teachers' conditions of employment might be resisted as violations of union contracts. However, all the LFR schools secured union support (or tolerance) for the specific "time banking" arrangements they proposed. A teacher from the same elementary school mentioned above gave this account:

And so we went to them [the teachers' union] and said, "You know, we keep reading in our union newspapers that restructuring is a big deal and we're talking about doing that. What do we have to do to satisfy you folks?" And they said "Well, if 80 percent of your staff says they'll give up two minutes a day of their time to do this thinking . . ."—and that's what it worked out to is we gave up two minutes; we all worked beyond contract anyway, so it was sort of a moot point with us—"then we'll support you." So we went back to the staff and said, "Well, we can do this if 80 percent of us or more sign," and all of us signed.

As a supplement to "banking" provisions, some schools provided teachers with additional compensation. As a high school teacher reported:

Our House coordinators got compensated so I now . . . well last year I compensated myself and all my House teachers for their meeting times. This next year no one gets compensated but I get a release period. I would prefer to give people money for participating, but the district would prefer that I take the time because they want to make me do more work.

To supplement "banking time" as a resource for change efforts, all LFR schools have depended on substantial contributions of teachers' personal time. A high school teacher provided the following example: "We went through twelve hours of training on site-based management. . . . And we took actual decisions that we needed to make and walked them through the process and did it with the committees that needed to have them. And all this we did on our own time after school."

Contributions of personal time by some teachers characterized change efforts at all LFR schools. However, these contributions were irregular; teachers who made them one year might not make them the next year. As a formerly active teacher noted about his reluctance to become more involved in a new program: "I was involved with other things. I was doing a Teacher Ed. program at _____ College, I was really busy, I needed time with my family and I saw this as a major, huge time commitment, which it was. So those were the kinds of reasons I was holding back."

As outlined in restructuring proposals and plans, the "extra" time that LFR schools created for teachers was usually regarded as a means for developing or designing new programs. The following account by an LFR high school teacher is an apt illustration: "The board made a commitment to give us five weeks out of the classroom, and they hired subs to go into our classes, long-term subs, so that we could spend . . . for five weeks we just went into our own office and worked out how we would design this program."

However, despite initial expectations that planning time was a means to design programs, school members frequently found such time valuable in its own right. This perspective is illustrated by another account from the same high school teacher noted immediately above:

> One of the things that struck the four of us was the power of collaboration among teachers and having the time to sit down with other teachers and share feelings, ideas, experiences and talking about "What could we do to create really powerful experiences with kids?" We were overwhelmed by how good that experience was, how powerful it was. And it became real obvious how much that's lacking in the traditional system. And we tried to communicate that to other teachers. "You're going to love this. If you can have a half hour a day or a couple of hours a week to sit down with the other teachers you work with and talk and communicate and connect and solve problems and innovate, it's incredible. It'll change your whole attitude about your job."

As this comment illustrates, the intrinsic value to teachers of "extra" noninstructional time was tied closely to increased opportunities for collegiality and reflection. In several LFR schools, small amounts of in-contract or compensated "extra" time for teachers enriched relationships among teachers. These enriched relationships were then rewarding enough to elicit additional contributions of teachers' personal time.

A parallel set of arrangements was designed at several schools to increase the amount of time that individual teachers spent with their students. At the elementary level, they involved multi-age classrooms in which students might stay with the same teacher for more than a year. In middle schools and high schools they took the form of "block scheduling," increased teacher and student involvement in long-term group projects, and the creation of "houses," "academies," and other "schools within the school."

LFR schools developed these arrangements to achieve three related goals: providing opportunities for students to become more engaged with teachers and with other students in their school; creating instructional blocks of time in which it would be easier for students to undertake long-term and open-ended inquiries; and deepening interpersonal relationships between students and teachers. As one teacher noted about the creation of these core programs, "When you have got a high school of 2,500 students, you start figuring out that one of the big issues is personalization."

For each of these goals, the organization of time in school was seen alternatively as a problem or a solution: former arrangements made the school less productive, and new arrangements would enable it to be more productive. In a generally positive account of such "new arrangements," a high school teacher characterized this contrast as follows:

What we're finding is although we won't be able to cut our classes down, at least in 85 minutes you have time to go around and talk to all your kids. You have time to do something more than take roll, give instructions, and send them out the door. So there's some real value to that.

Arrangements that enabled students and teachers to develop deeper relationships inside school also could elicit additional contact between teachers and students outside school. In terms of both student and teacher relationships, bureaucratic time was allocated as a resource for creating nonbureaucratic relationships. To the extent that this succeeded, the logic of reform proposals within LFR schools was at least partly sound.

"Scheduled Time" and School Planning

Changing the school schedule was an important vehicle at LFR schools for emphasizing different kinds of activities and relationships and for creating what appeared to be "extra time" for teaching or for collaboration. LFR participants were quite deliberate and self-conscious in these efforts. Indeed, as one teacher characterized the primary substance of her school's restructuring initiative, "What we did was we moved people's time." But they also found "school schedules" to be a useful artifact for understanding how their own restructuring efforts compared with those undertaken by other schools. As a high school teacher noted: "We wanted to change the schedule. Now what are we going to change it to? And so these people looked at seven jillion schedules, talked to a million different schools, talked to transportation, talked to the district, tried to figure out what they could do."

Judging from the example of LFR schools, the distribution of different "school schedules" was one of the most fully developed exchanges that occurred among restructuring schools. Schedules were passed around across district, regional, and state lines. However, in designing scheduling changes, no LFR school chose to implement fully a schedule developed elsewhere. Rather, teachers and administrators took particular features of how another school organized time—an extra period or block period arrangement, alternative day formats for longer class periods, "banking" time provisions, and so on—and incorporated them into schedules tied closely to local contexts and traditions.

Indeed, some of the most pressing scheduling problems noted by LFR participants referred less to substantive schoolwide change in how time was allocated or organized than to preferences of individual teachers. Some of these "personal" scheduling issues had important implications for curriculum and instruction. As one teacher noted:

And myself and my teaching partner, Renee, who is a lit teacher, who I have been teamed with ever since I came to [this high school], she and I had the luck of having our classes the first two years back to back. First and second period I had history kids, and she had the same kids in lit. So we started saying, "Oh, I know, let's go to the library... let's do all these things," and so we created this family of learners, of sixty kids. The following year, scheduling got screwed up, and we weren't able to do that, and we really noticed the difference. And we said, "Wait a minute, we have to find a way to force this to happen for us."

As this comment illustrates, changing schedules could create problems as well as solve them. That said, the notion of using schedules to "force" or "encourage" desired interaction was very much evident in all LFR schools. Here's an illustration drawn from one of our LFR discussions:

STEVE. We have this really significant meeting time every week, and we invited the whole staff, including maintenance people, secretaries, all the teachers and administrators all broke up into different committees and tried to figure out how could we design, restructure, and create our ideal school.

NOLAN. So then people volunteered for the separate committees?

STEVE. They had no choice. You're here for this hour and forty-five minutes. Which committee are you going to be on?

Some scheduling issues also emerged in LFR schools in response to changes in school organization or classroom instruction. For example, in some LFR elementary schools, annualized grade advancement was replaced by some form of multi-age instruction. In most LFR high schools, provisions were made for teachers to "stay with" some of their students for more than a class period or more than a year. In other schools, student assessment schedules were altered as new assessment instruments and strategies were introduced—for example, portfolio reviews, standards-based performance rubrics, long-term "investigations" in mathematics and science, and so on.

By and large, the scheduling changes being developed in LFR schools were regarded positively by school members, but they were also quite modest. Class sessions within the day were lengthened or abbreviated, or the daily schedule varied during a given week, or additional staff development days were scheduled just after or just before the regular school year. However, none of the LFR schools departed fundamentally from prior multiyear expectations for student achievement. High school was still a four-year proposition organized around grade-level specific courses and course sequences. Elementary school arrangements involving multi-age classrooms did not alter the number of years students would spend at a school. The school day may have been extended by a period or so, but not much more than that. In recognition of how modest these changes were, one teacher lamented, "What happened about that vision of the school that was going to be open from 8 'til 8?"

The "Dramatic Time" of Living Through Change

In contrast to the kind of rational-bureaucratic time characteristic of reform proposals and project planning, the accounts LFR members gave of *how changes were actually occurring at their schools* were organized around the drama of extraordinary events and episodes. The scope of these dramas was revealed to us in two different ways. First, LFR meetings provided lots of time for school members to describe changes at their sites in terms of key decision points, antecedents, and consequences. Second, repeating some features of LFR meetings over the course of several years (i.e., similar questions about the same schools asked and answered by the same cast of characters) helped highlight continuity and change in participating schools.

As representations of "dramatic" time, the change accounts of LFR participants illuminated series of related events, episodes, conflicts, and contrasts that were meaningful to school members. Units of dramatic time were defined by key events, transitions, and other things that "happened," and they differed substantially from the undifferentiated months, minutes, and days that appeared in "proposal" time. Sequences in dramatic time differed from those in proposal time as well. Rather than a linear plot through the school day or year, with compartmentalized activities associated with a given point or block of time, activity sequences in dramatic time were "smeared" across clusters of related events.

Some changes described by LFR participants in "dramatic" time happened quickly but were modest in scope. For example, at one elementary school a meeting among teachers to discuss how to evaluate student work led to fundamentally different arrangements for "open house" and "parent conferences," arrangements that were implemented in the space of a few weeks. As a teacher from that school described this process: "Well, we left out of our time line a big explosion that we had, a wonderful explosion, in a different way of doing parent conferences. They're not parent conferences, they're parent/student/teacher demonstration dialogues now."

Some schools went through far-reaching changes in priorities and organization that occurred almost as precipitously. For example, one

LFR elementary school had been developed over several years as an "experimental school" under the watchful and protective purview of the district superintendent. Cumulative changes at this school occurred over and above the casual resistance of the school's principal, encouraged through a special reporting line between teachers at the school and the district superintendent.

At our first LFR meeting, this school appeared to have implemented and institutionalized several key restructuring elements, and that appearance held true through our next three meetings. However, during the second summer after the LFR project began—a good eighteen months after the first meeting—the superintendent was recalled. The school's special status in the district was subsequently rescinded. The school principal, acting now with the support of the new superintendent, undid in six months' time some innovative features that had taken several years to develop and implement—for example, lead teachers with mentoring and instructional responsibilities for each grade level, cross-grade instructional teams, authentic assessment strategies, and so on. In response to these changes, several of the most active teacher-leaders left the school to take positions elsewhere, thereby completing a "turnaround" of the school in the space of a single year. As one LFR participant who left the school noted, "Fruitvalley Elementary, the Fruitvalley Elementary School we have been telling you about, is no more."

Some of the more substantial changes in LFR schools—as described by school members in "dramatic time"—had origins in outside events and circumstances, including changes at the state and district levels that were occurring throughout the first few years of the LFR project. At the state level, an active and influential State Superintendent of Public Instruction was removed from office in midterm. The state first adopted, then precipitously abandoned, a new and radically different assessment system, and California schools were left without a statewide assessment system for the first time in years. And a state budget crisis created extraordinary uncertainties and disruption for both teachers and districts. Compounding these changes at the state level was substantial administrative turnover in the schools. Only one LFR school district had the same superintendent in 1996 as in 1992, and ten of the twelve LFR schools changed principals during that same time.

In some cases, these changes created opportunities for schools to move ahead on thoughtful agendas for reform. However, they also revealed how change agendas set by individual schools were vulnerable to changes at higher institutional levels. An elementary school principal described impending district changes that would affect his school profoundly but fell completely outside the school's own restructuring proposal:

We're going through the middle of a reconfiguration process which was prompted by a seismic issue at a number of our sites. Our school has been considered to be seismically unsafe, therefore in the next couple of years we'll have our building completely torn down and rebuilt. But as part of that, the superintendent decided, "Well, since we're going to have to rebuild this anyway, let's go for [grade level and zone] reconfiguration as well. And since the school district needs to be restructured in some way, let's do it all at the same time while the schools are being rebuilt."

In many LFR school change accounts, precipitous change within a school was tied to issues that crossed boundaries between the school and its district or community. For example, at one LFR high school, teacher energies that had peaked around the process of developing an ambitious restructuring proposal for state funding dissipated when the proposal was unsuccessful. A school member noted that, in the wake of this disappointment, "the staff pretty much crashed as far as any type of vision of where we're going." For months after, reports from this school confirmed the impression that restructuring initiatives and planned change were dead. As an LFR teacher described it:

We kept having the Friday meetings, but the Friday meetings instead of having any direction, had no talk of restructuring except some discussion of how we need to integrate curriculum. . . . Basically, it was just long staff meetings and we got these long reports about who's done anything in sports, this team did that and this team did that. It was really a waste of time. It was like a year off as far as any kind of progress.

However, a widely publicized incident at a high school dance created a school-community crisis that led in a matter of weeks to an invigorated restructuring effort and a focused agenda for school change. A teacher from the school gave the following account at an LFR meeting:

Most of you have probably heard about the publicity our school got, not only nationwide, we were on CNN and it was in the *London Times*. It got on the news wires and just went everywhere. We had a Halloween party for the seniors and it was on campus in the gym and our principal and assistant principal were there. Three students came up and two of them—it was a group—and two of them on the outside were dressed as Klu Klux Klan, and the guy in the middle was a white kid with black face and a noose around his neck. And the noose was this long and hanging from his neck.

The assistant principal is the one who tried to talk them out of it, said it was inappropriate, and they said, "Hey, are you going to kick us out of here?" Essentially challenged him. And he said, "Well, if you take the hoods off, and the kid in the middle has to take the noose off his neck, then I'll let you in." Compromise. So he let them in. And they won a contest for most popular outfits, costumes.

Okay. So the senior class, or the portion of the senior class that was there, felt like this was worthy of electing them, and when they took the picture to receive this award, the picture for the yearbook, they were allowed to put the hoods and noose back on.

And if you don't know, in our community there is an active Klan. They have paraded in outfits down main street of the town and there are minority people who have had rocks thrown through windows with KKK written on the rocks and people have been threatened. So it's not just a reference to the past. For the minority people in our community it's a very real threat, and there are people who were not angry, but very upset because it seems like the school was condoning this image of a lynching. . . .

That has sort of become an opportunity for change, in a sense. I was really discouraged last summer, we didn't get our grant, and it seemed like we hit a brick wall, the staff went back to normal. So now this crisis hits, and all of a sudden we have a community group, we have sixty people who showed up at a meeting, and they're demanding that the school get it back together. And we've got to have some kind of conflict resolution program. We have to have some kind of anti-bias program. We have to change, transform our curriculum. We have to transform our discipline system. . . . There's a new student group that's formed. And the student group is a pretty radical group of kids and it's the first time there's ever been a radical group of kids active on our campus, so in that sense I'm more optimistic than I was last summer that maybe some things are going to happen.

Observations and subsequent accounts confirmed that the crisis did lead to changes in both the tenets and substance of the school. A school planning council was put in place that was largely teacher-led and included the principal as one of its members. Though created initially to respond to the post-Halloween crisis, this group quickly moved to address other school issues, including curriculum integration and block scheduling. A new citizenship participation class with a strong action research component was created for all freshmen, and an extensive program of community service was instituted as an integral feature of student participation in the school.

The detailed, multiyear accounts by school members of how changes actually occurred in their schools stand in stark contrast to the change process represented in restructuring proposals and plans, and a key component of this contrast emerges from fundamentally different orientations toward time: In proposals and plans, time is a fungible resource that can be managed and organized according to agreed-upon increments and units—seven minutes banked from a day, or an eighty-five-minute period instead of forty-seven minutes, or a weekly school planning meeting. In the lived experience of change in schools, time is organized as well, not by administrators or planners, but extraordinary and somewhat unanticipated events, unevenly distributed over the days, weeks, months, or years. Decisions are made quickly in the heat of a crisis, despite months of weekly meetings in which no decision could be reached. Groups mobilize or dissolve precipitously around issues that have been issues for decades. Policies that no one had considered for years are created or repealed in a flurry of urgent activity. While time marches on evenly through proposals and plans for how change is supposed to occur in schools, it lurches forward in fits and spurts within practitioner accounts of how change actually happens.

"Disjunctive" Time and "Follow-Up"

The challenge of pursuing reforms "over time" was a third perspective on time that shaped LFR change accounts. This perspective reflects the more general challenge of sustaining any kind of coherent social life.[8] As Nespor (1994, p. 6) frames the issue: "How is activity in one setting (such as a classroom) related to activities in settings distant in space and time (other classrooms or workplaces)? All of our notions of learning, development, teaching, curriculum and reproduction can be read as answers to this question."

Observations of the LFR project encourage me to add "notions of planned school change" to Nespor's list. Indeed, LFR school change accounts were replete with questions about how connections between past and future reform initiatives could be supported over time. How could information presented or decisions made at one point in a school's history be called on at other points? How could discussions stimulate cumulative planning and development? And how could teachers know whether the changes they made were effective in preparing students for the future?

As one illustration, consider the following exchange between Kathy, an elementary school teacher, and other LFR participants. Kathy, begins by commenting on what she is learning about high school from participating in the LFR project:

> KATHY. Well, this [the LFR project] is one way for us to get across the bridge. I don't want to give that up. I want to come across with the kids. I don't know what—my first, first-graders are ninth-graders right now. And I only know what's happened to a couple.
>
> JON. That's a pretty powerful thought .
>
> KATHY. I want to know what happens to them and right now there's very limited mechanisms for me to know what happens to the kids that I had.

IRENE. When they come back and start teaching with you, you'll know.

BOB. You'll know it's time, that's what you'll know. And when they become your deputy principal and your learning director you'll know.

IRENE. You'll know it's too late.

Kathy's concern builds into her elementary school classroom an awareness of time separations between her students and their futures and the implications of that separation for her own work as a teacher. Later in the same discussion she comments:

> What I got to do [through the LFR project] as an elementary school teacher was get a clearer picture of what's ahead for my students. But I really felt like there is this huge grand canyon and the only people who go across it are the kids. . . . It was a real eye-opener to me as far as this grand canyon. The kids pass through but somehow we as professionals stumble.

The time frame of this particular "canyon" involves a disjuncture of several years between Kathy's work and evidence about its effectiveness, but LFR participants also referred to similar "gaps" that were only weeks or months in duration, and some that involved a matter of days or hours.[9] Here's how one LFR teacher described trying to get a school principal to bridge planning activities over a period of a few days.

> I was saying, "Well, what's the next step? Are we going to work with these ideas that we've brainstormed and come to some decisions and maybe prioritize and talk about actions?" And he said, "Well, if there's a group of teachers that want to volunteer to meet after school and do something with this, that's fine." But there was no plan. And I went in and talked to him and I said, "This isn't how you do things. You need to have some follow-up." And he didn't get it. . . . He just didn't understand it. So then I said, "How about if we call the leadership team together and see if the leadership team can come up with a way to follow up?" And he said okay. I mean it was logical. He couldn't really deny it, that that's an appropriate thing to do. . . . It hadn't occurred to him to call the leadership team together, but now that it was being suggested, he didn't see anything wrong with it. So the leadership team picked up right away and he was just silent.

In this and many other examples, LFR participants affirmed the need for "follow-up." "Follow-up" involved deliberate efforts to build social connections among moments past, present, and future, and LFR schools exhibited three primary vehicles for doing this: preparing oral and written accounts of past or proposed activities; designing routines and rules to replicate key settings and contexts at different points in time (e.g., regular meetings); and building social networks through which individuals linked multiple settings and periods of time.

All of these vehicles were valued, but also problematic. For example, as illustrated by international distribution of a written account of the Halloween party, "follow-up" was not something that could be easily controlled. Follow-up responsibilities also gave some individuals the power and opportunity to represent or misrepresent the work of others. An LFR high school teacher shared her concerns about this:

> Our note taking [at restructuring meetings] was pretty bad, and I don't even know if we've gone to a tape recorder yet. We still have these sort of interesting secretarial-type people taking notes, and often I read the minutes and I have to come back and I say, "What? We didn't do that, or we didn't say that or that's not really true." And nobody's altered the record, it's just that they're clueless in terms of what's going on because they're not connected or they're not transcribing.

The same teacher was much less concerned about the power of misrepresentation when individuals entrusted with representational tasks were highly engaged in the social networks they were expected to represent.

> We have a billion grant writers, like four—three to four grant writers; they write all these pieces, they bring them back to our 1274 committee, we take it out to our other committees, you know, the sort of . . . committees, come back, suggest changes. Finally, people drop by the wayside: "I'm never going to write this!" People's feelings are sort of hurt, then we apologize. . . . And finally one person says, "Okay, I'm writing it." And it's written, we edit it, we go out to dinner, and it's over, we turn it in.

In some cases these representational challenges were tied to the ideal of getting students over time to "understand" the school they attended—understand what adults in that school wanted them to do—and documents were created for just that purpose. However, in other cases, representational trajectories and documents went in both directions:

> IRENE. So yeah, we're teaching and we're taking stuff back to kids, we're taking stuff back to meetings. Our students . . . Renee and I gave our students all the change literature we could find and we said, "You have $500,000, what would you do to change your school?" And they wrote essays about the kinds of changes they would make, they looked at schedules, they looked at . . . you know, what they talked about was they wanted more teacher–student connections, they wanted more student–student connections, they wanted more freedom in terms of when they went to school, dot dot dot. It was interesting stuff, and we shared that with the committee.
>
> KATHY. Did any of that actually end up incorporated? Any of the student input?

NOLAN. What's happening to all this stuff?

IRENE. It's being written up and it's in somebody's file somewhere. Hopefully somebody has an extra copy because I keep throwing mine away. No, that kind of stuff has gone into other programs.

References by LFR members to using oral and written accounts to link activity over time were complemented by references to using *routines and rules* for much the same purpose. Regular staff meetings arranged through "banking" time in LFR schools were valued by many LFR members as opportunities to guide and develop school programs over time. A third strategy noted by LFR members for linking activities over time involved *interpersonal networks*. In the following passage, a high school teacher responds to a question about how this kind of representation occurred:

NOLAN. So one person was basically translating and organizing everything that . . .

IRENE. Right, and she kept coming back and saying, "Is this what you want me to say? Is this what you guys intended?" We turned it in and we made it to the interviews. Our experience with the interview was the same thing. We had been living in each other's pockets. First of all, most of us had been at the school for three years so we'd been living in each other's pockets at all of those meetings because we were all on the same committees, or at least two of them. Everybody was on two committees.

The strategies used by members of LFR schools to support continuous collective action across separations in time and space were not ones that could be pursued arbitrarily or across the board. Instead, effective strategies for bridging gaps in time linked particular representations with individual actors and social settings. Different "follow-up" efforts were regarded as more or less effective depending on the school change contexts to which they were applied. And—as described in the following section—school change contexts themselves were defined in part by multiple dimensions of time.

Indexing Activities to Time in School Change Accounts

LFR school members spoke explicitly about conceptions of bureaucratic and dramatic time. They were also clear that "follow-up" was necessary to move change efforts forward over gaps in time. However, these orientations are only a few of the many ways in which issues of time were represented in their accounts of school change. Consider the following transcription of an oral presentation from an LFR meeting. The speaker, a high school teacher, is describing the circumstances surrounding a shift in the change orientation and planning priorities of several members of his school:

The committee who had done the planning, they took responsibility of running those weekly meetings. They formed what became the restructuring committee. Those people, Clarice Frank was the leader, she is a teacher, she and another group of teachers—at that point I still wasn't involved, early last school year—they organized these meetings. They were trying to get more and more teachers to buy in and get groups to formulate a plan that could end up being the proposal that would relate to our community and school and kids, etc. About halfway through the year, December, there was a blueprint of the plan, there was a core idea of the plan that would involve taking eighty kids and four teachers and doing a pilot.

Embedded in this relatively brief passage (a typed transcript of the ninety-minute discussion in which this comment appeared is about thirty pages long) are numerous references to different conceptions of time. As illustrated in Table 8.1, these references can be isolated somewhat from each other, but they cut across multiple dimensions of time articulated by Hall (1983), Hargreaves (1994), and others. References of this sort confirm that time does not appear as a unitary feature within the school change process but as a cluster of dimensions—contested and confounded, variously neglected and attended to—that shape and are shaped by social life of any sort, including the social life of changing schools.

Among the many dimensions of time referenced within practitioner accounts are historicity, duration, sequence, ephemera and immanence, frequency, pacing, scheduling, and so on, each of which can be differentiated further according to different time scales, reference points, and units of analysis or measurement. For example, within "proposal time" alone we can think of *duration* in terms of "six months of meetings," "meeting from September to March," "a dozen meetings of two hours each," or "twenty-four hours of meeting time." Even when these different representations of duration are consistent with each other, they do not mean the same thing. Six months of meetings might not do the trick unless they were held September to March, involved twelve separate meetings of two hours each, and twenty-four hours of total meeting time. Similarly, twenty-four hours of meeting time might or might not be better spent in six months than in three or twelve or forty.

Different features of dramatic time can also be used to characterize duration. For example, meetings might last until "we all got too tired to disagree," "someone finally got a bright idea," "Jackie finally left," "everyone had a chance to speak," "we had read everything there was to read," "we finally got the superintendent's okay," "the test data arrived," "we got the proposal out the door," and so on. Duration also can be characterized quite differently in terms of overcoming gaps in

TABLE 8.1
References to Time in a Teacher's School Change Account

Account	Annotation
The committee who *had done* the planning. They took responsibility of running those *weekly* meetings. They formed what *became* the restructuring committee. Those people, Clarice Frank was the leader, she *is* a teacher, she and another group of teachers, *at that point* I *still wasn't* involved—*early last school year*—they organized these *meetings*. They *were trying* to get more and more teachers to buy in and get groups to formulate a *plan* that *could end up being* the proposal that would relate to our community and school and kids etc. About *half way through the year*, *December*, there *was* a blueprint of the plan, there *was* a core idea of the plan that would involve taking eighty kids and four teachers and doing a *pilot*.	*had done* = refers to sequence, implicit and diffuse past *weekly* = notes frequency of activity over time, specifies "normal" unit of duration *became* = implies development and evolution over time *is* = implicit present, implies continuity over time, stability of identity as a teacher *at that point* = locates personal agency in larger event history *still wasn't* = implies continuity with past, but intimates impending change in status *early last school year* = locates activities within institutional school calendar *meetings* = "normal" time-activity unit involving synchronous communication *were trying* = persistence of effort over time (contrast to "tried") *plan* = artifact for organizing activities over time *could end up being* = development leading to changed status in the future *half way through the year* = experiential time linked loosely to school calendar *December* = location on Gregorian calendar *was . . . was* = parallel construction implies synchronicity of referents *pilot* = implies sequence, subordinates one activity (pilot) to next activity in sequence

time. Meetings might continue until "we finally had a plan we could distribute to others for comment," "we created a new committee that could take over the functions of this group," "we selected a representative to take this proposal to the board," "we scheduled another meeting," and so on. What distinguishes these different representations of time from each other—within and across proposal time, dramatic time, and disjunctive time—are the different configurations of social activity they entail.

Linking representations of time to social activity takes other forms as well. In some change accounts by LFR participants, time is used as a placeholder for other activities, "work," for example, or "learning," "communication," or "planning" (e.g., we didn't have enough "time" to reach consensus as a surrogate for we did not "meet together long enough" to reach consensus). As a valued "commodity," time is also used in these accounts to indicate the significance of different program components, themes, or activities—a version of what Hargreaves (1994) calls "socio-political time." A teacher might note that "it was clear they didn't care about that because of how little time they gave for it." Or, we noted that in reform proposals from LFR schools, teachers were more likely to be allocated "preparation" or "planning" time than they were "reflection," "research," or "debriefing" time. Some activities in LFR accounts or proposals were categorized explicitly on the basis of how long they took: meetings were shorter than retreats, but longer than conversations; assignments were shorter than lessons, and lessons shorter than units.

In trying to account for the process of change in schools, LFR school members referred routinely to these and other kinds of time as an "index" for specifying relationships among activities, actors, ideas and events. In these accounts, time does not provide a unitary axis on which to plot school change activities or a unidimensional resource to be allocated among them. Rather, different conceptions of time are used together to construct detailed and precise accounts of the school change process.

To the extent that references to time represent relationships among school change activities, actors, events, and so on, they also reflect implicit theories about school change itself. Why is it important that meetings occur over six months? Why is it important that they be two hours each? Why do they have to occur from September to March? Inviting school members to answer questions such as these can help make explicit the social theory that is implicit in their accounts of school change. As we struggled to do just that in the LFR project, we learned that practitioner theories of school change, even when they appear to be implicit, can be extremely precise and thoughtful.

Enriching School Change Research and Practice

I have tried to illustrate some of the ways in which school teachers and administrators use different conceptions of time in proposing and accounting for changes occurring in their schools. These illustrations also suggest that representations of time are important to practitioners in supporting school change over time and in addressing the challenges of "follow-up," however that might be defined.

These illustrations help frame two challenges for those interested in studying or guiding school change. First, there is the challenge of preparing representations that are adequate to account for the school change phenomena we want to examine or guide—in Nespor's words (1994, p. 7), accounts that can make "'absent' spaces 'present' in textual form." Second, there is the challenge of distributing these representations among settings in which power can be exercised to change the schools and engaging individuals in those settings to use these representations wisely.

Within the LFR project we stumbled over these challenges in almost everything we did. However, from that experience we also learned something about how to enrich the quality and utility of our investigations of school change. Some of that learning can be stated in terms of the following recommendations and cautions:

Resist Using Time as Placeholder for Social Activity

Time and time again, we came across references—in practitioner accounts and in our own research discourse—in which time itself was characterized as a social activity. Invariably, these references presented time as a surrogate for a distinctive social activity that took place over time. When left unchallenged, references of this sort keep us from understanding or describing social life with detail and precision. They also keep us from noticing the implicit social theories that both shape and are shaped by descriptions of this sort.

As a special case of this recommendation, we caution against using "official" or "institutional" timekeeping as the primary template for investigating or describing school change. Certainly, scheduled time matters in school, and it also matters in finding ways to support school change. All LFR schools gave thoughtful attention to scheduling and managing time to support school change. However, attending to "dramatic" time and "disjunctive" time may be equally important. And, according to LFR members, while revised school timetables might make some things possible, that alone did not make them happen.

Use Theory to Time Data Collection

Related closely to the recommendation above is the need to collect data from schools according to the kinds of time in which change actually occurs, which may or may not correspond to school calendars or school change proposals and plans. Part of the challenge here is the difficulty of conducting longitudinal studies of any sort. However, even within longitudinal studies, data collection intervals can be too short or too long to capture phenomena we are interested in.

For example, we can certainly learn something about school change from data collected at the end of each school year or at the end of different policy implementation phases. But this will not generate much information about what is happening during each year, or between implementation phases, for which reason some researchers have tried to complement annual surveys or interviews with ongoing observation—see Smylie, Lazarus, and Brownles-Conyets (1996) for a thoughtful recent example.

These concerns about the timing of data collection are closely related to what Strauss (1987) refers to as "theoretical sampling." If our theoretical perspective on school change treats the evenness and continuity of social life as unproblematic, it might make sense to collect data continuously, at random, or at regularly timed intervals. However, if our theory regards continuous social life as problematic, we need to identify key turning points and disjunctions and subject them to close examination, regardless of where they fit within institutional or annual calendars.

Preserve Time-Indexing in Practitioner Accounts of School Change

There are many features of change we can examine without attending to practitioner accounts. However, to understand school change phenomena we need to know how practitioners regard change processes in their own schools. Ideally, research would be informed by the most credible and detailed practitioner accounts that we can find, identify, enable, and help others construct.

Practitioner accounts of the sort elicited by the LFR project reflect extraordinary detail and precision in the temporal indexing of activities, events, actors, and the confluence of dramatic and bureaucratic time. We need to attend to this detail to do good research—and attend to more of it than can be found in the brief passages cited here. Detail of this sort is also valuable, and in some cases necessary, if we want our analyses to make sense to school practitioners within local networks of power and knowledge that shape planned change in individual schools and districts. And yet data analysis and reporting conventions make preserving this kind of detail throughout the research process extremely problematic.

For example, converting practitioner accounts to correlations among school change variables has its attractions within what some call "normal science" (Argyris, Putman, & Smith, 1985). However, changing, reducing, or deleting practitioner representations of time can substantially alter the substance of a school change account. When I called explicit attention to time considerations embedded in a transcript presented earlier—through the annotations and underlined words in Table 8.1—I interrupted the narrative stance, the voice, and the intelligence of the original speaker. This fragmented and undermined the teacher's account from which the transcript was derived, and it also changed what that account was apparently about. Dropping these references completely in favor of "timeless" propositions about different factors contributing to school change would represent an even more fundamental change in theory (Becker, 1992).

In some cases changes of this sort may be warranted. However, in other cases, temporal detail is reduced primarily to construct accounts that are easier to distribute among other researchers (Nespor & Barylske, 1991), and this can occur at the cost of theories that might make more sense. When we lose precision in how practitioners index activities to each other over time, we also lose the theoretical perspective embedded within that precision by school practitioners themselves. In moving from long stories to short ones and to cases or causes we may gain universality. But we may also lose the schools and the experience and theorizing of those who work in them.

To balance fidelity to practitioners' accounts with transportability among researchers and other colleagues, we explored within the LFR project a variety of strategies for extending data analysis activities into research reporting itself. Along those lines, we structured some research reports as invitations to LFR members and other colleagues to examine detailed practitioner accounts and explore with us their implications for understanding or guiding school change.

Consider Multiple Media and Formats
for Collecting and Reporting Data

Efforts to record and preserve detail in practitioner change accounts run up against the constraints of conventional reporting formats and media. These limit the kinds of data that can be represented in a research report. As one example, instead of presenting practitioner accounts of school change, I have presented here the results of my examination of how practitioners represent time in such accounts.

Formats and media also constrain relationships between theorizing and data representation, and, as a result, the kind of theorizing we do, or at least the kind of theorizing we do when we are doing educational research. As Becker notes from his examination of "causes, conjunctions, stories, and images" different kinds of reports support different kinds of theorizing (1992, p. 213) :

> Professional social scientists typically use only a few of the very large number of possible ways of representing social science results, those few being part of "packages" of theories, methods, types of data, and styles of analysis and representation which have been conventionalized in some working group. Like other agreed-on parts of a scientific package, such conventions of representation facilitate sociological work. But they also hamper it because, while they make communication of some results easy and efficient, they make communication of other kinds of results difficult or impossible.

Within the LFR project, we have worked primarily with paper copies of written text, but we have used a variety of reporting formats, as noted above. In addition, we are currently examining how extending data analysis opportunities to multiple audiences might be enriched by videotape, multi-media, and hypertext.[10]

Index Research to Local Change Through Practitioner Networks

One intriguing outcome of engaging practitioners in some LFR data analysis activities has been that research reports become "events" that are indexed by practitioners to local change initiatives. Written texts are still an essential part of this process. However, practitioners participating in data analysis sessions have transcribed LFR research accounts into school activities and events. Accounts of these activities and events have been subsequently distributed within local networks in which individuals shape and implement school reforms.

For conventional research reports to inform school decision making, they must be carried "piggyback" on time-indexed accounts and local representations of school members active in that setting. This same requirement applies to the kinds of research reporting supported through the LFR project. However, engaging members of LFR schools in a professional network involving researchers and members of other schools has made that task easier. As events of the LFR network became real to participating school members, the substance of LFR investigations also became real in members' reports about that network to their colleagues. Conversely, when LFR activities became too infrequent or attenuated, the LFR network and the substance of our investigations— however real they might be to university researchers involved with the project—faded away for our practitioner colleagues.

In linking educational research to practice, these observations underline the value of preparing reports as activities and events that involve networks of practitioners—or, if they do not already exist, helping to build networks of that sort. Along these lines, researchers studying school change can enrich both their own work and practitioner accounts by bringing together teachers and administrators from different schools to examine school change phenomena. Achieving these dual ideals also can be facilitated through joint efforts by practitioners and researchers to collect and archive evidence about how change is occurring in schools, a process made more feasible by the increasingly routine use of electronic media in support of school-site communication, planning, and reporting.

These recommendations will not resolve fundamental dilemmas of representing social life, nor will they institute a new paradigm for connecting school change research to practice. However, they could enrich the knowledge that researchers and practitioners develop and are enabled to report about time and school change. That could have some payoff within individual schools and within networks involving other schools and researchers. All this would take time, of course—and require attention to different dimensions of time—but then again, what doesn't?

NOTES

1. This report is based on data generated through the "Learning from Restructuring" (LFR) project supported by funds from the University of California Educational Research Center, Fresno. I shared LFR leadership with Professor Sandra Murphy, and the two of us worked closely in the early stages of the project with Professors Rosemary Papalewis and Theresa Perez from California State University, Fresno. I value greatly the assistance of these and other colleagues, including the elementary and secondary school teachers and administrators who joined us in the LFR project—and whose words appear in bits and pieces within this essay. Our LFR work was facilitated by Marcia Goodman and Rose Bachini from the CRESS Center at UC Davis and by three expert and thoughtful research assistants: Rich Hansen, Janet Hecsh, and Ting Sun. My work through the LFR project also was enriched by ongoing discussions with Judith Warren Little and her colleagues at UC Berkeley who have been evaluating California's SB 1274 school restructuring initiative (see Little, 1996).

2. Hall comments as follows about the conflict between "monochromic" time and "polychronic" time (1983, p. 45): "Complex societies organize time in at least two different ways: events scheduled as separate items—one thing at a time—or involvement in several things at once. The two systems are logically and empirically quite distinct. Like oil and water, they don't mix."

3. Hargreaves associates Hall's conception of "monochronic time" with the perspective of administrators and "polychronic time" with teachers. However, data generated through the LFR project reveal that both teachers and administrators referred to monochronic time in describing the challenges of managing or supervising others, and both referred to polychronic time in articulating their resistance to being managed or supervised. Thus, within hierarchical communication between teachers and administrators, teachers might appear to administrators as polychronic miscreants and administrators to teachers as monochronic tyrants. However, in hierarchical exchanges with students, teachers can become the monochronic tyrants, just as administrators can wax polychronic in exchanges with supervisors of their own.

4. For a more systematic and extremely well-conceived examination of how schools have participated in this statewide initiative, see Little (1996).

5. These two programs are: the Ph.D. program in Education at UC Davis and an Ed.D. program offered jointly by faculty from UC Davis and other University of California campuses and faculty from California State University, Fresno.

6. In the early stages of the project, we conducted site interviews of administrators and teacher leaders who had been involved in preparing SB 1274 proposals and other reform documents. In these interviews we asked about the proposal preparation process, change initiatives under way at the school, the goals of restructuring efforts, anticipated problems and opportunities, and expectations for implementing change over time. In later stages of the project, we pursued these same questions in LFR meetings themselves.

7. Little (1996) provides a extended and thoughtful analysis of similar arrangements among a large sample of California schools, all of which received SB 1274 grants.

8. The "disjunctive" dimension is not mentioned by Hall in his examination of time. This is curious because by defining monochronic time as "one thing at a time," and polychronic as "many things at once," Hall invites us to speculate about other forms of this equation: "one thing at many times," for example, or "many things at many times." Indeed, the notion that "one thing"—for example, a particular social relationship, a process of development or growth, a person's identity, an institution, etc.—can occur at many different times is an essential feature of organized social life, and a notion worth investigating further.

9. Had we probed about this in more detail, I am confident that the same problematics of "follow-up" could be identified between shifting micro contexts of an individual meeting or conversation—such as those examined by Erickson and Shultz (1981) in their videotape analysis of classroom lessons.

10. New opportunities are presented by this technology for representing both researcher and practitioner accounts within the same "document" as hypertext-linked files. An excellent example is an electronic publication by Glass (1997) . As the abstract notes:

Vol. 5 No. 1 is a uniquely reported multi-site qualitative study. Data on which the study is based are drawn from 37 interviews. The interpretive framework drawn from these interviews is illustrated by selected quotations. Each quotation is hyperlinked to its original location in the interview from which it was drawn. The full text of all interviews is available to any reader to be downloaded.

REFERENCES

Argyris, C., Putman, R., & Smith, D. M. (1985). *Action science: Concepts, methods and skills for research and intervention.* San Francisco: Jossey-Bass.
Becker, H. S. (1992). Cases, causes, conjunctures, stories and imagery. In C. C. Ragin & H. S. Becker (Eds.), *What is a case? Exploring the foundations of social inquiry,* (pp. 205–216). New York: Cambridge University Press.
Erickson, F., & Schultz, J. (1981). When is a context? Some issues and methods in the analysis of social competence. In J. Green & C. Wallat (Eds.), *Ethnography and language in educational settings,* . Norwood, NJ: Ablex.
Glass, S. R. (1997). Markets and myths: Autonomy in public and private schools, *Educational Policy Analysis Archives* (Vol. 5,): http://olam.ed.asu.edu/epaa/.
Hall, E. (1983). *The dance of life: The other dimensions of time.* New York: Anchor/Doubleday.
Hargreaves, A. (1994). *Changing teachers, changing times.* New York: Teachers College Press.
Little, J. W. (1996). *The SB 1274 School Restructuring Study: What are we learning? An interim progress report.* UC Berkeley, Graduate School of Education.
Nespor, J. (1994). *Knowledge in motion: Space, time and curriculum in undergraduate physics and management* (Vol. 2). Washington, DC: Falmer.
Nespor, J., & Barylske, J. (1991). Narrative discourse and teacher knowledge. *American Educational Research Journal, 28* (4), 805–823.
Smylie, M. A., Lazarus, V., & Brownlee-Conyets, J. (1996). Instructional outcomes of school-based participative decision making. *Educational Evaluation and Policy Analysis, 18* (3), 181–198.
Strauss, A. L. (1987). *Qualitative analysis for social scientists.* Cambridge: Cambridge University Press.

CHAPTER 9

Time(s) for Educational Reform: The Experience of Two States

Audrey J. Noble
and Mary Lee Smith

When one talks about educational reform, a fundamental proposition holds: Time is relative. The clock does not run at the same speed for everyone. After examining reform initiatives in two states with similar aims and instruments, we identified three sorts of clocks of educational reform. These are the political clock, the professionals' clock, and the teacher clock; they are differentiated by where the impetus for reform arises. One must know the source of reform to determine the time of day. Is the reform the instrument of government (hence, politics), the instrument of professions, or the instrument of teachers? The source of reform determines the speed of the clock, and the history of varied success of specific policies and initiatives is readily explained in this way.

THE POLITICAL CLOCK

We define political reforms as those that arise from official, governmental bodies and that are executed through legislation, regulations, or mandates. Both of the state reform policies that we have examined are of this type. The clock that paces political reforms runs fast, about the speed of the electoral process and political terms. The role of the political time clock should not be underestimated in any discussions about time for education reform. The more decision-making mechanisms are dominated by politics, the more likely initiatives will function to satisfy the agendas of politicians and the less likely are they to respond to the advice of professionals or to meet the needs of schools. The political system that focuses on elections and campaigns rarely provides sustained support for any initiative for two important reasons. First, to distinguish themselves, politicians must continuously put forward unique policies that will make their names known to the voting public. They build their reputations by coming up with new ideas. Showing continuing support for statutes already on record generates no public attention. Such action is counterproductive to their need to keep themselves in the public eye. Politicians who are seen as followers rather than leaders typically have short political careers. Second, because of the emphasis on reelection, politicians typically propose policies that can be used as campaign issues. These policies are designed to have immediate and distinct effects (Fuhrman, 1993) or to serve as symbols of forceful, effective leadership (Edelman, 1988), especially those initiated by one's rivals. Building on existing policies over time provides limited benefit to reelection campaigns. In the education reform arena, these efforts frequently result in "tinkering" with the system. Political reforms often manifest themselves as unfunded mandates that prescribe socially desirable outcomes without politically undesirable implications, such as higher taxation. Politicians can ill afford to commit to longer-term and complex change initiatives that rarely yield immediate benefit. Nor can they dedicate their energies to agendas that could demand additional and unexpected legislative action that might alienate the constituencies that reelect them.

Another reason why the political clock runs fast is that it is frequently measuring time afforded by mandates. The intended effect of mandates is compliance, that is, behavior as prescribed by some policy. Mandates typically set minimum standards and, consequently, introduce disincentives to exceed those standards. They are used to create uniform behavior or reduce variations (McDonnell & Elmore, 1987). Since the required action is expected of all, regardless of differing capacity, the time for accomplishment of the desired outcome is typically the same for all. Those policy makers who attempt to foster change through the use of mandates see them as the quickest method to get things done. To the extent that time is money, mandating standards and assessments (the particular reforms we examined) is perceived as relatively fast and cheap, relative to alternatives such as lowering class size, retraining teachers, or lengthening the school year.

THE PROFESSIONALS' CLOCK

The professionals' clock keeps its own time, usually varying by project and issue. Players that follow this clock operate outside the arena of government, although states sometimes look to private associations and coalitions for guidance. These change efforts typically represent private, voluntary groups that are based in higher education settings or professional associations. The New Standards Project fell into this category. It was a voluntary association of states and school districts that focused on school restructuring by developing standards for student performance and assessments that support curricula. In April 1995, the project's twenty-four partner states and schools were involved in piloting standards and assessment systems. The program acted as a mentor to school personnel who volunteered their participation and wanted to rethink their approaches to teaching and learning. The Coalition delineated a set of common principles that provided focus for the school change effort. The Coalition staff worked closely with schools to help them through the redesign process. Part of its mission is to challenge policy makers to create a climate that favors school change and to influence the discourse about school change. The National Council of Teachers of Mathematics (NCTM) is another high-profile nonprofit association that adheres to the professionals' time clock. As a professional organization it offers support for the improvement of mathematics education through conferences, journals, books, software, and research. It also sponsors national committees and task forces dedicated to instructional improvement in mathematics. Schools or states participate in their programs if they so desire. The association's support promotes improvement by capitalizing on schools' expressed interests and inherent motivation to change. Each of these groups follows a clock much different from the political or teacher clock.

Another group that often tends to follow the professionals' clock comprises those individuals involved in providing support service to facilitate change at the school level. Typically, they serve as consultants or service providers who offer their expertise to move the process forward. They model instructional methods, develop instructional materials, or facilitate school change processes. They are involved in the process of change but rarely are held accountable in any way for the end result.

THE TEACHER CLOCK

The clock that captures teacher change runs slowly. It keeps time in years rather than terms. In the current standards-based and assessment-driven reforms, the teacher clock runs at a slower pace because of the complexity entailed in reaching the outcomes proposed by the initiatives, that is, deeper levels of student learning resulting from new models of instruction. For many teachers the expected change is of a conceptual nature that requires complex and exacting work. Some of the issues that add to the intricacy of instructional change involve teachers' beliefs. It is common knowledge that teachers vary in their views about how students best learn. While some see students as depositories of information, others believe that pupils should be viewed as active creators of knowledge. Teachers also see their instructional roles from varied frames of reference. Teachers as sources of information versus teachers as coaches of learning are diverse postures that trigger decidedly different approaches to instruction. These diverse perspectives cannot be described as following a continuum; their differences are not incremental, but conceptual. Consequently, this type of change is not brought about merely by providing more information. Conceptual change or cognitive restructuring is fundamentally different from the acquisition of new facts.

> "It has taken me ten years. You have to understand the rationale for what you are doing; it's more than just adding to your kit bag."

This Arizona teacher's statement verifies the extraordinary complexity of the change proposed by education reformers. To make this change is not a matter of simply acquiring new skills, but of requiring a change in ideological orientation.

Another essential factor in effecting conceptual change is what cognitive scientists refer to as intentional learning, that is, learning that is desired and controlled by the learner. An individual's construction of new knowledge depends heavily on one's sense of being in charge of one's learning (Bereiter & Scardamalia, 1989). Consequently, when teachers perceive that they are in control of their professional lives, they are more likely to question their deep-seated beliefs (Richardson, 1990). On the other hand, when teachers see themselves as targets rather than agents of change, it is less probable that they will make genuine efforts to change their behaviors, that is, how they teach. This doesn't happen overnight or even within a legislative session.

Another determinant of teacher change is the environment within which teachers work (Cuban, 1988; Fullan & Hargreaves, 1991). The culture of schools and the level of organizational support have direct implications for the amount of risk a teacher is willing to take in attempting change. Environments that encourage and foster teacher growth and development involve supportive leadership that provides time as well as financial and human resources.

Therefore, educational reform directed toward instructional improvement when monitored by the teacher clock entails confronting the challenges presented by conceptual change. The differing levels of ability as well as the diverse belief systems of teachers influence their receptivity to change. In addition, allowing for teachers' sense of agency to grow is pivotal to movement toward authentic change. But this is change from the ground up and not from the top down.

An example of an intervention that followed the teacher clock was a project conducted by CRESST at the University of Colorado that was designed to examine the assumption that authentic assessment will improve instruction. The aim of the year-long program was to free teachers from the constraints of standardized testing and assist them in developing a system of performance assessment. "The hope was that the refocus of assessment on performance, understanding, and higher order thinking would, in turn, have a positive effect on instruction" (Flexer & Gerstner, 1993, p. 2). The project design involved extensive interaction between the classroom teachers and the university researchers who had expertise in the content areas, pedagogy, and performance assessment. Schools and teachers participated on a voluntary basis. Fourteen third-grade teachers met with a team of researchers for one-half day per week for an entire school year. Their interactions included hands-on development of assessments and scoring rubrics, classroom demonstrations and modeling small-group and individual assessment, regular sessions for reflection and feedback, and journal and record keeping. The researchers defined organizational support as "very strong" at the building and district levels. Teachers had the benefit of extra planning time and additional funds for instructional materials and the support of their administrators. Project professionals believed that simply providing performance tests is insufficient to change the way teachers think about and teach mathematics. Instead, intensive capacity development in pedagogy strategies and content knowledge is necessary. At the end of the year the researchers contended that "change is slow and nonlinear. And the more profound the change, the slower" (Flexer & Gerstner, 1993, p. 24). Even with the great amount of time that teachers and researchers committed to the project, the results illustrated the complexity of effecting change in instruction. The researchers reported that "for some teachers the real struggle was not in learning how to use performance assessment, but in believing that it was a useful thing to do" (Flexer & Gerstner, 1993, p. 27). Overall, the project revealed teachers varied significantly in how they ultimately integrated the ideas about performance assessment into their repertoires. Some grappled with their beliefs and moved toward conceptual change. Some adapted the ideas according to their own established beliefs and revised them to be more like their own. Others found too much discord between their own ideas and the new ones and chose to reject the new notions. Some just felt overwhelmed.

The CRESST project honored the teacher clock. It revealed that the teacher clock not only runs slowly but that it runs at different speeds depending on individual teachers' beliefs, experiences, and environment. Moreover, the profoundness of the proposed change has implications for how teachers will respond and how long the process will take.

NATIONAL AND STATE AGENDAS TO REFORM EDUCATION

A tension exists in regard to the time that many educators believe is needed to change schools and teaching, the professionals' and teacher clocks, and what policy makers believe it should take according to their political clock. The current national and state agendas to reform education through the use of standards and assessment is the present target of the time debate. Discussions of the time needed for reform are commonplace. The question of how much time it should and will take to reform education is frequently asked because of its political and financial implications. Those who accept the political time frame complain that it is taking far too long. Others, typically those who adhere to the teacher clock, argue that improving the current schools within the time frame proposed by the political clock watchers is unlikely.

The following descriptions provide brief histories of the education reform initiatives in two states. Each has embraced the prevailing reform model of standards and assessment. To illustrate the idea of conflicting clocks we describe the efforts of two states to reform their schools through mandated standards and assessments. The findings in the Arizona case derive from three sources of data: a policy study conducted at the outset of the Arizona Student Assessment Program (Noble, 1994); a two-year study that investigated the response of educators to ASAP that employed both long-term qualitative and extensive survey data (Smith et al., 1996); and a third set of policy interviews and document analysis that provided evidence on the end of ASAP and the beginning of the next phase of the Arizona assessment policy (Smith, Heineke, & Noble, 1997). The Delaware findings are based on a series of studies conducted during the beginning years of the reform and included case studies conducted at the district level, interviews with policy stakeholders, document analyses of curriculum development efforts, and statewide surveys of educators' response to the reform (Noble, 1996, 1997; Brown et al., 1996).

New Directions for Education in Delaware

In 1992, Delaware initiated an agenda to reform its public schools primarily in response to two political forces. The initial propellant for the current education reform agenda was the well-known *Nation at Risk* message. In response, the National Education Goals generated by the president and the nation's governors at the historic Education Summit of 1989 set the stage for further external critique of public education. Pressure to change schooling also stemmed from the private sector as corporate leaders demanded that schools better prepare students for the workforce of the twenty-first century. The demands of the private sector materialized at the state level through a study sponsored by Delaware's Business/Public Education Council, which argued that many of the state's most prominent employers saw a significant gap between the skills they required and those possessed by graduates of Delaware's public schools.

The state's response was a standards- and assessment-based initiative called New Directions. The strategy, proposed by the then Superintendent of Public Instruction intended to link the national and state reform agendas. From the beginning, New Directions was predicated on a participatory model designed to foster involvement and commitment from leaders of education, business, community organizations, and the state legislature. One key dimension of the plan entailed setting higher academic standards for all students along with the development of academic performance indicators. The second part was the development of an assessment that could be used to measure progress toward the learning goals.

By 1995, content standards had been written and approved in four areas: language arts, mathematics, science, and social studies. These documents were developed by state curriculum framework commissions that typically included about fifty participants, including practicing teachers from public and higher education, community members, and business leaders. Their work was strongly influenced by similar undertakings at the national level, for example, the NCTM standards. In 1993, Delaware revoked the state's standardized testing program and initially administered statewide performance assessments in reading, writing, and mathematics. These assessments, developed by Riverside Publishing Company, were given on an interim basis as the state developed its own assessments. The Delaware State Testing Program implementation began in the 1997–98 school year. Delaware's initiative to improve public school education is

> based on the conviction that to significantly improve our schools we must answer three apparently simple but actually complex and interconnected questions: One, what is it that all students must know and be able to do? Two, how will we know when students have accomplished the task? And, three, what are the best ways to enhance student learning? (Hicks, 1992, p. 6)

The state had answered the first question with its release of the state content standards in 1994–95. It has begun to address the second with the implementation of the state testing program. Question 3 is left to those actually responsible for student learning, the schools, specifically, the classroom teachers.

Arizona Student Assessment Program

The legislative passage of a testing mandate in May 1990 demonstrated Arizona's commitment to top-down reform as it established assessment as the means to leverage educational change. Arizona Revised Statute 15–741 directed the State Board of Education to adopt and implement a performance-based assessment plan aligned with the state's curriculum, the Essential Skills. The Arizona Student Assessment Program (ASAP) was the Arizona Department of Education's (ADE) response to the legislation.

Two primary constituencies supported the test mandate. Each group had its own ideologies and interests and saw the change process very differently. One constituency was dissatisfied with the norm-referenced test, concerned that it only covered one-fourth of the state's legislated curriculum framework and thus promoted inappropriate test preparation. They were unhappy with the use of norm-referenced, standardized tests as accurate accountability measures and argued that "they don't measure what our teachers teach." They wanted to force districts to align their curriculum to the Arizona Essential Skills. A policy maker who represented this group discussed the concern.

> The Department of Education and the state legislature had learned that simply having the state Essential Skills in no way was serving as a catalyst for districts to align their curricula. An assessment program, they felt, was a way to do that. It would compel districts to finally do what they were supposed to have been doing for years.

Another group opposed the past standardized testing program because of its deleterious effects on students, teachers, curriculum, and instruction. It hoped to change the kind of pedagogy that schools adopted. They believed that the performance assessment would encourage teachers to adopt a holistic, constructivist pedagogy that in turn would result in more meaningful learning for students: "We really want to change curriculum so that the students are vitally engaged in their learning process and beginning to create their own knowledge." The ideals and intentions of the two constituencies varied greatly. Their views of what effected changes and the time that it took varied as well. Yet despite their differences, their political interests converged in the creation of the Arizona Student Assessment Program (ASAP). The Superintendent of Public Instruction, C. Diane Bishop, made ASAP the centerpiece of her administration, the goals of which were not only to increase districts' accountability to the state's curriculum frameworks but also to move schools and classroom instruction toward greater emphasis on higher-order thinking, complex problem solving, subject matter, and application of basic skills. To accomplish these goals, the state's Department of Education reduced the emphasis on standardized tests and instead commissioned the development of performance assessments aligned with the state curriculum frameworks, the Arizona Essential Skills. The state assumed that familiarity with the tests would be enough to enable teachers to change their modes of instruction. No state funds were available for professional or curriculum development toward ASAP goals, however, and Arizona districts differ drastically from one another in their financial capacity to respond to unfunded mandates. There were several accountability mechanisms attached to ASAP measures that were intended to further motivate educators and students to improve achievement.

The political and professional clocks were ticking at different speeds from the outset. The State Board and the legislature wanted results—fast. To comply with their demands, the Department took some shortcuts in test development. For example, the interim between the award of the contract to develop the statewide assessment and its administration was three months, allowing no chance for pilot testing or revision (Smith, Heinecke, & Noble, 1997).

Within two weeks of the third scheduled administration of the statewide performance assessment, time ran out for ASAP. Citing inadequate technical features of the test, the newly elected State Superintendent announced that she was suspending it. Soon after, she and the State Board decided that the program as a whole would be substantially revised. The rationale given was that the ASAP failed to provide adequate accountability of schools to basic skills. Thus, a new political actor imposed a new agenda for state education reform in Arizona. The new initiative, the Arizona Student Achievement Program, was born.

RAMIFICATIONS OF DIFFERENT CLOCKS ON THE CHANGE PROCESS

Through our case studies in Delaware and Arizona, we found interesting ramifications of the three clocks ticking at different speeds during the implementation of the state's initiatives. Both states assumed that imposing high standards and assessments would result in improved instructional strategies and better performing schools. Judging whether either was successful depends on which clock one follows.

State Standards Affect Local Curriculum:
Different Clocks at Work

In the Delaware case study we examined the assumption that higher academic standards will trigger local curriculum alignment that would ultimately lead to instructional improvement. We found that each of the three clocks had been running at different paces throughout the state's process of developing academic standards and aligning local curriculum.

The ideas behind the reform of the state's educational system came from the then State Superintendent of Public Instruction, who could be characterized as following the professionals' clock. He had been described by many of the leaders of the Delaware education and business communities as visionary.

> What (he) did was to create the images of change and the vision of what the future should look like. . . . We have benefited tremendously from having a well-known educator (who) came from outside the state and brought a wealth of ideas and a bundle of energy to help us formulate plans and goals. . . . (He) came here with a mission. (Letters to the State Superintendent, 1996)

However, his professional clock did not always prevail over the political clock that mandated that he "fix our education system. We don't think that academically we're competitive with other states" (interview with a Delaware Legislator, 1996). His vision included a comprehensive program of standards and assessments along with a long-term commitment from the state to teachers' professional development. Four Curriculum Framework Commissions were appointed by the governor and the State Board of Education; however, the Commissions' work followed the professionals' clock. Their responsibility was to craft a content-focused curriculum framework based on national standards and contemporary research on how students best learn that particular subject. The fifty-member commissions, one for each content area, included individuals from public schools, higher education, business and industry, as well as national advisors renowned for their expertise. Over a two-year period with significant financial support from both the state and the business communities, the commissions produced the state content standards. These documents were not mere listings of goal statements but standards that include performance indicators, suggested instructional strategies, and embedded assessments. A recent national evaluation of the state standards conducted by the American Federation of Teachers judged Delaware's science standards as exemplary in the nation (American Federation of Teachers, 1996).

Upon completion of the state content standards, the political clock again began ticking. The State Board of Education approved the standards and required that each of the state's school districts align its local curriculum with them. As with most mandates, compliance and uniformity were anticipated by those following the political clock. Districts were required to align their curriculum and would be held accountable through their students' results on the state assessment. According to this group, the plan was clear. However, the differing capacities of districts and teachers became the concern of those following the professionals' clock, that is, some of the districts' curriculum directors and the support personnel from the state Department. Consequently, at the time when those on the political clock, that is, the State Board of Education, wanted to know the results of their directive, we found that results were far from uniform. The following provides a picture of what happens when clocks that run at different speeds are used to keep time. This snapshot was taken two years after the state content standards had been approved.

In an examination of half of the state's school districts, we found three different models of curriculum alignment. While curriculum directors used the phrases "gap analysis" or "discrepancy analysis" to describe their districts' activities, closer examination revealed that these terms, in regards to process and outcome, had very different meanings in different school settings. One model of curriculum alignment predominantly entailed districts comparing their own local instructional activities to the state standards, determining what was missing, and then filling the gap. This model typically prevailed in districts that, for all intents and purposes, had no curriculum prior to the release of the state standards. The approach was usually driven by the district's textbook adoption cycle and the gap was filled through the purchase of additional instructional materials and textbooks. Consequently, some continued to see the process as one of textbook selection. One curriculum director shared, "And I have had questions from teachers, 'Why are we doing this? When are we going to purchase a math textbook?'"

A second model of alignment revealed that districts used their own local curriculum as a basis for comparison and determined how the state standards fit in. Typically having had their own curriculum prior to the release of the state content standards, this process of curriculum alignment revealed little more than a cut-and-paste exercise. Their responses to those state standards not addressed in their curriculum varied from writing additional instructional materials, adding courses, changing course sequence, requesting state waivers, or ignoring the standard. Indicative of this perspective, one director stated, "I'm willing to go along with state standards if I see value and they fit into our curriculum and they meet our mission."

A third interpretation of gap analysis triggered a third model of cur-

riculum alignment. Those districts determined ideals through an examination of national standards, the Delaware state standards, and research
on how children best learn that specific content area. The gap was
defined as a comparison of these ideals to actual classroom practice.
Activities designed to fill these gaps included the development of new
instructional strategies and classroom assessments, provision of consultants and mentors to assist classroom teachers, new materials, texts, and
technology, and professional development around the new instructional
strategies for teachers and the administrators who evaluate them.

One might expect that financial and human resources available to
the districts would have had significant effect on how they chose to pursue curriculum development. However, this assumption did not hold.
Each of the three models was found in the wealthier districts within the
state. What did prevail in our analyses was that those districts in the
biggest hurry to comply were most likely to see curriculum alignment as
a glorified textbook review process or a mere cut-and-paste activity.
They saw their work as manageable and sufficient.

> We went through the standards and our current curriculum and we did
> a matrix for all of the curriculum. We looked at our curriculum, the
> standards, (and asked) where these standards were in our curricu-
> lum? . . . (Also) every student has a course of study laid out which is
> very good as far as the standards because we don't have to worry
> about students taking a myriad of elective courses.

These districts were proud of their progress and their ability to meet the
state's time line as far as completion of their curriculum alignment.

In contrast, those districts that were attuned to the teacher clock
saw the writing of the curriculum as only the first step in a long process
that would require intensive and sustained professional development.

> I am sure there are some teachers who don't understand how to make
> the standards happen in the classroom. . . . You're looking at changing
> a traditional classroom to a constructivist classroom. What's that
> gonna take? It takes a lot of patience, and a lot of modeling, and a lot
> of time. It's a massive undertaking but if it's done well, more children
> learn more things."

They expressed frustration with demands being made by the state that
they saw as unrealistic. They were concerned about premature judgments and potential criticism that would be made by those who
expected change to occur by the political clock.

> People are going to say that the idea of standards and assessment are
> no good because it didn't work. Because the assessment results will
> come out and the kids will not do well. People will not understand,

that it takes longer to implement than it does to create. Michelangelo knew you could fly but it was a long time before Orville and Wilbur got it off the ground."

The results of the curriculum alignment activity received mixed reviews by those who adhered to the political clock. Two years after the release of the standards, the good news was that all of the districts were responding to the mandate and were in the process of aligning their curriculum. The bad news was that none had completed the task. Those on the professionals' clock across the state worried that the ultimate goal of instructional improvement might be achieved by only a few. Despite the two years spent at the state level on the development of standards and the two subsequent years spent at the district level on curriculum development, those on the teacher clock typically felt overwhelmed by the implications: "At the elementary level, teachers are beginning to feel real frustration because they're asked to do so many things in so many different ways than they used to." Although the state had provided grants to districts to support curriculum activity and numerous professional development opportunities, the results, in many cases, were far from instructional improvement: "It's going to take a lot of work because teachers typically rely on the recipe in the teacher book rather than being driven by a set of standards."

Thematic Curriculum Affecting Instruction:
A Dysfunctional Side Effect

Another assumption of standards-based reform is that the provision of thematic, integrated curriculum will lead to changes in classroom instruction. Part of the Arizona Student Assessment Program required that the school districts provide the state with an annual report that delineated their goals for the subsequent school year, based on the results of all of the assessments. The report required that districts list their strategies for reaching these goals, budgets, and time lines for implementation. This annual report served as a compliance tool and was driven by the political time clock set by the Department of Education. One district's response to their students' low test scores in reading and writing as well as to their outdated social studies textbook supply was to purchase a series of textbooks based on thematic units and constructivist learning theory. In response to the political time line as defined by the mandate, the district made decisions about textbook adoption. However, actual change in instruction followed the slower teacher clock. We found that teachers' access to better textbooks and integrated curriculum models aligned with the state's goals did not ensure instructional change. This vignette provides a poignant illustration of the results of mandating a thematic curriculum for a teacher who lacked the conceptual understanding to utilize it as it was intended. What follows is a portrayal of a traditional, skills-oriented teacher's response to integrated, holistic curriculum.

Mr. Wilcox is a fourth-grade teacher at Valor School. Year-long observations of his classroom attested to a traditional approach to instruction. In his teaching of reading, he used a 1969 SRA basal reading series. All students were tracked in top, middle, and low ability reading groups. The same groupings were used for mathematics instruction. The class was highly structured, with reading, spelling, grammar, and mathematics instruction scheduled at the same time every day.

Most classroom activities involved the completion of worksheets. Mr. Wilcox held some very traditional beliefs about learning. He maintained that motivation and readiness and innate ability were the keys to student achievement. His beliefs about learning were strongly influenced by his own childhood struggles as a student. His teaching reflected how he was taught.

The Thematic Lesson

"Is social studies group #5 ready?" The children respond to the teacher's question with moans, "We're not even close!" Amid the confusion and pleas for more time, Paulina and Maria take their place in the front of the classroom, leaning against the blackboard for support. Mr. Wilcox announces, "they're going to lead a discussion on decision making." Paulina begins to read aloud in a muffled tone. The topic explores the responsibility of being the mayor of a city.

Mr. Wilcox interjects, "Now what do you need to do to make a good decision?" Billy calls out, "It's when you should think about all the things you do." Mr. Wilcox ignores his response. Jenny raises her hand and gives her interpretation. "You should talk to other people who have good ideas and find out more about it." Timmy laughs and says, "If you make a good decision you won't end up in jail." A look of disgust crosses Mr. Wilcox's face. Irritated at this point, he marches to the board and writes the words "correct answer = _____ ." "Now who knows the *correct* answer?"

Silence falls over the classroom. With heads down, most of the children furtively look to their friends with puzzled looks on their faces. Catherine timidly raises her hand and quietly says "e"? With a big smile on his face, the teacher writes the letter *e* on the board. "Be sure you write the right answer in the right space in your workbook."

Despite the holistic nature of this social studies lesson, the teacher altered it significantly. The teacher's definition of learning and its implications took precedence over the intent and the form of the curriculum. Higher-order thinking was diminished to finding the correct answer in a workbook.

Standards and their attendant curricula are only resources; their value derives from how they are used in the classroom. In this classroom, the teacher chose to "disintegrate" a thematic lesson. However, the goal of compliance set by those who viewed change according to the political clock was accomplished. The districts were purchasing and the teachers were using textbooks more in line with the state curriculum. The goal of instructional change hoped for by those who wrote the lessons, probably among those following the professionals' clock, was hardly attained. In lieu of instructional change came curriculum change. Combs (1991) attributed this sort of dilemma to the "partly right assumption" that grips much of educational reform, the manipulation of forces theory. Stemming from a behaviorist viewpoint, it proposes that change is a result of stimuli to which people are exposed. This vignette illustrates the danger of a partly right assumption, that is, change did result from the curriculum stimulus; however, the individual changed the curriculum rather than vice-versa. This demonstrates a flaw in an assumption that underlies standards-based reform, that curriculum aligned with high academic standards will change instruction.

In addition, in this particular scenario, the teacher's clock had just begun to tick. During a follow-up interview with the teacher, when asked what he could do to foster children's higher-order thinking, he responded, "I can't because I can't define it in my own mind." What's more, the teacher clock that sets the pace for instructional change ticks much more slowly than the political clock that mandates it.

Top-Down Education Reform: When Politics Calls Time

What happened in Arizona has striking similarity to the effect of the political clock on the national scene. Legislation for Goals 2000 created an oversight committee for the development of voluntary national content standards and to monitor those created by the states. Cohen (1995) portrayed this group, the National Education Standards and Improvement Council, as

> dead on arrival. Barely half a year after Goals 2000 was signed into law, Republicans took control of Congress. Although many Republicans had supported the legislation in the previous Congress, the new faces were generally more conservative and *had little use* for any sort of national school reform.
> (emphasis ours) (p. 752)

A comparable scenario was the dismantling of the Arizona Student Assessment Program. It was initiated by State Superintendent Diane Bishop in 1990 and rescinded by her successor, Lisa Graham Keegan, in 1995. Some of what we found (Smith, Heinecke, & Noble, 1997) during the four years we studied ASAP was that Arizona educators were fully cognizant of the reform although they defined it in different ways: as an assessment that was preferable to standardized assessment, as a way to change teaching in a constructivist direction, or as just another state mandate. Change in curriculum and teaching consistent with ASAP varied widely, depending on local conditions. Initially, the low rate of instructional change could be attributed in part to inadequate professional development. State support was characterized by familiarizing teachers with the need for performance assessment and training teachers in the use of scoring rubrics. The state failed to provide resources for teacher training, even though the reform implied fundamental changes in teacher knowledge and skill. This left the responsibility to the districts. Although a few devoted impressive resources to developing teachers' capacities and curricular changes, the average number of hours of relevant professional development reported by teachers was only about eight hours over a two-year period. Still, there was enormous effort exerted by teachers and administrators simply complying with ASAP testing and reporting requirements. There was evidence of a widespread increase in students writing more extended texts.

However, regardless of the pace of the teacher or professionals' clocks, the political clock prevailed. With the election of a new State Superintendent in 1994 came a new initiative. The state's multi-million-dollar testing program was scrapped along with the state's curriculum. The focus of the new agenda was the development of new standards, a different assessment, a return to mass standardized testing, and higher stakes to be placed on the results of the various assessments.

Edelman (1988) depicted an image of leadership that provides insight into the political decision making that characterized the shift in Arizona assessment policy:

> The term "leader" evokes an ideal type which high public officials try to construct themselves to fit. . . . The ability to create oneself as the ideal type maintain followings. . . . The leader must be constructed as innovator, as accepting responsibility for governmental actions . . . as successful in his or her strategies in contrast to the mistakes of earlier leaders." (p. 40)

A legislator justified Keegan's new course of action.

> [There were] constant complaints about the content of the test, about perceptions that the test wasn't valid, that it disrupted the classroom— just constant complaints and zero support [to keep it going].

At a similar point in time, a school administrator indicated that change at the classroom level was just beginning to take hold at the point when ASAP was suspended.

> They were just getting to the point where they were taking it seriously and gearing their teaching to it. The first year no one took it seriously,

because the district was convinced that ASAP was not going to last. . . .
The second year teachers were just starting to get going, but they didn't
have the understanding to do it well. By the third year they were ready
and eager to show what their students could do.

Just as those on the teacher clock of education reform were just beginning to make sense of the initiative and see the fruits of their efforts, the
political alarm clock went off and everything came to a halt.

When the Clocks Collide

When the political clock collides with the teacher clock, judgments of
each group's inadequacy are predictable. Political actors blame educators' resistance to change. They perceive change as straightforward and
readily accomplished, as the following statement by a Delaware legislator shows:

> If you talk to teachers, they'll talk about class size and all those other
> issues which we can deal with legislatively. They still talk about disci-
> pline. . . . I think we're on the right track and I think we just have to
> put these things in play and see how they do play out. . . . I don't think
> that there are major things that need to be done, just fine tuning and
> implementation.

On the other hand, those following the teacher clock frequently
express frustration and disparage reformers for being out of touch with
what schools are like and the complexity of the change process.

> Business has a couple wonderful things going for it. When they want
> GM to redesign the car, they shut down the plant, they retool the
> whole thing at whatever cost it takes, they retrain every person, and
> then they start up again. . . . What they've done is created these (stan-
> dards) and this assessment and they've forgot this part in the mid-
> dle. . . . And they think that you can hand somebody a document, and
> it is going to change them.

Sometimes those on the professionals' clock observe the collision
and try to temper the repercussions.

> Because one of the things that we've got to guard against is the notion
> that we've got standards adopted and all of a sudden things are going
> to happen as a consequence of having those things. . . . We've got a lot
> of capacity building to do in terms of getting teachers up to snuff in the
> classrooms to be able to start to work against those standards. . . . The
> legislature is going to say, "We're spending money, where's the
> progress?" That's a problem that's got to be managed.

Standards-based and assessment-driven reforms involve the compli-
cations of three clocks running simultaneously. Studies conducted at the

national level and within our two states explored the concept of teacher agency in regard to reform initiatives.

In 1993, a national study of school reform, conducted by the Ford Foundation, found that many classroom teachers see themselves as objects of others' efforts to improve education. Their findings indicated that "nationwide, 53% of the teachers feel they are the targets of reform, while only 37% feel they are the agents of reform " (Harris & Wagner, 1993, p. vi).

Although Arizona and Delaware have taken seemingly different roads to improve their schools, similar degrees of teacher skepticism prevail. Parallel questions asked of teachers in the two states at similar points in time in relation to the implementation of the states' initiatives showed that 34 percent of Arizona's teachers and 35 percent of the teachers in Delaware viewed themselves as agents of change. Most teachers in both states continued to see their state's reform efforts as being orchestrated by outsiders.

In addition, teachers saw the current efforts as following a political clock, thus judging them to be mere echoes of past politically driven initiatives. Just as the new math faded in short order, many classroom teachers saw their states' standards-based and assessment-driven reforms as fads that would disappear just as readily. Four years into the Arizona plan to improve schools through high-stakes assessment, about 80 percent of the state teachers saw the Arizona Student Assessment Program as a "passing fad." Likewise, four years into Delaware's plan to reform schools through higher academic standards, 81 percent of Delaware's teachers were skeptical that New Directions would take root.

Followers of the political clock would judge these data as the outcome of an intractable system invested in maintaining the status quo. They would likely see the findings as a reflection of teachers' resistance to change. According to the political clock that measures time in terms of office, four years into any reform should result in higher degrees of commitment on the part of those who have been the focus of the effort. If the reform has not worked, it must be time to find some other solution. At this point in time, any political player who had been an original advocate for either of these reforms would likely have gone on to support other plans to improve education. For their own political survival, they could not afford to have themselves seen as leaders of initiatives that had generated so little commitment from those who were the targets of the plan. In Arizona, the new agenda is vouchers and charter schools.

Those who adhere to the professionals' clock might critique the lack of teacher commitment as due to a lack of sufficient supports within the system to effect change. They might contend that making judgments about teachers' level of commitment or resistance to the reform was premature without having provided adequate opportunities for capacity building. They might criticize the professional development that had been offered, saying that it was inappropriate or insufficient. They would likely propose that professional development would need to be more in line with the standards, be more ongoing in nature, and provide teachers with more opportunities for active engagement and time for reflection. In addition, those operating on the professionals' clock might criticize the reform agenda as lacking coherence. They might rebuke policy makers for sending mixed messages to practitioners that led to teacher skepticism. They might assert that the flood of demands being made on schools and teachers created confusion and minimized the chances of generating commitment.

Those who keep time by the teacher clock would probably receive the results of these studies quite differently. They would tend to see the findings as unsurprising considering the complexity of the instructional changes being imposed by the reforms and the limited time allowed for their development. They would likely point to the lack of organizational support and limited professional development provided. In addition, they probably would have anticipated the low levels of teacher commitment to the reforms. They would attribute it to teachers' lack of genuine involvement in the creation of the reform agenda, asserting that it takes more than token participation to generate a true sense of agency among them. They would also point to the many short-lived, politically contrived reforms of the past that, according to their clocks, were never given a chance to work.

CONCLUSION

There is more than one clock that measures time for education reform. The lack of understanding of that simple principle has generated conflict and antagonism among groups involved in efforts to improve our schools. Difficulties ensue when judgments are made by groups on one clock of those following another and a vicious, unproductive cycle transpires. By way of illustration, in cases where education reform is driven by centralized initiatives that come with a promise of rewards and a threat of sanctions, teachers might attempt to respond to the political clock. Their results may prove satisfactory to political timekeepers but may be less than what was hoped for by those on the professionals' clock. At the same time, practitioners on the much slower teacher clock complain that policy makers are insensitive to the challenges they face and have unrealistic expectations. Consequently, within the time frame determined by those of the political clock, some form of change may have occurred. However, it is likely to be judged as insufficient or superficial to those adhering to the professionals' clock. And time has been called long before any change has had a chance to occur, according to those on the teacher clock. The outcome leaves those on the teacher clock susceptible to criticism by those on the professionals' clock. Then in response to their judgments, those keeping political time, in efforts to meet political needs, are likely to decide that the initiative is a failure and go on to propose another solution to fix education. And then, the cycle begins again.

REFERENCES

American Federation of Teachers. (1996). *Making standards matter 1996.* Item No. 265. Washington, DC.

Bereiter, C., & Scardamalia, M. (1989). Intentional learning as a goal of instruction. In L. B. Resnick (Ed.), *Knowing, learning, and instruction: Essays in honor of Robert Glaser* (pp. 361–392). Hillsdale, NJ: Lawrence Erlbaum.

Brown, P., Deemer, S., & LeMahieu, P. (1996). *Educators' perceptions of the conditions of education in Delaware.* Technical report T96.014.1. Newark: Delaware Education Research and Development Center, University of Delaware.

Cohen, D. (1995). What standards for national standards? *Phi Delta Kappan,* 76 (10), 751–757.

Combs, A. W. (1991). *The schools we need: New assumptions for educational reform.* New York: University Press of America.

Cuban, L. (1988). A fundamental puzzle of school reform. *Phi Delta Kappan,* 70 (5), 341–44.

Edelman, M. J. (1988). *Constructing the political spectacle.* Chicago: University of Chicago Press.

Flexer, R. J., & Gerstner, E. A. (1993). *Dilemmas and issues for teachers developing performance assessments in mathematics.* CSE Technical Report 364. Los Angeles, CA: National Center for Research on Evaluation, Standards, and Student Testing, UCLA.

Fuhrman, S. (1993). *Designing coherent education policy: Improving the system.* San Francisco: Jossey-Bass.

Fullan, M., & Hargreaves, A. (1991). *What's worth fighting for: Working together for your school.* Toronto: Ontario Public School Teachers' Federation.

Harris, L., & Wagner, R. F. (1993). *Testing assumptions: A survey of teachers' attitudes toward the nation's school reform agenda.* Study #930012. LH Research, New York.

Hicks, L. (1992). *New directions for education in Delaware.* Doveri Delaware Department of Public Instruction.

McDonnell, L. M., & Elmore, R. F. (!987). Getting the job done: Alternative policy instruments. *Educational Evaluation and Policy Analysis, 9* (2), 133–152.

Noble, A. J. (1997). *Curriculum alignment: Delaware school districts' response to the state content standards.* Technical report T97.003.1. Newark: Delaware Education Research and Development Center, University of Delaware.

Noble, A. J. (1996). *Letters to the state superintendent: A study of leadership transition.* Technical report T96.010.1. Newark: Delaware Education Research and Development Center, University of Delaware.

Noble, A. J. (1994). *Measurement-driven reform: The interplay of educational policy and practice.* Unpublished dissertation. Arizona State University, Tempe.

Richardson, V. (1990). Significant and worthwhile change in teaching practice. *Educational Researcher, 19,* 10–18.

Smith, M. L., Heinecke, W., & Noble, A. J. (1997). *Assessment policy and political spectacle.* Los Angeles, CA: National Center for Research on Evaluation, Standards, and Student Testing, UCLA.

Smith, M. L., Noble, A. J., Heinecke, W., Seck, M., Parish, C., Cabay, M., Junker, S.C., Haag, S., Tayler, K., Safran, Y., Penley, Y., & Bradshaw, A. (1996). *Reforming schools by reforming assessment: Consequences of the Arizona Student Assessment Program.* Tempe, AZ: Southwest Educational Policy Studies.

CHAPTER 10

Reforming Time: Timescapes and Rhythms of Learning

John Lofty

What are some of the ways in which time in school has been represented? In Peter Hoeg's novel, *Borderliners*, the male protagonist has been educated in Danish institutions since childhood. As a young adult, Peter finds himself at Biehl's Academy, an elite private school in Copenhagen. He and Katarina, an orphan girlfriend, slowly discover that the students there are subjects of an educational experiment designed to correct supposedly deviant social behaviors by reforming their temporal identities.

> The succession of days was an endless line, gray. They ran past you. Yourself, you were held firmly in place, you stood absolutely still and watched them running past, and there was nothing to be done about it. . . . Of course, it was only from the outside that the days seemed the same. Deep down they were meant to be different. It only seemed as though the same subjects and the same classrooms and the same teachers and the same pupils came around again and again. In reality, the requirement was that you should, with every day be transformed. Every day you should be better, you should have developed, all the repetition in the life of the school was there only so that, against an unchanging background, you could show that you had improved. . . . I know I cannot bring anyone to understand this. How our lives back then were totally saturated by time. (p. 226)

We recognize, of course, that here are characters, situation, and theme from a novel that contrasts with the "real" schools in which we teach. Yet in our own context, the school reform movement in North

America is very much an ambitious educational experiment. Like characters in Hoeg's novel, the learning lives of its subjects are being transformed, but they, too, have not volunteered and cannot withdraw easily. Our purpose, though, is not to reform students but rather to transform learning to ensure that time in school will be much more meaningful than a monochrome "succession of days" or the mere accumulation of credits toward graduation. As in the novel, the lives of teachers and students are "totally saturated by time"; it permeates learning at every level, from structuring the master schedule, to determining credit hours for course work, to allocating time for schoolwork and for teachers' own professional development.

Time's high visibility in education is well documented by the National Education Commission on Time and Learning in the publication *Prisoners of Time*. Reviewing the relationship between time and learning in the nation's schools, the Commission noted that "Unyielding and relentless, the time available in a uniform six-hour day and a 180–day year is the unacknowledged design flaw in American education" (1993, p. 8). A major direction of recent school reforms has been to attempt to solve the "design flaw" by restructuring the school day. One immediate challenge that faces school leaders is to use this opportunity to rethink how students learn and teachers teach. Anything short of directly facing this daunting yet exciting task will relegate the reform effort to the graveyard of quick-fixes that continues to plague our schools.

Block-plan variants that have evolved across the country typically offer teachers and students longer periods, fewer classes and changes, more instructional choices, and the promise of additional time for teachers to plan, collaborate, and continue their own professional growth. The initial success of these pioneering innovations is well documented. Innovative plans allow schools to use time more efficiently and in ways less fragmented than typically possible in the traditionally structured high school day. Reports such as the National Education Association's *Time Strategies* (Dalheim, 1994) suggest that teachers across subject areas and students, too, value and adjust to the new block plans more easily than anticipated. Few faculties have voted to turn back the clock even when offered the option.

Given the rapid expansion of all that we now must teach, our search for new ways to reconfigure the finite resource of school time is a critically important task. We rightly consider ways to provide teachers and students with additional time. This is important work, but my concern is that as high schools across the country swiftly adopt innovative schedules, teachers and principals are failing to scrutinize their core beliefs and values about the relationships between learning and the time structures of schooling. The challenging task of altering ingrained habits of teaching and learning requires us to examine basic yet seldom asked questions about the nature of time in school:

1. Are we considering the different kinds of time that affect teaching and learning? Do our representations of time encompass adequately the complexities of time in education?
2. What are the several different ways in which time is a major element in teaching and learning?

My concern is not that an experiment conducted under the banner of school reform is going to fail. The experiment, though, simply will not go nearly far enough for us ever to discover what reforming our relationships to time might accomplish in schools unless we stop regarding time only as a simple linear constant that determines the broad-brush architecture of the school day.

In this essay, I argue, then, that we must look more closely at time's complexity: its interiority, embedded values, and the personal and social rhythms that impel its motion. How students experience the quality of that movement—routinized or mechanistic on the one hand, and personalized and organic on the other—will shape in part how students engage and value education. I use the term "rhythm" broadly to refer to the tempo or pacing of an activity, its frequency or cyclicity, and the distinctive measures and segments of an activity's temporal duration. I explore these rhythms as they affect students' composing processes and invite readers to consider how time shapes the teaching and learning rhythms of subjects across the curriculum.

First, we need to identify and distinguish among several different ways of thinking about time that shape our work, whether in an English, science, or math class. Miriam Ben-Peretz and Rainer Bromme (1990) describe four categories: instructional time, curricular time, sociological time, and experienced-personal time. Instructional time is defined as "classroom time, allocated and prescribed by teachers and engaged in and used by students" (p. 64). Curricular time is defined as "time allocations and specifications of time use, prescribed by curriculum developers" (p. 67). Conversations about restructuring school time have focused on the first two, in part, because they are tangible and can be measured in ways that are widely accepted as quantifiable and objective.

Because the second two kinds of time can appear more abstract and hence harder to describe in concrete terms, they have figured much less prominently in educational conversations. The sociology of time studies are what Eviatar Zerubavel in *Hidden Rhythms: Schedules and Calendars in Social Life* (1981) describes as the "sociotemporal order which regulates the lives of social entities" (p. xii). Experienced-personal time, the least studied perspective on time, is defined by Ben-Peretz and Bromme as "the perception of the temporal order by individuals who perceive time in different ways and may be viewed as assigning personal meaning to time" (p. 73). Each kind of time has its own distinctive rhythms or patterns of organization that influence school and classroom life.

What can we learn about time values in education from studying the sociology of time and experienced-personal time? I will answer this question with reference to my teaching (1978–81) and subsequent research (1984–90) on an island off the Maine coast where I taught English to a group of middle-school students who enjoyed class discussion but who resisted writing (Lofty, 1992). I invite teachers, then, to compare their own contemporary observations about the influence of these kinds of time with those described below. My students wrote scant amounts in moody silence, responded indifferently to encouragement, and refused studiously to write more than a single draft. Their spare, thin prose was shorn of the rich descriptions characteristic of their talk. A small, very vocal group successfully disrupted writing sessions by asking, "Why do we need to learn how to write?" Their question not only challenged the way in which writing was being taught by a process approach; it echoed their skepticism toward the value of writing itself.

When my students described their lives at home, a set of cultural values emerged that contrasted significantly with the values taught in school. One of the most visible features of the difference was related to conceptions of time. While teachers now recognize that learning to write is influenced by students' sociolinguistic backgrounds, specifically by their oral language, we often overlook the influence of cultural frameworks so fundamental as learners' modes of perceiving time and space.

When Thoreau spoke of time as "the stream I go a-fishing in," he appropriately pointed to time as the stream of human activities in which we create self, for it is in the context of our daily lives that we construct and shape the contours of time to serve our primary needs. Central here is the idea that we perceive time as reified and seldom recognize the extent to which it is a social product grounded in part on biophysical rhythms and in part on social convention (see Zerubavel, 1981, pp. 42–43; Berger & Luckman, 1967, p. 26).

Thus, for many adults in the island community in which I taught, time is working at some fishing-related activity, while for students, time is both the experience of being at home and the experience of being in school. Here, I speak of time, then, as a measure of the location, duration, and rhythmicity of events and as a means by which members of a community create their identity. A significant part of my students' resistance to writing was embedded in the tension that they experienced between how time was constructed and valued in the respective settings of home and of school.

In island homes, life is attuned less to the uniform periods measured by a clock than to the fluid fluctuations of tide, season, and sun. The fishermen live according to "island time," and they define their personal rhythms of work and play in harmony with those of nature. Adults' time values reflect the ways in which work is done, and people seldom stop to consider the hour of day or day of week when planning their daily round of activities. Islanders will say, "We follow the sun until the job is finished." Men seldom watch the clock when they cut wood, haul lobster pots, or dig clams, nor do women as they work in home and garden, rake blueberries, and make Christmas wreaths. In contrast, the school day is part of the culture of clock and calendar. School time demands observance of the bell, celebrates punctuality, and organizes learning in units of time efficiently utilized for maximum productivity.

The island teachers applied practices based on assumptions about learning that had less currency in this community than they would have had in communities more directly influenced by bureaucratic, corporate, and industrial powers. The problems that I describe here are grounded in fundamental conflicts between the cultural values of home and of school and do not reflect on the professional skill, caring attitudes, and dedication of the teachers. During the three years that I taught on the island, I asked my students to hand in work on time, to allow sufficient time for reflection between drafts, and to work productively for a whole fifty-minute period. While these expectations appear reasonable to those of us habituated to the time order of the school day, they conflicted with the familiar temporal rhythms of life in many of the students' homes.

When these students wrote in school, they applied their knowledge of how they had seen adults in the community temporally organize their work. Their strategy was potentially rich because it drew on local knowledge, but in applying it, students imported practices and values that conflicted with the ways in which teachers asked them to prewrite, to revise, and to meet deadlines. My former students and those currently enrolled in school gave their views on these topics when I returned to study resistance to writing.

PREWRITING

A phrase that island people frequently use to describe their attitude toward work is "Do it until it's done." Whenever possible, labor is not distributed consciously into stages to reflect and to prepare for the next step. The stages of designing and making a project usually evolve together, as Jeff explained in his comments about building a barn.

> If I'd done it before, I'd probably just do it. If it's somethin' that I ain't never done before, I would talk about it. If it was somethin' simple that didn't take much, just do it in your head. Some people would have to draw everythin' out right to start with. Other people wouldn't have to draw nothin'. An island person would be more likely to just go ahead and do it.

When I asked Andrea, a former student now in her senior year, how she and her mother made a quilt together, she told me, "I did it all at once. We stayed up real late one night. My mother and I finished it. We just started it and did it all day. That's the way I am. When I get started, I never stop." My students wrote their papers in similar fashion. I wanted to teach them different ways to start writing such as making packing lists, freewriting, and provisional outlining, but these preliminary activities conflicted with their preferred one-shot approach. Andrea preferred to write intensely for short periods until her writing was completed.

> I don't wanna stop when I get started writin' a paper. I couldn't do it in any other way, 'cause if I kept stoppin', I'd like lose my train of thought, and I'd have all these sentences and paragraphs flowin' in my mind, and then I'd just lose them, if I just don't do it all at once.

Students' practice of writing a paper at one sitting led them to resist any kind of prewriting, preferring in Todd's words to "Get it off, get it over with. Do it once and get it right." Students argued that they already knew what they wanted to write and therefore should produce one finished copy without preliminary drafting. It was an argument grounded in their culture-based experience of completing an activity in one session, whenever possible, instead of prolonging its duration by interrupting its progress.

REVISION

Resistance to revision is by no means unique to students in this community. The reasons for their particular resistance, however, become more intelligible when we view that resistance in the light of local practices, rather than regarding it as typical student laziness. To make and remake writing within a short time period is a fundamental feature of revision, but islanders seldom revise their performance while telling stories, providing directions, or giving explanations. Islanders construct the material texts of their houses, boats, and fishing gear with clear conceptions of the final product that preclude revision. Islanders will say, "If it works, leave it alone. This is good enough—finest kind."

Minor changes in cultural texts occur in successive versions of artifacts, but those variations evolve over a period of years. The maker and user of familiar objects locates a creation within a far longer span of time than does the teacher whose temporal perspective anticipates a relatively brief process of making and remaking. Islanders tend to see events within a cycle of natural recurrence in contrast to a linear stream of unretrievable opportunities. This perspective suggests why my students were more willing to produce an altogether new paper than to go back and revise what they saw as completed writing.

When teachers asked students in the lower elementary school to revise their writing, these children readily complied and did not see revision as repetitious busy work. However, by grade 6, students were more acculturated to the community's time values, and many students were reluctant to write multiple drafts. In the upper high school, students often resisted writing more than one draft for the reasons that Jeff described.

> The way the stories are written, you have to go through all kinds of study. You just can't write the story. You have to have a draft and all that stuff. Takes quite a bit of time. If we could write them our way, it would be all right.

Writing papers "our way" meant using the approach that Ann described. "If it's due Monday, I usually do it on the Sunday before it's due. . . . I think everybody writes about the same way, just wait until the last minute." When I asked Dave if he ever began his writing well in advance of the due date, he replied negatively.

> I've done things over a long time, and I lose all the information, 'cause I keep most of it in my head. When I do my book report, I have two things to do in two days. So one night I just do all the research, 'cause I speed read. I take three or four books home, and I read them all that night, take my notes, then any page numbers I want. Then the next night I'll make the finished copy.

Students believed that to revise what was adequate for their purposes was a poor use of time and did not produce better writing or a higher grade, the final issue for students like Lynn who planned on college.

> Last year I had a teacher that we had to hand in our bibliography cards, hand in our note cards, and we got graded on every single thing. Rough drafts and every single thing we had to hand in. So we had to do it her way. I got an 86 on that, and the papers that I always do at the last minute, I usually get a 97 or a 98.

Because many parents needed their children's support by grade 9, the school's demands for homework took time away from the essential tasks of making money to pay for clothes, for transport, and in some homes to put food on the table. Students would say, "Time in school belongs to the teachers, but time at home should be ours." One major consequence of this attitude was that students allocated only sufficient time to write one draft at the last minute and revised only if a paper received a failing grade. Moreover, students often misinterpreted a teacher's encouragement to revise a paper as leniency toward failure, a second chance that the sea seldom offered to those who made mistakes.

TIME FRAMES AND DUE DATES

In school, students learned quickly that teachers expected writing to be submitted on time rather than to arrive in the students' own time. While some students believed that they would not write without the pressure of a due date, most resented it. Teachers frowned upon students who tried to negotiate paper deadlines. When I asked students for late papers, they would say, "Stop buggin' us. It's comin'." They promised to get their work to me when they could. The writing usually did arrive, often when least expected and not always during the same ranking period. If I protested that it was too late to count for that term, the reply was, "I thought you wanted this. Here, you better read it." When I became frustrated, students sympathetically advised that in time I would get over the frustration of not always getting work on time.

Andrea soon became irritated when I asked her how she used her time to write a paper. "I'll start my paper when I feel like it. If I feel like Monday, I wanna take the day off from school, that's how I work, whenever I feel like it." Andrea, who did not value her writing except for the grade she received, resented investing time in what she saw as a task only for the teacher. To assert her independence in school, Andrea therefore invested minimal time in writing at her own convenience and accepted the consequences of late work.

In the community, calendric deadlines seldom determine when work or a payment is due. For example, local bankers know that as soon as the ice leaves the bay and boats can begin fishing, winter loans will be paid, a flexibility essential to the islanders' survival. Fishermen deliver their goods and services according to a schedule controlled by the priorities of other work and ever-changing natural constraints. In contrast, rigid deadlines enforced by social authorities are the norm of school time.

My students' problem with meeting time lines that were set by convention rather than by the time needs of particular activities surfaced in response to the master schedule that then organized secondary-level education into a school day of seven fifty-minute periods. Sherrie, a seventh-grade student who enjoyed writing, described her experience of moving between classes.

> Here, when it's English, do your English, math, do your math, science, do your science, social studies, do your social studies. Then just cut right off in the middle of it, finished or not. And then you do it again, and you cover it up, and then you go home, and then you do the other half of everything. . . . If you're sitting down in English and the bell rings, there's no choice, you have got to leave. But if you're sittin' down at your house, and you are in the middle of your English, and supper is done, you could just say, "Well, could you please wait?" But you can't up here. It's just bang, the bell rings and you've gotta go, that minute, and you're all done.

The change was disorienting also for senior students like Greg, who related the confined time frames of learning to his difficulties in achieving a high quality of education in school.

> Cramming all those classes into one little short day is too much. In the elementary school, I don't think they had that many classes in one day. I might have had three subjects, and we worked on those for a couple of hours, and I think that was more comfortable. You'd have a lot longer time to work on a specific thing, and you could get it really embedded in your head.

My interpretation of resistance to writing in school from the context of the community's time values might suggest to the reader that the activity rhythms characteristic of this community caused students to act in similar ways when in school. While procedures and values learned in the home could be observed in patterns of student behavior in school, however, the influence was one of association rather than of direct causality. Students watched how adults at home organized their activities and expected to find some continuity of that approach in schoolwork. Instead, they discovered other ways of learning that often perplexed and frustrated them partly because these new approaches made familiar ways of proceeding invisible. Disjunctions between home and school are partially inevitable but can be generative, too, if students and teachers discuss the differences between home and school learning and the logic for each. Teachers also need to consider the significance of the differences when planning instruction.

I have argued that island students are caught in a tension between time values located at different positions on the spectrum of time: values conventionally ordered to serve an institution and those derived from the natural world. Although many of us do not teach in communities where time values are predicated on the activity rhythms of rural life, this example strongly suggests the possibility that other communities might also experience time in ways that are unfamiliar to us.

I turn now from sociological time differences between home and school to the category of experienced-personal or existential time. This experience is marked by a deep engagement in the activity at hand, whether in school or at home, which allows an individual to become a particular person. I observed times of intense concentration when lobstermen hauled, picked, and set their traps or dug for clams with rhythmic absorption. There were times, too, when students were so involved in their work that until the teacher or the bell stopped them, they were unaware of other ongoing activities. In colloquial terms, students would talk about "getting into the swing" of their work. An existential experience of time is available in school under the right conditions, but difficult to achieve in the fragmentation of time that results from a day of seven fifty-minute periods.

I began my essay by referring to school reforms that sought to solve the design flaw in American high schools by restructuring the time frames of the school day. I cautioned that for school reform to be successful, we needed to consider not only curricular and instructional time, as measured by clock and calendar, but also to recognize the importance of sociological and experienced-personal time as well. If as we attend to reform, we consider only the time constraints associated with curricular and instructional time, then we overlook the need to consider what I have described above as personal and social activity rhythms associated with the different times of home and school.

TIME'S VALUES

These rhythms are derived from, and in turn establish particular time values that govern beliefs about how work is best organized. We need, then, to consider values whose origins lie outside the classroom and in contexts with agendas sometimes, but certainly not always, very different from those of education. This is not to argue that schools are discontinuous with other social institutions and cannot and do not need to learn from them. But it is to observe that schools have inherited and transmitted to our classrooms values that establish a distinctive politics of time that does not always support and easily can subvert educational goals.

A growing body of literature documents time not only as a social and cultural construct. The literature also documents time as a primary way to demarcate and establish power relations and hence to control people's work lives. In *The Politics of Time*, Henry Rutz defines the field's interest.

> A politics of time is concerned with the appropriation of the time of others, the institutionalization of a dominant time, and the legitimation of power by means of the control of time. And above all, a politics of time is focused on the struggle for control and forms of resistance or acquiescence. (p. 7)

If we are not accustomed to thinking about the political implications of how we use time, we might well question Rutz's use of terms such as "appropriation," "institutionalization," and "legitimation." If, on the other hand, we routinely consider the political dimensions of institutional practices, then Rutz's critique, if not his perspective, will be familiar. Rutz's purpose is to critique practices that, though normalized, express political values over which individuals historically have had little, if any, control.

As high school students quickly will tell you, one defining feature of their time in school is that teacher and schedule control all features of their school day. In *Hidden Rhythms*, Zerubavel shows that the principles apparent in the monastic table of hours continue to influence the time values of the school day. Saint Benedict's bells coordinated the medieval activities of work, study, and prayer to ensure all time was devoted to the service of God. Bells serve to ring class changes but more fundamentally to make visible and audible the temporal scepter of school authority.

The National Education Commission's 1992 report opens by observing that "Our schools and the people involved with them, students, teachers, administrators, parents and staff—are prisoners of time, captives of the school clock and calendar" (p. 4). In *Discipline and Punish*, Michel Foucault argues that students in school, like inmates in a prison, have learned to regulate and monitor their own temporal behaviors. Students do so by internalizing the rhythms and time frames of the daily schedule, which functions panoptically to normalize a centralized set of codes and practices. Even though time is controlled by the central administration of the school, students become responsible for and direct their own movements through the time and space of a school day as though moving independently. By carrying the schedule within them, students thereby support its authority even as many resist unsuccessfully its domination.

As public institutions, schools have been regarded as instruments of the corporate state whose mission, in part, has been to prepare a labor force. Schools have attempted to reproduce in students time management skills and attitudes toward labor required by the workplace. Since the early 1900s, Frederick Taylor's time and motion studies have precisely measured a worker's efficiency in terms of production units. The locus and rhythmicity of workers' physical movement were monitored and tuned for the minimum time loss and hence maximum economy. Labor has been organized by a rational model of scientific management that related output to the efficient use of time for a task. Michael Apple argues:

> The most widely accepted models of curriculum planning still in use have their roots originally in Taylorism. Many of the techniques now being proposed in or standing behind the reports for evaluation and testing, for standardized curricula, for "upgrading" and rationalizing teaching e.g. systems management and management by objectives, competency-based testing and curriculum development, reductive behavioral objectives come from similar soil. (p. 140)

We cannot expect constructs of time derived from settings that feature uniform, normalized, codes of behavior to serve our mission of teaching students to acquire language skills adequate to participate in a democracy. The central standard time of the schoolhouse clock represents neither the diversity nor the evolving nature of time in school. As we prepare to enter the twenty-first century, we can see that schools will be less affected by time values originating in penitential and industrial contexts and shaped more by media, technology, and information science. Each will bring its own distinctive trajectories and rhythms of moving us through time and space. As we restructure time in education, we must consider its different kinds and how each affects teaching and learning. We must scrutinize also cultural time values that influence our work and accordingly shape values to support education, whether in a writers' workshop, a math class, or a science lab.

COLLEGIAL CONVERSATION

In my introduction, I noted that the block-plan variants that have evolved as part of school reform have promised not only to improve students' use of time but also to provide time for teachers outside the classroom. Although the need for teachers to talk with each other about their work has been long recognized, this part of the promise has yet to be fulfilled for the K–12 teachers and administrators with whom I spoke recently in three small rural schools in Maine. Teachers there are now in the initial stages of interpreting and developing indicators of performance for the Maine Learning Results, state standards approved in 1997 by the state legislature.

In my conversations about the effects of the new standards on English teachers' work, the issue of time emerged as a central theme. In this section, I feature quotations that begin to answer the following questions. Why is time for conversations with colleagues valued? What are the consequences for professional development when such time is limited or absent? What are some of the possible ways that teachers and administrators see for making collegial time available on a regular basis? Statements by both new and experienced teachers and administrators, too, are represented here.

Wendy graduated from a teacher education program and practice school in which teachers did talk a great deal about their work. In her first year of teaching, making the transition into a high school where talk about teaching was not valued was very isolating.

> That was a huge shock for me [in 1993] because I went from [a university and a school] where people sat around talking about books during their break time to meeting up with women who said, "Nice outfit today, where did you shop to get it?" I don't know if it was because I was experimenting so much, and they didn't appreciate or respect it. I would ask them some questions and made it a point to drop by their rooms occasionally, once every other week, just to chat. They always seemed so busy in order to get their work done, so they could leave at 3 P.M. It was very much a contract time for them. I didn't have any mentors. . . .
>
> I need time to step back and not just alone but with the department head, with a mentor, with somebody who is good at saying "That sounds nice, but why are you doing that?"

Most teachers recognize that new teachers need frequent and extended conversations about their classes to discuss their work, identify problems, and develop new strategies with the aid of their mentors. Administrators and department heads often—certainly not always—anticipate the need to provide support time. What happens, though, when Ashley, a former principal and very experienced classroom teacher, wants and needs to talk about developing new approaches to teaching writing in grade 6.

> When I get an idea at a theoretical level, I desperately need to be able to bounce ideas off someone and to get some suggestions on how to start doing it, and then start it the next day while I am hot, while I have got the energy to start it. And then as I stumble, to be able to go back to that person and say, "This isn't working. This is what is happening." And I cannot get those conversations about instruction in this district—so far. I have never been in that position in my life when I couldn't get a conversation about instruction. . . .
>
> My perception is that teachers think it's an imposition on their

time. We are talking about informing my practice by the curriculum, and I am saying that I need to inform my instruction by dialogue with colleagues, to support me in fledgling steps in new ways of instruct- ing. . . . One person who I can begin to get that from is, Sue, a teacher I started teaching fifth grade with. She is in her first year and me in my twenty-eighth teaching year. But she is a star, and I can do this with her, but the point is her time is very limited. It's like, "Yes, can we do it in fifteen minutes? I can meet with you next Thursday for fifteen minutes in the morning." And she isn't being uppity or anything. It's where she is. And "No, I can't do it in fifteen minutes in the morning next Thursday." I can start, but. . . .

Part of Ashley's difficulty here is created by a widespread and highly dysfunctional assumption that capable, experienced teachers do not or should not need such time.

You don't admit what it is you don't know how to do. You just avoid it. So you don't get honest conversations. What you get at best when you talk with teachers, and when teachers talk about kids and their teaching, you get war stories about the lessons that went well. You don't get much talk about the failures. . . . I feel like the lone ranger in asking, "How do you?" And the response I get at my age now is, "Well, you must know. You have taught this long." I don't know. So then it becomes almost a humiliation. . . .

This is the salient point in terms of curriculum change, and I have got to believe that there is at least some percentage of teachers out there that hang up as I do on "the best is enemy of the good." I don't feel I know enough to take the risk to do it, because I can't do it. I like to think I would do better with that if I had some collegial support.

Sharon, a highly experienced second-grade teacher, talks next about her problems of finding time to talk with fellow teachers in the elemen- tary school day.

Time needs to be made for these conversations to happen, or they don't happen. We are very isolated at the elementary level. I think we are more isolated than perhaps at the secondary level. . . . We seem to be so incredibly booked up for the entire day with students. . . . I want more time for dialogue with my colleagues. We have practically no planning time at the elementary level. I have two thirty-minute plan- ning times a week when my children have physical education. I have much less than in high school. We have all the subjects and the chil- dren in the class all day. We are expected to meet all their needs no matter what level they are, and we have forty-five minutes a week when our children have art and one thirty-minute-a-week slot when our children have music. So three days a week we have thirty minutes and one day a week we have forty-five and one day a week we have nothing.

Although the secondary teachers with whom I spoke had more planning time than Sharon, they did not report using much of it for professional development. Beth, a department chair, does recall, though, that when she taught in Nova Scotia, administrators and teachers created release time in the day and scheduled voluntary meetings after school.

> We did that all the time. We would take a book on education and then the faculty would meet every other week in the library and discuss the book and the ideas. It was always something progressive, something interesting. The message I got was that education is something that is alive and developing. We talked a lot about kids and kids' learning and how kids learn.

When Beth taught in America, however, fellow teachers did not value such conversations.

> I found that when I moved into high school there was a cynicism, "You don't need to tell me that stuff. That's all theory crap." I get that a lot. "This is the real world. This is what kids are really like." It's like the heavy weight of the practical that everyone is carrying around this big bulk. "This is the way it really is." It would be lighter if we talked about some broader concepts, the philosophy. What are we trying to do? Why are we doing this? Then I think we would feel better about things. The grind gets to them. . . . There is a lot of resistance to common study already. Teachers don't want to give up their class time. And they would rather meet Saturday. "Give me the money, and I will meet on Saturday."

With the new Maine Learning Results approved, the current challenge both for teachers and administrators is to develop performance indicators that show how the standards are being met. Teachers often will say that they are meeting the standards. "Yes, I am doing this already in my classes." The challenge, then, is for teachers to go the next level and to be able to document how, when, and where they are implementing the standards in their classroom practice, including their assessments of learning. For teachers to analyze their practice in relation to the learning results, though, teachers will need ample conversational time as George, a high school principal, explains.

> [T]he high school experience of individual classrooms can be such isolating experiences for teachers. There isn't the camaraderie. There isn't the time built into most schedules for the kind of collegial conversations that need to be taking place. So at least by default, if nothing more, teachers are left to their own devices within their classrooms, unless they really work to build bridges through teaming types of arrangements, collaborative teaching with other adults, where they then get to sit down and talk about what they are doing and what they are trying to achieve with students. If more of that could be built into

the structures of schools, it would help to implement more generalized goals or learning results for students. Without that conversation among the adults, the tendency is going to be to go in whatever direction a teacher feels most comfortable with and knowledgeable about.

Creating time for teachers to convene within the school day is difficult not only for logistical reasons, but also because the public perceives that the bulk of a teacher's time should be spent working directly with students, reading their work, or planning instruction.

> In this country, we have not placed value on adults having the time to work together. In school board and teacher association negotiations, all the time is this struggle over planning and preparation time. From the school committee perspective, the worst-case scenario, if you are not working with students, then you are not working.

In other professions, practitioners seldom would be expected to work in isolation from colleagues and especially so at those times when the critical reforms in progress likely would need careful monitoring, assessment, and subsequent revision.

Critics of the position that contact with students is the appropriate use of time for teachers have asked why the five days of time typically allocated for professional development are inadequate provision for such conversation. Sharon's answer illustrates well a politics of time in her school that continues to assume that decisions about the agenda for professional development should be made by the administration rather than by consultation with the teachers themselves.

> [W]e have five in-service days. But instead of leaving us alone and letting us plan our own in-service, although they are doing better about this now, those in-service days are often planned by the administration. It's not possible to have much professional development on five days of the year when one of them is the much ballyhooed, "go get 'em" first day of school speech, and then there is the parent conference day. That takes you down to three. . . .
>
> [O]ur present school board doesn't want to spend money on any speakers or to send anyone anywhere. We have now more leeway to come up with what we want to do ourselves because it's cheap. Essentially we say to them, "Give us this day to work on our writing continuum. Give us this day to work on our reading." . . . What makes a difference in my practice is reflection, new learning, involvement—the process of redoing a curriculum and dialogue with other teachers about new learning, dialogue about curriculum development. When you are writing the curriculum and working on it, that is how you do it. We sit down and we talk about it together. I would like to have much, much more time than I have to talk with my colleagues about behavior, about literacy about math.

The current arrangement of allocating five professional days for conversation was judged inadequate by most of the teachers with whom I spoke both in terms of the sheer amount of work to be done and because agendas were set or guest speakers brought in. Such provisions did not necessarily coincide with what teachers themselves needed to talk about. For promoting collegial conversations among faculty, how frequently do teachers need to talk? George replies from an administrator's perspective:

> Is once a month on a schoolwide basis enough? I don't know. I would hope that we would be able to develop schedules that would allow for that kind of at least touching-base-conversation to take place on a daily and weekly basis among faculty, among pairs of teachers; that the conversation would become interwoven with the life of the school; that it could take place very frequently.

Redesigning the structure of school time, whether at the level of the school day or the school year, is likely to prove difficult, though, given resistance to change both from teachers and from the community.

> How to build that kind of time and feeling of commitment to that process into a high school schedule seems overwhelming. There are so many variables that go into developing the master schedule—student time versus teacher time. Certainly pressures from within the school and outside the school that are both educational and political seems to make that a daunting task. Initially, time has to be scheduled, and it has to take place in the school day, whatever the definition of the school day.
>
> Certainly, there is a lot of experimentation around the structure of the school day, week and year. But there are just so many ingrained traditions. In Maine, we have two week-long breaks from school between the first of January and mid-June, when school is dismissed for the summer. Most states in the country have one. There are an extra five days we could use somehow without lengthening the school year, which seems to be anathema for many people. However, that would mean tinkering with the sacred institution of the February break and the basketball tournament for the state. That would be a difficult hurdle to overcome at best.
>
> We have talked here about looking at trimester schedules, so that some of the frequency and continuity for professional development work would be scattered throughout the year. There would be a break of say a week between trimesters where students would not be in class, but professional development would be a part of a teacher's work year. So there could be some of the kinds of conversation that we have talked about, some of the planning that needs to take place on a regular basis.

The need for collegial conversations is recognized by teachers at every level, by principals, and in this final quote by a language arts consultant with the state of Maine. Nancy makes the key point that educational reform and the professional development needed to support it takes place over time and is not a linear process. To transform practice and assessment, teachers need to generate their own questions.

> Many schools are moving toward the Maine Learning Results and making changes in their instruction and moving a few steps at a time— a few steps forward, step or two back. As they regroup and say, "Wait, wait! Things are going too fast. Stop the world I want to get off." Maine Learning Results is a conversational document. . . . What do you see here? What are you going to do with it? How will you align your curriculum with it? What does it mean in terms of assessment and instruction? What will your instruction look like? If this is what your second-graders should be able to do at the end of second grade, what does that mean for your kindergartners? What does that mean for you as first-grade teachers? If at the end of second grade one of the performance indicators is that children can choose books, what does that tell you about your first-grade classroom? Do you think they learn to choose books once in second grade and don't have any choice before that? There are lots of questions, and you can just start asking the questions.

TIMESCAPES AND RHYTHMS OF LEARNING

From presenting the perspectives of individual students, teachers, and administrators about the issues of time in education, I will conclude by considering the need for more complex representations of time than often we find in schools today. Each of us will recognize that different temporal rhythms shape how we engage activities at home. The cadence and pacing of activities such as planting a garden, making something by hand, preparing a meal, taking a walk, or talking with friends will vary widely. In school, we know that a technical education teacher needs at least ninety minutes for the cycle of students getting out tools and projects; for the teacher to talk about the work; for hand and eye to engage the making; and then time for materials to be put away. What rhythms, though, do our students need to become absorbed in a book, engaged in computations, or immersed in a science experiment? What rhythms do teachers need to talk with each other about their own work and that of implementing the new standards?

Time has dimensions other than the line metaphor of time's arrow. The terms that we use to talk about time are critical to educational restructuring because our language and concepts reflect and shape how we define time. I use the term "timescape" to suggest that as we draw the contours of time to suit the purposes of instruction, we must attend consciously to the rhythms of the work at hand (Lofty, 1992, p. 222). The term "time frames" focus on time as a set of outer limits between classes, as in our schedules. Timescapes, however, encompass the view of time as boundaries but always in relation to time as the interior spaces in which teaching and learning occur.

As a teacher, I find it useful here to think of the movement through or across the time-space of learning in terms of an analogy to music. One of the first pieces of information that a musician reads on a score of music is the speed or tempo at which the composer judges that a piece should be performed. The scale stretches from prestissimo, very fast, through andante, a walking pace, to largo, very slow. Although these pace markers can be referenced against a numerical scale and beaten out with metronomic regularity, the terms are interpreted in the context of composer and performers rather than being absolute. That we have finely graded, linguistic differentiations to describe time in music indicates the importance we place upon it.

Despite the performative aspects of teaching and learning, and our need to describe their temporal qualities, the available language is far less complex than for music; until recently, I would argue, the need for such language has gone largely unrecognized. We have spoken of a slow learner, of a teacher going too fast and leaving students behind— imagine this happening in an orchestra. If we apply the music analogy to teaching and learning, the tempo of a student–teacher conference will be scored and conducted differently from that of a class lecture; the pacing of dialogue between small-group discussants will be different than that in large groups and will vary in relation to the exchange of ideas and their complexity. The forward motion of a writer at work will not proceed at a constant pace. Rather, the rhythm will be marked by periods of acceleration and slowing down. Stretches of high activity likely will be punctuated by and alternate with pauses and rests. Similarly, the rhythms of reading will vary as students skim and scan, and on occasion, dwell within passages or stop to reflect on an image or an idea. Yet often as teachers we have set only one rhythm. Imagine if all music were performed at the same uniform pace. How would it sound?

The language we use in school defines time primarily as a quantity to be measured—by clock and calendar. We speak of "contact" and "credit hours" and "time on task." On the timescapes of school time, the contours of instructional and curricular time are most conspicuously marked. Metaphors of "investing" and "budgeting" time carefully and using it "productively" define "time as money." In *Time and the Art of Living*, a rich set of thought-provoking meditations on time from multiple angles, Robert Grudin observes:

> We still speak and think in clichés which suggest that time is outside of us, something we "passes," something we can "spend," serve" or "kill"; something which, though admittedly part of the natural order, runs a course of its own. While natural science has attained a temporal understanding which is not only realistic but strangely beautiful and evocative, our own more general awareness of time has changed little since the days when Galileo was hauled before the Inquisition. Our world of time is as flat and exclusive as some medieval map. (p. 19)

Conversations about restructuring time in school have tended to view time as a structure that needs to be reformed as one might reorganize the architecture of space. A concept as valuable as "restructuring" has focused on time as spatial forms that we fill with instruction. We turn to the clock to measure changes, add on minutes here, shave them off there. Remember Harlan Ellison's (1997) Ticktockman.

> And so it goes. And so it goes, And so it goes. And so it goes goes goes goes goes tick tock, tick tock, tick tock, and one day we no longer let time serve us, we serve time and we are slaves of the schedule, worshippers of the sun's passing, bound into a life predicated on restrictions because the system will not function if we don't keep the schedule tight. (pp. 25–26)

If the promises of school reform are to be realized fully, in part, through reconceptualizing time, then we need definitions of time that enable us to represent the complexity of how teachers and students do and might well experience time in school. The task of defining time adequately is admittedly difficult. If schools are to serve both students and teachers and to become places where possibilities for learning are realized, then as teachers "remodel" and restructure school time, they will be wise to heed the advice of Michael Halliday speaking in another educational context about definitions of language.

> The implication for a teacher is that his [or her] own model of language should at least not fall short of that of the child . . . a minimum requirement for an educationally relevant approach to language is that it takes account of the child's own linguistic experience, defining this experience in terms of its richest potential and noting where there may be differences of orientation which could cause certain children difficulties in school. (Halliday, 1973, pp. 9–11)

So, too, whenever possible, our models of time in school should take account of those of our students, especially where there are "differences of orientation," and consider time comprehensively, in its "richest potential" rather than in restrictive and limiting ways. We need to take full account of the importance of sociological and experienced-personal time.

With the above in mind, consider now another of Hoeg's descriptions of time in *Borderliners*.

> Time is a sphere made up of language, colors, smells, senses, and sounds, a sphere in which you and the world coexist, an instrument with which to put the world in order and comprehend it, one of the reasons for your survival. (p. 257)

We are reminded here of several features of time important for any discussion about time and school reform. First, despite our primary experience of time as the frame and measure of all that we do, it constitutes and in turn is constituted by our experience of the world—a good reason, then, to study its varied representations and rhythms. Second, time is socially and politically constructed by people to serve their purposes and to meet a range of needs and interests. Time is constructed not only of and by language, and therefore of all that language makes possible, including our identities, but also the whole sensorium; time is as visceral and material as it also is abstract. Third, it is by means of time that we order the world, position and orient ourselves within it as a tool for survival.

First and last, we need to think of time not only as a line or arrow—it is these representations, too—but also as a moving sphere or multidimensional timescape in which teaching and learning occur. Students need to explore and shape time's interiority, as in turn it structures them. It is only within time, and through the time within them, that students' being in school can be realized fully. Put another way, teachers set in motion learning rhythms that in turn are restructured by students as they find their own rhythms. Teachers, too, need to talk about the new learning rhythms that curriculum reforms promote and support as well as to develop timescapes for their own professional conversations and growth.

NOTE

To Patricia Gandara, my full appreciation for her encouragement to write an essay for this collection and for the gift of additional time in which to write it. For careful readings of my work and for her ever thoughtful revision suggestions, many thanks go to Ellen Westbrook.

BIBLIOGRAPHY

Apple, Michael W. (1986). *Teachers and texts: A political economy of class and gender relations in education.* New York: Routledge & Kegan Paul.

Ben-Peretz, Miriam, & Bromme Rainer. (Eds.). (1990). *The nature of time in schools: Theoretical concepts, practitioner perceptions.* New York: Teachers College.

Berger, Peter L., & Luckman Thomas. (1967). *The social construction of reality: A treatise on the sociology of knowledge.* Garden City, NY.: Anchor.

Dalheim, Mary. (Ed.). (1994). *Time strategies.* Westhaven, CT: NEA Professional Library.

Ellison, Harlan. (1997). *Repent harlequin* (pp. 25–26). New York: Underwood.

Foucault, Michel. (1979). *Discipline and punish: The birth of the prison.* Trans. Alan Sheridan. New York: Vintage.

Grudin, Robert. (1988). *Time and the art of living.* New York: Ticknor & Fields.

Halliday, Michael. (1973). *Explorations in the functions of language.* London: Elsevier.

Hoeg, Peter. (1994). *Borderliners.* New York: Farrar, Staus & Giroux.

Lofty, John S. (1992). *Time to write: The influence on time and culture on learning to write.* Albany: State University of New York Press.

National Education Commission on Time and Learning. (1993). *Annual report fiscal year 1992.* Washington, DC: U.S. Government Printing Office.

National Education Commission on Time and Learning. (1994). *Prisoners of time.* Washington, DC: U.S. Government Printing Office.

Rutz, Henry J. (Ed.). (1992). *The politics of time.* American Ethnological Society Monograph Series, No. 4. Washington DC: American Anthropological Association.

Thoreau, Henry D. (1960). *Walden.* Ed. Sherman Paul. Boston: Houghton Mifflin.

Zerubavel, Eviatar. (1981). *Hidden rhythms: Schedules and calendars in social life.* Berkeley: University of California Press.

CHAPTER 11

When Time Is on Our Side: Redesigning Schools to Meet the Needs of Immigrant Students

Laurie Olsen and Ann Jaramillo

Walk into almost any traditional comprehensive high school in this nation—from Florida to Maine, from New York to California—and you'll see something remarkably the same. Bells ring every fifty minutes, and students pour out of classrooms for a noisy, jostling few minutes of "passing time" as they make their way from one classroom to another, shouting greetings at friends, stopping at lockers to get their books. The bell rings again and the halls suddenly become quiet. Students have found their way to their next class. A new subject. A new teacher. Another text. Learning is sliced neatly into six or seven distinct "subjects," each granted a fifty-minute slot per day. Students pass through six or seven subjects each day. Teachers see a succession of groups of twenty-five to thirty-five students (depending on the state) passing through their classrooms each day—totaling a norm of 125 to 150 students per day.

These high schools are the tail end of the public schooling system that has been defined for almost a century as a thirteen year sequence from kindergarten through twelfth grade. Each year students pass from one grade to another. One grade-level curriculum in one year's time. A national textbook industry and strong national professional networks of educators have resulted in remarkable similarity of curriculum from state to state despite the fact that the United States does not formally have a national schooling system (Apple & Christian Smith, 1991). Tenth-grade teachers throughout the nation greeting students who are

225

fifteen years old assume that their students have received nine or ten years of prior schooling, and that they can base their curriculum on what that schooling has purportedly included. This is a lockstep system with expected age-grade relationships (Olsen & Chen, 1988; Slavin, 1987; Oakes, 1985). It's no wonder we have come to think about the large, comprehensive high school as a factory model.

It is a rational, aligned, deeply imprinted system. And yet this model of schooling is dramatically unsuited to our society today. As educators have grown more and more aware of the importance of interdisciplinary learning, and of making connections across the curriculum, there have been critically important movements within public schooling to rethink how we structure learning (Goodlad, 1984; Sizer, 1984; Gardner, 1985). There is growing awareness that the factory model approach to schooling is an awkward, rigid, inflexible, and inappropriate structure. This is particularly true for the increasing population of immigrant students.

During the 1980s, the United States experienced the largest flow of immigrants since the turn of the last century. Fully one-third of the population growth in this nation in the last decade was due to immigration (Portes & Rumbaut, 1990; First & Carrera, 1990; McDonnell & Hill, 1993). Nationwide, the foreign born population has reached its highest level in nearly seventy years—immigrants make up 9.3 percent of the U.S. population. In this decade, almost twenty-five million newcomers from every continent in the world have joined an already diverse population in the United States to form an unprecedented mixture of cultures, languages, national backgrounds, and ethnicities. Because of the youthfulness and high birth rates among immigrant groups, these changes are being felt most dramatically in the schools, where close to 3 million schoolchildren face the leap of cultures, national experience, adjustments of immigration, and the challenge of learning English (Hopstock & Bucaro, 1993). First- and second-generation immigrant children are the fastest growing segment of the U.S. population under age fifteen (Fix & Zimmerman, 1993). The 1990 U.S. Census counted 2.1 million foreign born children in the United States. If children born in the United States to immigrant parents are included, the total is 5 million (Fix & Passel, 1994). In California, the most impacted state, immigrants comprise close to one-fourth of the school population—language minorities almost one-third (California Department of Education, 1996).

NEWCOMERS, NEW CHALLENGES, NEW NEEDS

Public schools are required by law to create educational programs that assure full access to the curriculum for students regardless of whether they can speak, understand, or utilize English (*Lau v. Nichols*, 1974). This is out of recognition that lack of English proficiency constitutes a barrier to educational access and opportunity. One of the major hurdles facing immigrant students is the need to become English speakers, English writers, and English readers—in addition to the regular academic tasks students face of learning social studies, math, science, and all the other subjects. While most immigrant students learn conversational English relatively quickly, they generally need four to ten years to become fluent enough to really comprehend the language and use it as a medium of academic learning (Collier & Thomas, 1997). And it requires strong, sustained instruction and support in English as a second language to help them develop that literacy.

During these long years (sometimes almost an entire public schooling career) immigrant students also need a way of learning all their other subjects—or they will fall further and further behind academically. Immigrants, particularly those coming from war-disrupted nations or very poor and rural areas, are in greatest danger of being seriously hampered because they often begin school already academically behind. School districts all over the nation are reporting an increase in these "underschooled" or "preliterate" adolescents. When they enter the United States many middle school and high school students lack literacy in even their own languages, but they're still expected to perform literately, learn English, and somehow catch up academically to U.S.-born peers who have had at least seven years of schooling (Olsen, 1988).

Even those who may have been in U.S. schools since their early years often have not yet developed by the time they reach high school the strong English language literacy needed for full participation and success in English-taught secondary school classrooms. They haven't yet "gotten there" in terms of English literacy—and are effectively foreclosed from courses requiring a lot of reading and writing and critical thinking—precisely the gatekeeping courses that lead to further education. While these students have varying levels of oral English fluency and academic content knowledge, most schools report that the average continuing LEP student from elementary schools in the United States has a fourth- to sixth-grade academic skill level when she or he enters high school—far below the academic level expected for the standard ninth-grade curriculum (Minicucci & Olsen, 1992; Fleischman & Hopstock, 1993). Even when these students are orally fluent in English, they may be weak in reading comprehension and writing. Most achieve oral English fluency, but not the literacy needed to compete in challenging academic areas. Many are placed in remedial classes. Continuing LEP students have been gloomily labeled "ESL lifers." Within this group are immigrant students who have been classified as LEP since kindergarten but whose mobility and frequent school changes, and movement from one type of bilingual program to another without consistency, have left them without a strong literacy base in either English or their home language.

Compounding the challenge is that our school year doesn't correspond neatly to the patterns of migration of the large number of immigrants involved in farmwork and the migratory patterns of following the crops—nor does it fit well with the yearly migrations back to Mexico to spend the holidays with family and loved ones.

It is these students for whom the rigid curriculum and program structure of a traditional secondary school simply doesn't work. Addressing the needs of these students requires approaches to developing basic literacy in an accelerated fashion, more time spent in instruction and support to accommodate the extra academic tasks they face, instructional approaches that support comprehension and language development throughout the curriculum, mechanisms for filling the gaps they often have in academic content, and readjustments of the school calendar to meet their real-life needs.

The extra language challenge all of these immigrant students face—of developing full literacy in English, and needing ways to make the curriculum comprehensible to them either in their native language or in special instruction through English—simply takes time. Not only do they need to continue to learn everything their English-fluent and U.S.-born peers are learning, but they have to develop in English at a faster rate than one year's growth in one year's time if they are ever to close the gaps between themselves and their English-fluent peers (Collier & Thomas, 1997). And most have to accelerate their studies in the content subjects of the curriculum—to overcome gaps, to catch up to the content taught in the U.S. curriculum.

Jumping from subject to subject in fifty-minute intervals. Trying to learn from six to seven different teachers in a day—none of whom has time to get to know the students. Trying to decode the language, absorb the content in a not-yet-comprehensible language while sitting in fifty-minute classes that offer little time to ask questions, to slow the teacher down to clarify what is happening—is a recipe for frustration. Secondary school curriculum is based on assumptions that the students have basic literacy skills, are able to read and write, and have had exposure to the basic curricular concepts. These assumptions simply don't hold for many of the immigrant students in our schools.

And so, thoughtful educators, witnessing the high school failure rates and dropout rates of immigrant students, have had to rethink how we go about structuring schooling for this new population. In doing so, they have had to grapple as well with a complex array of needs that go beyond academics and language.

All newcomers face adjustment to new culture and language, but the size of gaps they have to bridge, the resources they can bring to the adjustment, and their success in making the transition differ enormously; some are far more at-risk than others (Ima, 1995; Olsen, 1988). Children from war-torn nations are often plagued by post-traumatic stress syndrome, with deep emotional scars from being victims of the chaos and violence. There is a high incidence of physical disabilities among them as well. Without good bilingual and bicultural counseling supports, referrals and availability of health and mental health services, and staff who can recognize such trauma, these students are unable to really participate in their schooling. Mobility is very high for many immigrants—both within the United States as their families pursue economic and support niches in the new land, and movement back and forth to their homeland to see family left behind. For students from Mexico this movement back and forth can be and is more frequent—and seldom coincides with the particular whims of the academic school year calendar. Crucial units of the curriculum may be missed, credits toward graduation may be lost because of attendance problems, and the student faces the difficulties of adjustment and transition with each move. The initial adjustment for newcomers is particularly difficult.

Even our schools are foreign. Here immigrant students face the social challenges of coming to understand themselves and others, as well as challenges in comprehending the schooling system. Some adjustments are simply the immediate orientation to a new society. Many students are in large industrialized urban areas for the first time. Many of our schools have populations larger than the villages or regions from which immigrants have come. In large schools, they have to learn the oddities of bells ringing, lockers, and cafeteria lines. But the most important difference is that our teaching approaches, school structures and expectations, and the very processes of teaching and learning are different from schooling systems in many parts of the world. For example, the relationship between U.S. students and teachers is more informal than that in many Asian countries. U.S. students are expected to voice opinions during class discussions (Olsen, 1997). The tests that are given are relatively insignificant, and don't determine the direction of one's future, as they often do abroad. Another big adjustment for many immigrant students is being expected to speak up in class and voice their opinions and perspectives. Many schooling systems have students recite as a group and discourage individuality. There is a tremendous need for orientation, for help in connecting to the new world and the new ways. And this, too, takes time and deliberate structures that are more human-scale.

ADJUSTING THE SCHOOLS TO MEET THESE NEEDS
REQUIRES TIME—IT TAKES TIME TO CHANGE

The impact of the immigration wave has been felt strongly in public schools nationwide, as teachers and students face each other across divides of culture, language, and national background. Teachers, mostly ill prepared for the challenges of diverse classrooms and seldom sharing a language with their immigrant students, are often baffled by the cultural implications of teaching and learning, and many don't know how to communicate with children with whom they don't share a language. While the challenges are increasingly clear, we have yet to create a schooling system that truly addresses the problems of an increasingly diverse population, including underachievement, lack of access, and the need for strong social and educational support. The current school reform movements have done little to address these barriers (Olsen et al., 1994; Gándara, 1994; Olsen, 1995). Our schools, which were designed for a more homogeneous population, and with little flexibility to meet the kinds of needs immigrants present, have become caught in a time warp. Too few teachers are trained in bilingualism and second language acquisition, and even fewer have knowledge of their students' cultures (National Center for Educational Statistics, 1997; Gándara & Sun, 1986; Olsen, 1990). Rarely do schools offer limited English speakers good language access to curriculum, nor do they provide strong multicultural curricula that speak to the experiences of diverse communities.

As educators have become caught up in the dilemma of trying to teach without the full capacity or sets of skills and strategies to reach their new student population, in schools structured in ways that mitigate against addressing their needs, they have turned their attention to trying to change that structure (Olsen & Mullen, 1990; Raywid, 1993; Watson et al., 1992). One of the things they have discovered is that change takes time. Time to engage in professional development. Time to collaborate with other teachers. Time to sit and try to reach consensus about shifting how the school day is structured. Time to inquire and reflect on what is not working and on what their students need.

It is for these reasons that when California Tomorrow, a nonprofit organization working to help schools adjust to the demographic changes of immigration, was invited by the Andrew Mellon Foundation to partner with high schools to develop new models of "immigrant-responsive" secondary schools, the issue of "time" was central to the agenda. This essay focuses on the experiences and lessons from that demonstration project—and shares how some schools have attempted to meet the challenge of re-creating schools to serve immigrants by creating the time that educators need to change their practice and to change the nature of the program they offer their students—and by taking on the rigidity of the traditional high school and structuring time differently within the instructional program in order to better meet the needs of a diverse population.

The California Tomorrow project began with an understanding that the challenge was not to define a single, static programmatic or structural model of a secondary school, but to develop in schools the habits and structures that would result in ongoing responsiveness and accountability for meeting the needs of whichever mixes of languages, cultures, and immigrant groups enrolled in the school. Their approach identified a complex of six interdependent process "principles" at the core of immigrant-responsive high schools.

- Change takes time. How time is used in schools must be rethought and restructured to allow educators to develop the skills and understandings to respond to immigrant students' needs, and time must be rethought and the school day and year restructured around the needs of students.

- Responsiveness requires capacity. Investment in ongoing, sustained professional development in collaborative and individual formats is at the center of responsive schools.

- The challenges of teaching and schooling in this era of complex cultural, linguistic relations require immersion in inquiry and reflection, as educators seek to work with students across cultural, language, and national experiences.

- Accountability for inclusion and access for immigrant students, and deepened understandings of the needs of immigrant populations requires data systems and processes of analyzing data about student achievement, participation, and progress through school.

- Much is already known about effective schooling for language minority and immigrant students—and schools throughout the nation are engaged in cutting-edge development of new models to address new challenges. A responsive school is engaged in reading and assessing the research, and checking out the models of what others are doing for potential replication or transfer of experience.

- Responsive schools elicit and respond to the voices and concerns of their immigrant students, parents, and communities.

None of these alone is sufficient. The California Tomorrow project has demonstrated a powerful impact on building the capacity of schools to respond to their immigrant students and on improving student outcomes. This essay illustrates the interrelationship of the principles and the central role that the rethinking and re-creating of time in high schools plays.

TIME AND STUDENT NEEDS: MAKING TIME WORK FOR US

Four years ago, the faculty from Alisal High School in Salinas, California, sat in a retreat together and hammered out their ideas for changing their school. Alisal is a school of almost all Latino language minority students, situated in a rural agricultural community in Central California. Over half of the students are immigrants who are limited English-proficient—many are farmworkers themselves, or the children of farmworkers. The faculty of Alisal are dedicated teachers with many ideas. Some had been excited about increasing the uses of technology in the school. Others felt the real emphasis ought to be on better guidance systems for the students who were on the verge of dropping out. One group had been to conferences together, and engaged in many excited conversations about the school-to-work transition and the possible creation of career-oriented "academies" within the school. The conversation was full of many reform ideas and possibilities, but little coherent vision. One idea seemed as good as another, until the group stopped and listened to their students.

A panel of six students from the school, supported by a group of the reform-oriented teachers, had run a series of focus groups with a cross-section of classes at the school—from AP to mainstream to ESL, ninth grade through twelfth grade. Filled with the concerns and voices of their peers, these students stood in front of their teachers and counselors and presented the findings to the faculty, who were instructed to "simply listen." The students shared a litany of comments, concerns, hopes, and fears about proposed changes for Alisal High School. Deeply moved, the educators who were present began to work on the "problem" of time. Consistently throughout the more than three years since that definitive retreat, staff at the school have credited the student focus groups and panel with sharply focusing their reform energies and motivating the changes to come. In an extraordinary exchange between students and educators, the reform plan came to be shaped.

One area of concern for this largely farmworker school was the traditional six-period day. Students spoke of how hard it is to keep up in all their subjects, and voiced ideas such as, "we have jobs after school, and with six classes a day it's impossible to concentrate enough on each one." They expressed concerns that "lots of kids work" and "when you're working, you can't do your homework for six different subjects every night—you have to make choices and then you get behind in something." Students also indicated strong dissatisfaction with the teaching being done within the six-period day. Complaints ranged from the more typical "classes are boring" to "my teachers just talk and talk and I can't keep it all in my head and after a while the English gets too hard to just be hour after hour trying to listen and understand" to "we need higher expectations: things need to be more challenging" to "some teachers think they are like doctors where they give us a pill and then send us away." And there was a general awareness that many students were not doing well, that some came to school to "kick back" and were allowed to disrupt or not be involved in class. The overriding concern, however, was that students believed they were not learning what they need to learn: "We're not learning what the kids over at Salinas High are learning." "We get second-grade stuff." Embedded in this fear was the unspoken realization that the expectations at Alisal High did not represent the demands of the real world beyond this community. Students felt they were being failed by the school and that their preparation needed to become more rigorous.

The idea of changing how time was used emerged from what had been a long list of possible reform ideas for the school to become a centerpiece. When shown by their teachers a possible block schedule format with three ninety-eight minute blocks per day, students were excited. They felt it would be great to be able to concentrate on just three subjects a semester, and to do homework for just a few subjects each night. They also recognized that block scheduling had the potential to really enhance science classes—a beginning recognition of the rich potential longer periods might hold for how teaching and learning could occur. "It would be great to have a long period where you could really get into a lab experiment and finish it! As it is now, we have to set it up, do a little bit of the experiment, put it away, and then the next day reset it up, try to remember where you are, do a little more, put it away, and then pull it out again the next day. Like that. Three days in a row. And it wastes all this time getting it out and putting it away over and over, and if you have questions or don't understand—too bad, no time!"

Conversely, students recognized that merely having a longer class period would not fix the teaching of an already disorganized or ineffective teacher. They were afraid that classes that were boring as fifty-minute periods would be "deadly" if they were ninety-eight minutes long. They told the teachers that they hoped classes would become more interactive, with a variety of projects and activities each period. They even thought students might be more focused with longer periods—and they might learn more, and have more of a chance to really connect with their teachers. This last point was important—another major student concern was they wanted their teachers to "know" them and care about them.

Intergroup relations was another issue raised by the students, in particular the ESL students. They felt "isolated" and "categorized into a group of our own"; "no one else talks to us" and "we can't make American friends." Newly arrived immigrant students expressed hurt and dismay that "there is so much discrimination—among our own people—the Mexicans who have been here don't want to be with Mexicans who just got here." "Most students here are Mexican and can speak Spanish, but they pretend sometimes that they don't speak it when they are around us." Additionally, the ESL students felt afraid and insecure about not knowing English and unaware of how to get information about clubs, sports, and other school activities—and very unsure whether they would be welcomed in those activities that are so central to this high school. "Help us make friends and be part of the school," they pleaded.

These student voices were crucial in defining how the restructuring of Alisal High evolved. A block schedule was created, and the school year was changed to address their concerns and the reality of their lives. For example, latecomers—immigrants who enter the school after the school year has started—and students who leave for extended periods to go to Mexico to be with family during the Christmas holidays or who have to follow the crops as migrant farmworkers are a large part of the Alisal student population. These students were frequently left with incompletes in their classes because of missed schooling, perpetuating patterns of falling further and further behind their peers in school and not progressing toward graduation. The new block schedule (condensing a term into a shorter time period by doubling the content through ninety-eight-minute periods) was coupled with a change in the school year calendar. The first term now ends around the beginning of November, permitting students who leave to accrue credits at that point.

The clear need for more academic support for a student body with large numbers of failing students led to another new use of time. A tutorial for each "block" was added to the regular school day so that students could have in-school time each week to complete homework and catch up in their classes. Their actual course teachers now run the tutorials, so there is a formal structure for getting more help and clarification.

A twice-weekly enrichment (advisory) period was also instituted. The enrichment period fulfilled several purposes, and spoke directly to the concerns of students about the need to break down the intergroup barriers that existed at the high school. Each enrichment class consists of students across the four grade levels (9–12), and is representative of the language proficiency levels at the school. Each enrichment class has Special Education students, "honors" and "GATE" students, ESL students, and others. One enrichment period a week was also set aside for club meetings and activities. Placing these activities prominently within the school day, at a set time, has provided far more students the opportunity to participate and heightened awareness of ways in which students could become more meaningfully connected to their school experience. For newcomers, this is especially important—for many of their parents want them to come immediately home from school, and do not understand the importance of extracurricular activities in the U.S. high school. For students who work after school, this arrangement also provides an avenue for their involvement.

The final addition to the new schedule at Alisal was a collaboration time for teachers at the end of the day. A faculty subcommittee had struggled with the competing elements of "minutes of instructional time" mandated by the state, and with teacher contract issues that mitigated against any extra unpaid time for teachers, and the very real need to carve out some time in the schedule when teachers could meet and collaborate on a regular basis. They compromised with the creation of a "voluntary" collaboration time of a half hour placed at the end of each school day. As the faculty designed the new schedule, they also made a compact that would strongly influence the success of the effort: Instructional time would be kept sacred, with none of the typical interruptions that eat up class periods, such as attendance slips, announcements on the intercom, issuing school passes, and so on. This compact was upheld loyally, and the teachers were amazed at how it strengthened the focus on learning in their classrooms.

School opened in the fall of 1994 to this new schedule with a sense of tremendous excitement. But the schedule itself was not enough to deliver on the promise. It was a shell, an opportunity. The challenge now was to use that time, and Alisal began to realize the deep levels of work it would take to realize its potential.

Close examination of many secondary classrooms reveals wasted minutes, time ill-spent on attendance or tardies, and a general lack of a sense of urgency about the preciousness of each moment of the class period. Moreover, for many classrooms, there is no overriding focus, no principles that guide teachers in effectively structuring their classrooms for wiser use of time. This was as true for Alisal in the new schedule as it was in the old. The simple creation of collaborative time for teachers does not mean that this time will be used either wisely or productively. Teachers need a reason to collaborate, a reason to begin the difficult but rewarding process of critically examining the restructuring of classrooms to leverage the structural opportunities that longer periods or

OLD	NEW
Summary Features:	*Summary Features:*

Summary Features:

Six periods per day of fifty-four minutes each; semester courses run from September through January, and January through June. Students take six subjects at a time; Teachers teach approximately 180 students per day. Clubs are after school. No collaboration time for teachers. No tutorials.

Bell Schedule:

8:15–9:09   Period One
9:15–10:09 Period Two
10:15–11:09 Period Three
11:15–12:09 Period Four
12:09–1:04 LUNCH
1:04–1:58   Period Five
2:04–2:58   Period Six

Summary Features:

Three class periods per day of ninety-eight minutes each. A one-semester course runs approximately 2.5 months. Students take three subjects at a time, with a weekly tutorial in each course in addition. Teachers teach approximately sixty to ninety students per day. Tutorials are built into the day. Clubs and enrichment are built into the day

Bell Schedule:

8:00–9:38   Block I
9:38–9:51   Nutrition Break
9:51–10:29 Tutorial (Block I tutorial on Monday, Block II tutorial on Wednesday, Block III tutorial on Friday). Enrichment Advisory on Tuesday and Thursdays
10:39–12:17 Block 2
12:17–1:07 Lunch
1:07–2:45   Block 3
2:45–3:15   Voluntary Collaboration Time

Benefits:

Teachers see fewer students per day and for longer periods of time so closer relations are possible
Stronger academic focus
Fewer subjects to concentrate on
More interactive, intensive teaching and learning are possible
Built-in tutorials provide essential academic support
Clubs and extracurricular life of the school are built into the day, maximizing participation by all students
There are regular structured ways of "mixing" students across grade levels, language proficiencies
Collaboration time is built in for teachers

blocks of time afford. The challenge facing Alisal was to find a way to use the opportunities created through the new schedule, to answer to their students' concerns. The classes would need to be focused, interactive, and interesting. They needed to figure out how to use tutorial time to provide the kind of academic support their language minority population needed, and to create relationships with students. And the large educational task was to find ways to address the literacy needs of their students.

The summer preceding the fall of 1994 school-opening was preparation time: dialogue about creating an academic focus, training in new consistent discipline approaches across the school—professional development in project-oriented and interactive instruction—and a frantic down-to-the-wire effort to schedule students into a new master schedule template. But even this was not enough. There was some immediate payoff for the students and teachers at the school, but it would take several years for dramatic shifts in how instruction was being delivered. A contrast between classrooms in the spring of 1994 and the spring of 1997 illustrates how time in a classroom can be used in radically different ways—a change from where the focus is unclear, to a focus where emphasis on literacy is the heart and soul of every moment, from where students engage in a series of fragmented tasks to where they are immersed in multiple approaches and ways "in" to their learning.

Scenario 1, Spring 1994:

The tardy bell rings, and five or six students shuffle in from the hall to Mr. Hagen's third-period "sheltered" literature class. Of the twenty-seven other students already in the classroom, ten are seated at their desks; the others are milling around, chatting amiably in their primary languages. Several are in line to sharpen pencils; others are fiddling around with their binders or notebooks. One looks bored, staring blankly into space, slumped in his chair. Five girls are seated in a circle, laughing and sharing some secret. Two hold mirrors, lipstick, eyeliner, and mascara in their hands, carefully reapplying makeup.

A quick visual survey of the room reveals a bright, well-lit classroom with thirty-five desks placed in rows. Colorful posters with motivational slogans line the walls: "You can do it!" A small bookcase under the window holds an assortment of magazines, teacher curriculum guides, and novels. One bulletin board boasts an "excellent student work" space. Five student essays, three paragraphs each, are tacked up for display. The teacher stands at the front of the classroom, pulling various stacks of papers out of his briefcase, consulting his roll book, and writing the date and several other items on the chalkboard. He talks and jokes pleasantly with Lorena, Gilberto, and Sandra, who stand grouped around his desk.

Six minutes into the forty-five minute period, Mr. Hagen calls out genially to the group, "Okay, class, it's time to get started. Time's a wasting. Jose, sit down please. Angelica, would you please pass out the books? Also, everyone please get out a piece of paper for a journal topic." Five more minutes pass as students get seated, shuffle through their binders to find a paper, or ask their neighbor for a piece. "Class, your journal topic is on the board. I want you to write about what you did this weekend." Mr. Hagen sits down at his desk and begins to look through some student papers, raising his head occasionally to remind the class to be quiet. One student calls out, "Mr. Hagen, I don't get it, you mean everything we did this weekend, all of it?" As the teacher crosses the room to consult with the student, he notices two students appear to be doing some math homework instead of their journal writing; several students stop him and tell him they either don't have a paper or a pencil. Another calls out, "Teacher, I didn't understand the homework last night so I didn't do it." Mr. Hagen ignores him and again admonishes the class to write. Finally, ten minutes later, most students have written five to six lines on their paper, a few have filled a page. Some have written nothing.

Twenty-three minutes into the period, Mr. Hagen says, "Class, save your papers until Friday. I'll pick them up then. Open your books to page 62. We're going to read a story today and you're going to really enjoy it a lot." Over the course of the next fifteen minutes, the students take turns reading aloud from "The Circuit," a story by Francisco Jimenez about the life of migrant farmworkers who must pack up, move on, and leave behind their homes over and over again as they follow the harvest When students stumble over a word, Mr. Hagen gently corrects them. Three students refuse to read when called on, and the teacher moves to another student. In the course of the fifteen minutes, eight students get the opportunity to read. Domingo and Mario at the back have their eyes closed and are obviously napping; Juan is working diligently on writing a local gang name in Old English script. Most of the others appear to be listening to the story, if not actually following along. Mr. Hagen stops occasionally to ask a question: "Who is the character? What is he doing? What does that word mean?" With seven minutes left in the period, Mr. Hagen tells the students to close their books and to pass them to the front. "For homework tonight, just finish your vocabulary paper you were working on yesterday. If you have it finished, you don't have homework." The students spend the last five minutes of class talking to friends, lining up at the door, and getting out money to buy sodas and chips at the snack bar.

Mr. Hagen's classroom in 1994 may at first seem entirely appropriate and better off than many. He is obviously organized and cares about the students—and the students are working. But ask these questions about the use of time in Mr. Hagen's classroom: How many students are actually engaged in literacy tasks, and for how many minutes? Is there any connection between the assignments? How much time do many of the students spend doing nothing connected to learning? Now consider these questions when reading the next scenario, Mr. Hagen's classroom three years later.

Scenario 2, Spring 1997:

The tardy bell rings and Mr. Hagen quietly shuts the door. Of the thirty-two students in this Block 3, ninety-eight-minute sheltered literature class, twenty-nine are seated at their desks, which are arranged in groups of four. The other three are thumbing through paperback books on a revolving bookcase in the corner of the room. Most of the students have their individual paperbacks open and are already beginning to read. Mr. Hagen announces to the class, "The bell has rung and you should be reading now." He then moves to the three students at the bookcase and assists them in picking out new reading material. To one he suggests, "You've been reading books by Gary Soto. Here is another one you might like." He reminds another student how to peruse the back cover of a book to see if it holds interest. Within about five minutes, the three students have chosen a new book to try.

For the next twenty minutes, all students in the class are reading, except for Maria and Teresa, who are both fidgeting and seem unable to concentrate. Mr. Hagen spends some time conferencing quietly with each one. After some conversation, Maria begins to read. Teresa is encouraged to try another book—it turns out she thinks the one she began last week is "really boring." Twenty minutes into the period, Mr. Hagen rings a small bell and announces, "Please get out your reading logs and work on them for the next few minutes." All students spend the next five minutes recording the number of pages read and fill out the part of the log that asks them to "summarize what happened on the pages you read today."

As students finish writing their reading logs, Mr. Hagen asks individuals in each group to help in passing out the journals for the group. He turns on the overhead projector to display the journal topic, "Write about a time when you had to move and leave someone you loved, or something you loved behind." Nine or ten students have the topic written already, and are beginning to write. Some look like they are stuck, or don't quite understand the prompt. The teacher speaks, "Let's put a few ideas here on the overhead for those of you who can't think of something right away. I'll put the first example. One time when I was eleven, we moved from California to Texas. I had to leave behind my best friend."

He writes *"best friend"* on the overhead, and then asks the class for three or four other examples. *"My grandmother," "a pet," "a house you like," "a school"* are subsequently written up for all to see. As the students begin to write, Mr. Hagen circulates and quietly assists students who need help with a word or idea, or are just slow getting started. As others work, he is able to spend a solid ten minutes with one student who appears to be having difficulty with vocabulary—and to suggest that they work together on this assignment again at the tutorial the next day.

A rapid tour of the classroom this time around discloses a much different environment than the prior three years. Student work covers almost every inch of available wall space. The work appears to be grouped in different categories: Under the sign *"Interacting with Text"* are examples of dialectical journals, with quotes from *"The Pearl"* on one side and student responses on the other. Brightly illustrated *"Open Minds"* dominate one section: the directions above each graphic say: *"Show what Kino was thinking and feeling at the end of the book. Use symbols, graphics, and quotes."* The side wall closest to the door reveals a collection of student-constructed plot outlines and graphic organizers for three or four pieces of literature. The printed sign above reads, *"Schema Building—How are these pieces of literature all the same?"* Next to the window stand two revolving book stands stocked with a wide selection of interesting, age-appropriate but readable fiction and nonfiction paperbacks. In boxes labeled *"Reading Logs"* are class sets of folders—a survey of several shows that students are engaged in free voluntary reading three times a week, and are responsible for summarizing the stories as they proceed. Manila folders in boxes labeled *"Portfolios"* contain collections of student-selected and teacher-selected work, similar to the work displayed on the walls.

Forty minutes into the block, Mr. Hagen asks students to finish up their last sentence in their journals, and to have one student from their team replace the journals in the appropriate box. He then says, *"Remember, I will be reading and commenting on your journals this weekend. You will have my comments and your points on Monday.*

"Now please open your books to page 62. We're going to read a story today titled 'The Circuit.' The journal topic you just wrote about is connected to this story in some ways." Over the course of the next six minutes, Mr. Hagen asks the students to predict what the story will be about from the title, and from the title of the journal topic. He then asks

for a student volunteer to come to the front to help him model a strat-egy, telling the class, "Look at our reciprocal teaching strategy poster on the front wall. Which of the strategies have you learned how to do?" Twenty hands shoot up, and Maria calls out, "We know questioning." "That's right, Maria," Mr. Hagen responds. "Today I'm going to model for you, and you are going to practice the next one, summarizing." Over the course of the next ten minutes, Mr. Hagen and Diego, the volunteer, model how to read aloud a paragraph of the text with a partner, with one person reading and the other summarizing what is read. He then tells them that they are going to read the first two pages of the story with their partner, using the summarizing strategy. Students appear to be familiar with pair work; several complain that their partner is absent. Mr. Hagen quickly pairs them up. As the students read aloud to each other, the noise level in the room rises considerably. Several pairs pull their desks to the side of the room so they can hear each other better. The teacher circulates to keep students on task, although it seems that they all are reading. Students participate in the reciprocal reading activ-ity for the next fifteen minutes.

With about twenty-five minutes left in the period, the teacher passes out a dialectical journal form that asks students to summarize in the left-hand column, and to create questions that are "on the surface" and "under the surface" in the right-hand column. He tells the class, "I'm going to model for you how to complete this dialectical journal. You will be practicing summarizing the story, and we will be working hard on how to ask questions that are 'under the surface' of the story, questions that are 'hard' and for which there might or might not be an answer." Mr. Hagen reads page 3 of the story aloud, paragraph by paragraph. He calls strategically on students to summarize the different sections, and writes on the overhead on his copy the summaries. He asks students to think of "under the surface" questions for each section, giving them time to think. Twelve different students offer questions to the group—each is recorded in the right-hand column, and all students copy them.

With five minutes left in the period, Mr. Hagen says, "Okay. Thank you. Nice job. Please put these dialectical journals in your binder. Tomorrow we will continue with the story. You will be reading more of the story in your groups, except you will be summarizing, asking the questions, and recording them without my help. Your homework for tonight is to read again the first two pages, and write down ten good questions, just like you do when you use the questioning strategy with a partner." He models two questions on the overhead, and just as he fin-ishes, the bell rings. The students cram their books in their backpacks, say good-bye, and rush out the door. In their next class, the social stud-

ies teacher, who has worked closely with Mr. Hagen, will again use reciprocal reading, summarizing, and dialectic journals—this is literacy throughout the curriculum.

The second scenario shows what can happen when a teacher, with the focus of accelerating literacy for ESL students, transforms his classroom into a place where every minute counts. The 98-minute block served as an essential vehicle for Mr. Hagen to accomplish what he and his colleagues had identified as the focus for their in-classroom efforts: acceleration of literacy in primary language and English for students enrolled in English as a Second Language, Specially Designed Academic Instruction in English (SDAIE or Sheltered), and Spanish content classes. They had to come to a deep understanding of literacy development, and then developed teaching strategies that integrated multiple literacy skills into whatever they teach. The students in scenario 2 were engaged in learning through almost the entire ninety-eight minutes—and the learning drew on their own life experiences in the farmworker community.

THE USES OF TEACHER TIME
TO GET FROM "THERE" TO "HERE"

Of course, for Alisal teachers to get from scenario 1 to scenario 2 itself took *time—a lot of time, and time well spent.* Time is an essential ingredient of change. A group of teachers at Alisal had to choose to spend intensive time together over the course of several years to identify, define and operationalize an "accelerated literacy" approach for their students in the bilingual program. After all, how time spent with students can be improved is dependent on the amount, nature, and quality of the time teachers spend together.

Spotlighting literacy as the focus at Alisal involved a series of collaborations in which teachers used their time in different and interesting ways outside the classroom. Ensuring that literacy remained the focus in classrooms required a series of activities that involved use of teacher time both in and outside the classroom. The story of the transformation of "Mr. Hagen's" classroom is a journey on those two, simultaneous paths, one in which teachers began to explore what issues or content they might collaborate around, and one in which teachers engaged in looking at how well they were individually and collectively implementing the agreed-upon "what."

After the first year of block scheduling, a core group of teachers, including Mr. Hagen at Alisal High School and dubbed the "Working Group on Language and Culture," began a year-long exploration into what a quality education might look like for immigrant and LEP students. The actual path the group took evolved over the course of the year, but began with a kickoff Saturday retreat in September in which the teachers met with two teachers from International High School in New York City who shared their vision for working with immigrant students. This retreat provided one day where the working group could look at a structural, curricular, and pedagogical model that operated in a very different context from their own. It opened their eyes to other possibilities, to other ways of doing business that went beyond just creating a new block schedule and included ways of restructuring the inner workings of classrooms.

The retreat led to a series of voluntary after-school meetings in which the group continued to read research, review other models of curriculum and instruction, look at samples of their own students' work, and engage in conversation about the implications of their inquiry. It was through examining his students' writing that Mr. Hagen, for example, really began to see there was a literacy problem for most of his students. The after-school meetings were scheduled for two-hour slots for six consecutive weeks so intensive work could go on. The teachers had long since recognized that the voluntary collaboration time built into every school day was hardly ever used for collaboration and instead was usually used up for tidying up the various loose ends of a teaching day. More time was needed. Although the teachers had initially committed to the after-school time, consistent attendance suffered from the perennial overcommitment syndrome of the best secondary teachers: coaching, university courses to fulfill credential requirements, parent meetings, all intruded on the process. Additionally, the time was unpaid time. Without the carrot of pay, many secondary teachers are unwilling or unable to give the extra time.

Nevertheless, for a period of time before more formal extended collaboration time could be arranged, the series of meetings served as a valuable springboard for another day-long retreat to review and rethink the bilingual program at the school. For this event, teachers were released for a whole school day. They, and the school, realized that serious visioning and planning were necessary—and a legitimate use of teachers' time. It was through the creative combination of the short, daily built-in collaboration time, sometimes whole-day release time from classrooms, occasional retreats, and intensive summertime collaboration that the teachers put together a schedule that could support their innovation. They used this time in different ways. Teachers examined data on the students in their classes, data that included information on the students' primary language proficiency, oral language proficiency in English, and reading and writing proficiency in English. The student concerns about lack of literacy, voiced in the focus groups a year and a half previously, surfaced once again via the cold, hard reality of individual student scores reflective of the struggle to acquire a second language as well as content in a short amount of time. It was the first opportunity many of the content teachers had ever had to look hard and deep at these data on their students. There, Mr Hagen began to question whether his teaching approaches were really appropriate for the group of students with low levels of English proficiency. The day culminated in the formulation of some guiding principles for redefining the bilingual program, principles that centered around the need to accelerate the literacy of the students, both in English and in Spanish, and to give teachers time to work together in teams for student success. Of special concern to the group were the students who arrived at the school "underschooled," with little, no, or interrupted schooling in their primary language, as well as those students who were moving into all-English (sheltered) instruction for the first time.

In the same time frame in which the working group was meeting outside school in various formats, the professional development coach at the school spent time in each teacher's classroom to begin to get a picture of what was really happening across the bilingual program, from ESL to sheltered to Spanish content classes. The coach provided each teacher with extensive, written, private feedback, much of it in a questioning sort of format. She asked Mr. Hagen: What do you view your role to be in promoting literacy for your students in your sheltered literature class? Is it the same or different from a mainstream English literature class? Most of the teachers had already been through extensive staff development (five days) aimed at providing teachers with various strategies they could use in classrooms that would make on-grade-level content accessible to English Language Learners. The well-documented phenomenon of nonapplication of strategies learned in workshops had occurred at Alisal (yet another illustration of how merely providing teachers with the time to acquire new strategies via workshops is almost never sufficient to changing classroom instruction). And the teachers freely admitted that although they had been through the training, strategy-use was spotty at best.

During their spring break of that year, ten of the teachers visited three small public high schools in New York City noted for their innovative approaches to curriculum and instruction: International High School, Central Park East Secondary School, and El Puente Academy for Peace and Justice. The visit solidified the group's desire to attempt to "remodel" their instruction within the constraints of a large public California high school—large class sizes, yearly uncertainties around staffing, and master schedule, pressures to conform to a whole-school ethic where self-reflection and reevaluation is not valued or practiced. Actually "seeing" schools in action that had made such major changes, and having the foundation together of the year of intensive examination of the issues at their own school, combined into a powerful reform energy.

The year ended with the teachers spending eight days together after school let out to work on the nitty-gritty of an accelerated literacy approach. This was paid time, funded out of the school-site state-granted funds for the program for Limited English Proficient students. The group worked together to identify common categories of strategies (schema building, metacognition and reading process, bridging, etc.), and common routines to be implemented (free voluntary reading, journal writing, binder upkeep, beginning class when the bell rings, etc.). The group acknowledged the need to up the ante of classroom instruction, to really take a risk and try to define what their classrooms should look like in terms of quality instruction with an accelerated literacy focus.

The next year began with a core group of teachers ready to jump in and implement an approach to accelerated literacy that was based on the very best they could distill from the research, models, visits, staff development, feedback from the professional development coach, and their own, rich experience. They understood that accelerated literacy requires more time, and a different use of time—and teaching approaches that provide multiple ways in, multiple forms of skill development, and multiple comprehension checks. Their excitement about the block schedule structure grew—what originally had seemed like a good restructuring idea now became in their minds an absolutely essential structure for supporting the work of literacy. Creative and varied uses of time to convene teachers for reflection and planning, such as Saturday retreats, school day release time, after-school hours, vacation time, and paid summertime was key to the progress made.

Helping the teachers to implement what they had so carefully defined and outlined became the job of the professional development coach. Joint questions arose: How can we (the teachers) be encouraged to try what we said we wanted to try? How can we get a picture of what is happening across the program as a whole? What would be the evidence that there is an accelerated literacy approach in individual classrooms? How can we heighten the sense of urgency around the use of time in a ninety-eight-minute block format? How would we have assurance that the strategies are being used across the curriculum (in science, math, social studies, ESL) and across the various bilingual classroom formats (SDAIE, ESL, primary language content)?

The teachers had said many times that they believed that "peer coaching" could make a difference, and that they never had the chance to observe their colleagues in action. But the group felt that they needed a tool to assist in the coaching, and that the tool had to be intimately linked to what they hoped to accomplish. Thus the teachers and the coach sat down together shortly after school began to hammer out an observation log, an "evidence check" for implementation of the agreed-upon strategies and approaches. How would an observer know, for example, that the teacher had the students engaged in tasks that could help them establish the connections that exist among concepts (schema building)? He or she would search for evidence on classroom walls, in portfolios, in binders, or in the instruction of content organizers, concept maps, compare/contrast matrices, story maps, or Venn diagrams. Spending time constructing the observation log helped teachers view more clearly the categories they themselves had created.

It was at this point that teachers like Mr. Hagen really concentrated and operationalized their notions of literacy development. The relationships of what had been a miscellaneous collection of teaching strategies began to make sense.

Over the next several months, a whole series of observations occurred. The coach first observed in all of the classrooms, for one full block and then provided feedback to the teachers as a whole on implementation. The teachers were also released for a day to view their colleagues, again for the full ninety-eight-minute block each time. The goal of observing for the entire block was for teachers to get a grounded, real sense of how students' time is spent throughout an entire block and throughout an entire day. They came away with fresh recognition of the need to use every minute as wisely as possible, to vary activities, and to provide a common focus of strategies for the students that revolve around literacy tasks.

The observations also took a slightly different twist on the commonly practiced pre-observation conference/observation/post-observation conference cycle of classic peer coaching. Again, the issue of time was key to redefining the peer coaching model. Fitting pre- and post-observation cycles into teachers' already stuffed, crammed days felt cumbersome and unworkable. So the model evolved so that a teacher could go to a colleague's classroom with the observation log/evidence check in hand and simply observe. The goal of the observation in this model was not to attend a classroom to critique the teacher's lesson or style, but for the observer to regard the teacher in the class as the "coach" in order to learn what the teacher is doing that is effective and/or innovative. The result was the observers got a clear picture of the range of implementation of literacy tasks and strategies. It was with some relief that the teachers and the professional development coach discovered, after using the model this way, that it mirrored the latest research done on peer coaching (Joyce & Showers, 1996).

The in-classroom observations were coupled with weekly lunchtime meetings, and various other opportunities spread out throughout the year (district staff development days, after-school time, and paid summertime again) that allowed teachers to reflect, revise, and plan for the future of the program.

By the beginning of the second year of working together, Mr. Hagen's classroom had begun to take its new shape. He and his colleagues were excited about how much more effective they felt in their teaching—and they felt connected to something larger than their own classroom. Many now say they would be appalled if required to return to a six-period day.

The process of finding and creating time for teachers to collaborate remains challenging, but central to the issue of redesigning schools to meet the needs of immigrant students (Fullan & Miles, 1992; Rosensholtz, 1989). But as the Alisal experience reveals, neither extra time for teachers nor extra time for students in classes is sufficient guarantee of quality education for immigrant students. A critical look at time use in schools must show how teacher collaborative time is linked to improvement in classroom use of time. And the classroom use of time needs to circle back to what the teachers define as quality instructional practices based on the best research.

CONCLUSION

Alisal High School took one approach to the restructuring of time in the school day and year. It was based both on their understanding of student needs and concerns, and on their own need for time together to respond to those student needs. The exact model they devised may or may not be appropriate for other schools, the process they went through, however, is absolutely relevant. California Tomorrow has worked with other schools in the state on similar kinds of restructuring efforts. While Alisal ended up creating a schedule that lessened the number of academic courses a student and teacher grapple with per semester, built in tutorials, and emphasized literacy, other schools have taken a different route in the reconfiguring of time to meet the needs of their language minority and LEP students. Based on listening to student concerns, examining data about student needs, reading literature and checking out models of other schools, and then using those as a springboard to reexamining the uses of time, each school has found a schedule and framework of time that meets their particular needs. Interestingly, all have recognized the need for longer class periods.

In the traditional secondary school, the structures of how time is used often work against student success—particularly against the achievement and successful participation of immigrant and limited English-proficient students. To create schools that work for immigrant students has taken a willingness of educators to rethink that basic structure, to think "outside the mold." Alisal High today is a much different school than it was five years ago—and the payoff for the hard work and creative restructuring is beginning to show in student outcomes. Fewer students are referred for discipline. Limited English proficient students are gaining English literacy proficiency at a faster rate than before. There is evidence that more students are staying in school (the ninth-grade return rate for tenth-grade enrollment has improved) (Olsen, Jaramillo, McCall-Perez, White & Minicucci, 1999). These substantial improvements were made possible by the switch to block scheduling and the creation of collaborative time for teachers—but it has been in the uses of that block scheduling for project-oriented instruction that speaks to the needs of comprehension and literacy development, and in the uses of collaborative time to build a joint vision and a research-based pedagogy that the promise has been realized.

Alisal is one of many high schools in this nation rethinking the use of time. And there are many creative approaches to creating time—time for students to use in learning, time for teachers to use in building their skills and capacity and shared visions. But time in and of itself is not the answer. It is a resource to use. And the creative and thoughtful use of that precious resource involves other elements as well. It took leadership at the district level in one district to switch the calendar of the school year to better match the patterns of families returning to Mexico for the holidays. It took active advising and advocacy to involve the LEP students at another high school to make use of the opportunity that an extra block of time presented for doubling the amount of ESL newcomer students could take in one year. It took skillful facilitation and a process of eliciting and listening to student voice for the teachers at Alisal High to pinpoint the student needs that were the imperative for changing the uses of time in the school; it took professional development coaching and support and a plethora of collaborative formats to help teachers at Alisal High make different use of instructional time in the classroom. And all of that came about because these school faculties and administrators were willing to invest a host of related resources (time among them) to achieving the real goals they knew they wanted to achieve—schools restructured to truly support the academic achievement of their diverse student population.

REFERENCES

Apple, Michael, & Christian Smith, Linda. (1991). *The politics of the textbook.* London: Routledge.

California Department of Education. (1996). *Language census.* Sacramento.

Collier, V., & Thomas, W. 1997). *School effectiveness for language minority students.* Washington, DC: National Clearinghouse for Bilingual Education.

First, J., & Carrera, J. W. (1988). *New voices: Immigrant students in U.S. public schools.* NCAS Research and Policy Report. Boston: National Coalition of Advocates for Students.

Fix, M., & Passel, J. S. (1994). *Immigration and immigrants: Setting the record straight.* Washington, DC: The Urban Institute.

Fix, M., & Zimmerman, W. (1993). *Educating immigrant children: Chapter 1 in the changing city.* Washington, DC: Urban Institute Press.

Fleischman, H. L., & Hopstock, P. J. (1993). *Descriptive study of services to Limited English Proficient Students. Volume 1. Summary of findings and conclusions.* Prepared for the Office of the Under Secretary, U.S. Department of Education by Development Associates, Inc. Arlington, VA.

Fullan, Michael, & Miles, M. (1992). Getting reform right: What works and what doesn't. *Phi Delta Kappan,* 745–752.

Gándara, P. (1994). The impact of the school reform movement on Limited English Proficient Students. In B. McLeod (Ed.), *Language and learning: Educating linguistically diverse students* (pp. 45–70). Albany: State University of New York Press.

Gándara, P., & Sun, A. (1986). *Bilingual education: Learning English in California.* Assembly Office of Research, Sacramento, CA.

Gardner, H. (1985). *Frames of mind: The theory of multiple intelligences.* New York: Basic Books.

Goodlad, John. (1984). *A place called school: Prospects for the future.* New York: McGraw-Hill.

Hopstock, P. J., & Bucaro, B. J. (1993). *A review and analysis of estimates of the LEP student population.* Arlington: Development Associates.

Ima, Kenji. (1995). Testing the American dream: Case studies of at risk Southeast Asian refugee students in secondary schools. In W. Cornelius and R. Rumbaut (Eds.), *California's immigrant children: Theory, research and implications for education policy.* San Diego: Center for U.S. Mexican Studies, University of California.

Joyce, B., & Showers, B. (1996). The evolution of peer coaching. *Educational Leadership, 53* (6), 12–16.

Lau v. Nichols, 414 US 563, 39 L. Ed 2nd 1. Decided January 21, 1974.

Leiberman, A. (1995). Practices that support teacher development: Transforming conceptions of professional learning. *Phi Delta Kappan, 76* (8), 591–596.

Little, J. W. (1982). Norms of collegiality and experimentation: Workplace conditions of school success. *American Education Research Journal, 19* (3), 325–340.

Lucas, Tamara. (1997). *Into, through and beyond secondary school: Critical transitions for immigrant youths.* Washington, DC: Center for Applied Linguistics.

McDonnell, L., & Hill, P. T. (1993). *Newcomers in American schools*. Santa Monica, CA: Program for Research on Immigration Policy, Rand Corporation.

Minicucci, C., & Olsen, L. (1992). Programs for secondary limited English proficient students: A California study. *FOCUS: Occasional Papers in Bilingual Education*, No. 5. National Clearinghouse on Bilingual Education.

National Center for Education Statistics. (1997). *A profile of policies and practices for Limited English Proficient Students: Screening methods, program support and teacher training (SASS 1993–94).* Statistical Analysis Report, U.S. Department of Education Office of Educational Research and Improvement. Washington, DC.

Oakes, Jeanne. (1985). *Keeping track: How schools structure inequality*. New Haven, CT: Yale University Press.

Olsen, L. (1997). *The invisible crises: The educational needs of Asian Pacific American youth*. A report from Asian Americans/Pacific Islanders in Philanthropy.

Olsen, L. (1995). School restructuring and the needs of immigrant students." In W. Cornelius & R. Rumbaut (Eds.), *California's immigrant children: Theory, research and implications for educational policy.* Center for U.S. Mexican Studies, University of California, San Diego.

Olsen, L., & Chen, M. (1988). *Crossing the schoolhouse border: Immigrant children in California Schools.* San Francisco: California Tomorrow.

Olsen, L., & Mullen, N. (1990). *Embracing diversity: Teachers' voices from California classrooms.* San Francisco: California Tomorrow.

Olsen, L., Jaramillo, A., McCall-Perez, Z., White, J., & Minicucci, C. (1999). *Igniting change for immigrant students: Portraits of three high schools.* Oakland, CA: California Tomorrow.

Olsen, L., Jaramillo, A., Minicucci, C., & McCall-Perez, Z. (1998). *Portraits of school change.* San Francisco: California Tomorrow.

Olsen, L., et al. (1994). *The unfinished journey: Restructuring schools for a diverse society.* San Francisco: California Tomorrow.

O'Neil, J. (1995). On schools as learning organizations: A conversation with Peter Senge. *Educational Leadership, 52* (7), 20–23.

Portes, Alejandro, & Rumbaut, Ruben G. (1990). *Immigrant America: A portrait.* Berkeley, CA: University of California Press.

Raywid, M. A. (1993). Finding time for collaboration. *Educational leadership, 51* (1), 105–109.

Rosenholtz, S. J. (1989). Workplace conditions that affect teaching quality and commitment: Implications for teacher induction programs. *Elementary School Journal, 89* (4), 421–439.

Sizer, T. (1984). *Horace's compromise: The dilemma of the American high school.* Boston: Houghton Mifflin.

Slavin, R. E. (1987). Ability grouping and its alternatives: Must we track? *American Educator, 11* (2), 32–48.

Watson, A. M., Buchanan, M., Huyman, H., & Seal, K. (1992). A laboratory school explores self-governance. *Educational Leadership, 49* (5), 57–60.

CONTRIBUTORS

Lorin W. Anderson is a Carolina Distinguished Professor at the University of South Carolina.

Judy Fish is Assistant Superintendent for Educational Services in the Palmdale School District in California.

Patricia Gándara is Associate Professor of Education at the University of California at Davis, and Associate Director of the University of California Linguistic Minority Research Institute.

Ann Jaramillo is a trainer and ESL/Bilingual Resource Specialist in the Salinas Union High School District, and an Associate of California Tomorrow in San Francisco, California.

Carolyn Kneese is an Assistant Professor of Education at Texas A&M University at Commerce.

John Lofty is Associate Professor of English and Education at the University of New Hampshire.

Catherine Minicucci is President of Minicucci Associates in Sacramento, California, and Associate to the Center for Research on Excellence and Diversity in Education at the University of California, Santa Cruz.

Audrey J. Noble is a Senior Research Associate for Evaluation and Policy Analysis at the Delaware Educational Research and Development Center, University of Delaware.

Laurie Olsen is Executive Co-Director of California Tomorrow, a nonprofit research and technical assistance agency fostering diversity in San Francisco, California.

Allan Pitman is Associate Professor of Mathematics Education at the University of Western Ontario

Susanna Purnell is an Associate Researcher with the RAND Corporation in Washington, DC.

Robert Reichardt is a Ph.D. student at the RAND Graduate Institute in Santa Monica, California.

Thomas Romberg is the Sears Roebuck Foundation-Bascom Professor in Education and Director of the National Center for Improving Student Learning and Achievement in Mathematics and Science at the University of Wisconsin at Madison.

Mary Lee Smith is Professor of Education at Arizona State University at Tempe.

Jon Wagner is Professor of Education at the University of California at Davis.

INDEX